*The Dawn of Belief*

# THE DAWN OF BELIEF

Religion in the Upper Paleolithic of Southwestern Europe

D. Bruce Dickson

THE UNIVERSITY OF ARIZONA PRESS   TUCSON

The color plates reproduced in this book were made possible through a grant from the College of Liberal Arts of Texas A&M University.

The University of Arizona Press

Copyright © 1990
The Arizona Board of Regents
All Rights Reserved

This book was set in Trump Mediaeval.
⊗ This book is printed on acid-free, archival-quality paper.
Manufactured in the United States of America.

94 93 92 91 90    5 4 3 2 1

**Library of Congress Cataloging-in-Publication Data**

Dickson, D. Bruce.
    The dawn of belief : religion in the upper Paleolithic of southwestern Europe / D. Bruce Dickson.
        p.   cm.
    Includes bibliographical references.
    ISBN 0-8165-1076-8 (alk. paper)
        1. Paleolithic period—Europe, Southern.   2. Religion, Prehistoric—Europe, Southern.   3. Europe, Southern—Antiquities.
    I. Title.
    GN772.22.F854D53 1990
    291'.042'094—dc20                                                89-38911
                                                                       CIP

British Library Cataloguing-in-Publication Data are available.

To my father, Don,
and to the memory of my mother, Bess

# Contents

# Illustrations

# Acknowledgments

I deeply appreciate the willing assistance of the many people who made this book possible. First and foremost, I want to thank my wife, Mary Ann Dickson, for her patient help and advice at every stage of this work. Thanks are also due to Catherine Muller-Wille, Norbert Dannhaeuser, and Vaughn M. Bryant of the Department of Anthropology and Jon Alston of the Department of Sociology of Texas A&M University. These colleagues critically read all or parts of the manuscript and provided me with invaluable suggestions on ways to improve it.

The illustrations included in this volume were made possible through the aid and cooperation of a number of people. I especially want to thank Dean Daniel Fallon and Associate Dean Charles Stoup of the College of Liberal Arts at Texas A&M for providing the generous subvention that has underwritten the publication of the color plates.

I am also indebted to Alexander Marshack, Associate in Paleolithic Archaeology at the Peabody Museum of Harvard University, for allowing me to publish the diagrams he developed to illustrate his original interpretations of Upper Paleolithic mobiliary art. One of Professor Marshack's illustrations, that of the La Marche palette, appears as the frontispiece of this volume.

Professor Denise de Sonneville-Bordes, Directeur de recherche au C.N.R.S., Institut du Quaternaire, Centre Francois Bordes, Universite de Bordeaux I, was equally generous in allowing me to publish her illustrations of the key tool types that characterize the southwestern European Upper Paleolithic industrial traditions.

Madame Yvonne Vertut kindly granted me permission to reproduce the late Jean Vertut's classic photographs of the Chinese Horse from Lascaux and the modelled clay bison from Tuc d'Audoubert.

I am also grateful to Seymour Hacker of Hacker Art Books for allowing me to publish the original illustrations from the Abbe Breuil's monumental *Four Hundred Centuries of Cave Art*, as well as to Nina Cummings of the Photography Department of the Field Museum of Natural History in Chicago, who was particularly helpful.

Thanks to the Minnesota Museum of Art and the American Museum of Natural History for permission to reproduce photographs from their collections. The map of southwestern Europe that appears with the text was drawn by Cartagraphics, Inc.; Christopher Muller-Wille, the Director of Cartagraphics, was instrumental in its composition.

Ms. Celinda Stevens cheerfully and efficiently typed the original manuscript.

Finally, I would particularly like to thank the many students who have taken my classes in archaeology and anthropology at the University of Tennessee and at Texas A&M University. These bright, articulate young men and women have taught me a great deal over the last seventeen years. I remain most grateful to them.

COLOR PLATE 1. Upper Paleolithic artifact: A *déroulée*, or unrolled drawing, of the La Marche bone shows two sets of tiny marks and horses that have been repeatedly reengraved. Alexander Marshack interprets the tiny marks as evidence of a formal system of calendric record keeping or notation. *Courtesy of Alexander Marshack.*

COLOR PLATE 2. The celebrated biste yellow "Chinese Horse" outlined in black from the Axial Gallery of Lascaux in the Dordogne, France. This horse is approximately 1.4 meters long and is surrounded—and presumably associated with—a number of other images. Directly above the horse's withers is a red quadrilateral figure. Four lines drawn perpendicular to this figure descend toward the animal suggesting a trap or net. The Abbé Breuil (1979: 109) interpreted the two feathery lines below the horse's neck and belly as "flying arrows . . . one has stuck in the croup." Mithen (1988: 300) identifies the two black lozenges just below the horse's muzzle as representing horse's hoof prints. *Photograph by Jean Vertut and supplied courtesy of Madam Yvonne Vertut.*

COLOR PLATE 3. Two bison modeled in clay against a rock in the cave of Tuc d'Audoubert on the Volp River near the site of Les Trois Frères in the Ariège, France. The bison on the right is .61 meters long. These clay sculptures represent one of the masterpieces of Upper Paleolithic art. *Photograph by Jean Vertut and supplied courtesy of Madame Yvonne Vertut.*

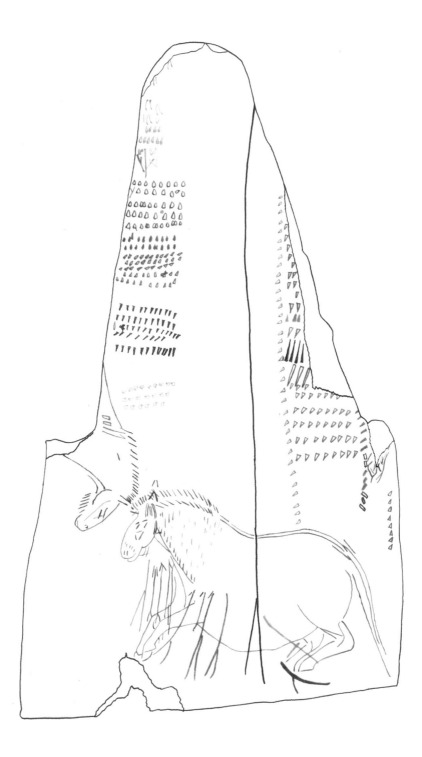

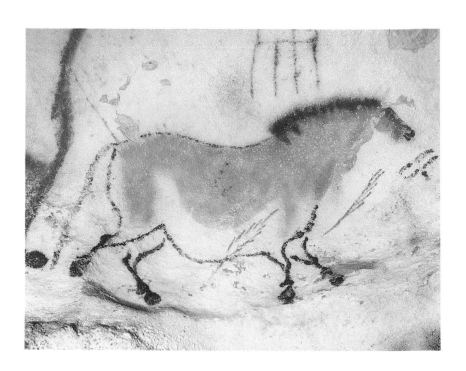

# 1. Humanity, the Gods, and Archaeology

*Time present and time past*
*Are both perhaps present in time future,*
*And time future contained in time past.*
T. S. ELIOT, BURNT NORTON

Archaeology is a discipline obsessed with things, with the ages and origins of things, and the places that things fill in the overall scheme of culture growth and change. Stratigraphic profiles, potsherds, building foundations, post molds, skeletal remains, pollen—the list goes on and on. This preoccupation is natural, perhaps inevitable, in a science that seeks to learn about the past by studying its material remains. However, preoccupation with material evidence can lead us to lose sight of the real objective—gaining knowledge and understanding of the ways human beings behaved in the past.

Reconstructions of the past generally work upward from the bottom, that is, they begin with the elements of culture most directly traceable in the material remains: subsistence and diet, settlement patterns, skeletal pathologies, technology, and such. The more daring among prehistorians venture on to inferences about social and political organization. Deductions about ideology and religion from such data are made only by the most foolhardy. With the writing of this book, I find myself in this latter camp.

Beyond this, however, the perspectives utilized in this book are entirely conventional. They include the views that 1) the abstraction that anthropologists call "culture" is the proper unit of analysis for prehistorians; 2) that cultures have become measurably more complex through time; 3) that societies form systemic wholes; and 4) that social institutions are interrelated, purposive, and nonrandom in their growth and change. Needless to say, I believe that the holistic perspective does not necessarily impede the study of change or prevent comparisons across cultures and through time. Finally, the anthropological perspective on religion, which tends to emphasize strongly both functionalism and comparison, is followed throughout the book.

## PREHISTORY

The term "prehistory" refers to that vast portion of the human career that took place before the development of written records. It is, therefore, a discipline whose practitioners must attempt to reconstruct the human past through the systematic examination of the surviving remains of human activity rather than through study of contemporary accounts or other literate documents.

Prehistory in the broadest sense of the term refers to the attempt to answer questions such as "where did humankind come from?" and "why is the world arranged the way we find it at present?" It is safe to assume that prehistory conceived in this broad sense has been a human concern from the very earliest times. Certainly, the worldwide occurrence of stories and fables explaining the origins of mankind, of society, and of the gods attests to this interest, even if such accounts often seem designed as much to legitimize an existing social order as to satisfy the demands of pure human curiosity about the past. The earliest recorded example of such prehistory is found inscribed in cuneiform on Sumerian clay tablets dating to the third millennium B.C. in Mesopotamia. The Sumerians envisioned a vast primeval sea that engendered both heaven and earth (Kramer 1959: 84). From the union of these entities was begot the air god, Enlil, who subsequently created man and all the works and institutions of Sumerian civilization. Although such a story may have made both the past and the present seem more intelligible to the Sumerians, it is of a distinctly mythic variety.

A far more adequate form of prehistory seems to have emerged from a mythic base with the rise of the Greek philosophical tradition. The Greeks constructed many scenarios of the past by using formal logic and common sense rather than by merely relying on imagination and emotion. Although supernatural cause was sometimes invoked, it was seldom the only cause to explain the present. Aristotle's account of the origins of the state is such a "philosophic prehistory." Aristotle believed that the family was the simplest and earliest form of human organization. In time, families combined to make a village and the state emerged when several villages combined to create a self-sufficient entity. This growth from simple to increasingly complex institutional forms was, he believed, both a natural and inevitable development for human society (Jowett 1943: 52–54).

Aside from his teleological and vitalistic assumptions, Aristotle's account of the prehistory of the state makes no use of supernatural cause and is logical in its structure. However, the point to recall is that, whatever the logical strength or internal consistency of Aristotle's prehistory, he had no method to determine whether it was true or false. For that matter, the same could be said of the prehistories of St. Augustine, Montesquieu, Herder, or Hobbes. No matter how rigorous the argument or compelling the logic, such philosophic forays into the vast time before written records remained untested and untestable hypotheses. What may be referred to as "scientific prehistory," that is, prehistories based on or tested against some physical evidence, did not exist until the late eighteenth century.

Scientific methods and techniques for learning about the prehistoric past have emerged in geology and paleontology and in antiquarian and humanistic studies only in the last two hundred years. The development of the means of assessing relative time through the Law of Superposition and the formulation of the concepts of association and of artifact seriation were especially critical in the rise of scientific prehistory. Important also was the evolution both of rigorous field methods for data collection and of stringent canons for data evaluation. Of course, twentieth-century developments in absolute dating have further strengthened the enterprise of prehistory. As a consequence of these developments, our theoretical and conceptual picture of prehistory has altered radically. It is now possible to compare formulations about the past against material evidence and, if not to determine which are true, at least to reject or falsify formulations which do not agree with that evidence.

This is not to say that modern scientific prehistory is entirely free of mythic elements. Our reconstructions of the past surely contain their share of nonrational notions sanctified by tradition or prejudice rather than evidence. We must also recognize that a large part of even the best reconstructions are philosophic prehistories, which have yet to be tested against any evidence. This is especially true of renderings of such complex processes as the emergence of agriculture and the rise of the state. Gaps in theory and data will always force the prehistorian to connect the dots and fill in the image as best he can. I freely admit to having followed such a procedure in reconstructing the religious systems discussed in this book. However, like all scientists, prehistorians must structure their research so that—at least ultimately—their conclusions can be evaluated against the data.

Further, by being entirely candid about the incomplete and prefactorial nature of the reconstructions, prehistorians encourage the recovery of the data they lack. It is in this spirit that I offer my outline of the religious system of the Upper Paleolithic period. While this outline is both tentative and incomplete, it is nonetheless a scientific, as opposed to a merely philosophic, prehistory. Its statements about the past have been evaluated against existing evidence—or can be so evaluated in future research—and they can be falsified or provisionally accepted on grounds other than their internal consistency.

## CULTURE

The concept of culture, which may be the most significant idea in anthropology, developed more or less simultaneously with scientific methods for studying the past. This concurrence was by no means accidental, because the idea of culture gives coherence to the study of prehistory, while prehistoric studies provide abundant examples of cultural stability and change. By expanding the number of known cultural systems, prehistoric studies have increased the basis for cross-cultural comparisons and generalizations.

Unfortunately, the term "culture" has never been defined precisely. The extent of the inexactness that surrounds its definition is reflected in Kroeber and Kluckhohn's "Culture: A Critical Review of Concepts and Definitions" (1952), wherein the authors reviewed and evaluated 164 definitions and valiantly proposed a new one of their own. In consequence, anthropologists have customarily selected or formulated definitions of culture appropriate to their subject matter or to the level of abstraction with which they have chosen to work. David Bidney's solution to this dilemma, and the one that we adopt here, is to recognize that culture consists of two "irreducible constituent categories" which he refers to as "theory and practice." That is,

> a culture must be understood in its practical and theoretical aspects. Normative, impersonal, ideational culture has no existence unless it is practiced and influences men's behavior and thinking in social life. Practical, real, or actual culture—the actual behavior and thought of men in society—is not intelligible apart from the social ideals which men have created or discovered from themselves and endeavor to realize in their daily lives (Bidney 1953: 30).

The distinction between a culture's theory and its practice is a useful one and has been observed throughout this book. Culture is here considered to consist both of symbolic, learned, and shared patterns of thought and of actions which express these symbolic understandings in material and behavioral terms. Since cultures consist of both theory and practice, thought and action, both realms must be treated in any valid ethnographic account of a cultural system or subsystem (whether that system be an extant or prehistoric one).

In any event, definitions of the kind that we have been discussing are static in that they tell us what cultures are without stating what they do or why they developed in the first place. Perhaps the most succinct theory of the nature of cultural dynamics and cultural evolution is provided by Leslie White in *The Science of Culture* (1949b). According to White, cultures are formulated and transmitted symbolically, and they evolve through time to higher and higher levels of social and technical complexity. The evolution of culture occurs through the systematic development of more and more sources of energy or of ever more efficient modes of energy generation. In White's view, culture is man's extrasomatic means of adapting to his environment (White 1949a: 363).

Following White's definition, I view human societies as accommodating themselves to their physical and social surroundings through both theory and practice available in their cultural system. As Geertz notes, the interaction between theory and practice—what he prefers to call " 'patterns of meaning' and the concrete course of social life" (1973: 250–51)—is a complex dialectic process. At a very crude level this dialectic may be diagrammed as a kind of cybernetic or feedback relationship in which success in the sphere of collective behavior reinforces existing symbolic structures, while failure leads eventually to their modification or elimination. Adaptation is the product of such dynamic interaction.

Part of this adaptation is accomplished by the techniques and the organization of subsistence, production and distribution, and reproduction, or what Harris (1979: 51–54), modifying Karl Marx, refers to as cultural "infrastructure." Another part of this adaptation takes place through patterns of internal arrangement of society, its social and political structure, its modes of acculturating its young and recruiting them into social roles, and so forth. Harris (1979) refers to this second level as the "structure."

Cultures also include a third level that not only contributes to their adaptation but transcends it. Harris calls this sphere the "super-structure," but it might also be referred to as the sphere of meaning or significance. It consists of the set of values and the vision or theory of reality which provides the members of society with a shared set of goals, strategies, and expectations about the world. In large measure, it is through these cultural screens that the world is viewed and reality is interpreted. Like the rest of culture, these elements are transmitted from generation to generation symbolically through learning. In other words, human cultures both interpret the world and create it for each succeeding generation.

However, lest we conclude that people live exclusively in cultural glass houses of their own creation, let us recall that these houses are surrounded and permeated by corporeal reality. It is to this corporeal reality that people, by means of culture, must accommodate themselves. Ultimately, their mental constructs, strategies, categories, ethos, and worldview must enable them to do that. Cultural superstructures which depart so widely from physical reality that they impede this adaptive process tend to disappear over time along with their bearers. Lévi-Strauss sees the internal logic of culture and the events of the material world as the Scylla and Charybdis between which humanity, like Odysseus, must steer. "Native institutions," he says, "though borne along on the flux of time, [must] manage to steer a course between the contingencies of history and the immutability of design and remain, as it were, within the stream of intelligibility" (1966: 73–74). This observation would seem particularly germane to that sphere of the human culture which we class as religious.

## THE ANTHROPOLOGY OF RELIGION

While any number of definitions of religion exist in the anthropological literature, these definitions, like those of culture, tend to follow either an idealist's or realist's perspective. For example, a dialectical materialist works from the ground up and regards religion as a rather insubstantial evanescence—an epiphenomenon whose nature is determined by the grittier forces of subsistence, economy, technology, and production. From this vantage point, Marxists dismiss religion as an opiate, a cloud hiding the grim realities and injustices within human societies. Realists of a functionalist persuasion tend to be more indulgent in their view of religion. While still regarding it as derived from, or closely related to, the material conditions of life, they tend to see religion as an important social lubricant which aids the articulation of social and economic institutions with the environment (for example, cf., Rappaport 1968). Yet merely granting that religion can be both a form of fraud and adjunct to social policy hardly exhausts or does full justice to the subject.

Alternatively, idealist definitions such as the one proposed by Clifford Geertz are built from the top down. According to him religion is "(1) a system of symbols which acts to (2) establish powerful, pervasive and long-lasting moods and motivations in men by (3) formulating conceptions of a general order of existence and (4) clothing these conceptions with such an aura of factuality that (5) the moods and motivations seem uniquely realistic" (1973: 90). By symbols, Geertz means the cultural patterns which serve as blueprints for the institution of the social and psychological processes that shape public behavior (1973: 92). Religion for Geertz is the mental template or model from which ongoing "public behavior" is derived. Certainly, his notion that religion consists of mental and symbolic organization is a persuasive one. Yet, is it enough? Or must any definition of religion also include physical and behavioral expressions of that mental organization? After all, the set of symbols that Geertz considers the creator of those "powerful, pervasive and long-lasting moods and motivations" can effect the transfer and redistribution of huge quantities of material goods and services, can guarantee the persistence of a set of social relations while masking their essential inequity, can trigger critical social or economic events, and can sometimes even revitalize a disintegrating moral and social order.

Perhaps Durkheim's handling of the problem is more satisfactory. According to him, religious phenomena consist of two fundamental categories: beliefs and rites, or "states of opinion," and "determined modes of action," respectively (Durkheim 1961: 51). He advances the proposition that a single common characteristic enables us to distinguish religious opinion and actions from the ordinary kind. To Durkheim, religions

> presuppose a classification of all the things, real and ideal of which men think, into two classes or opposed groups, generally designated by two distinct terms which are translated well enough by the words profane and sacred (*profane, sacré*). This division of the world into two domains, the one containing all that is sacred, the other all that is profane, is the distinctive trait of religious thought. (1961: 52)

Once he has made this distinction, Durkheim is free to define religion as "a unified system of beliefs and practices relative to sacred things, that is to say, things set apart and forbidden—beliefs and practices which unite into one single moral community called a Church, all those who adhere to them" (1961: 62). Durkheim's definition has great utility. We can identify as religious those social institutions, cultural patterns, and individual behavior which we observe to be organized around the sacred. Religion becomes both the plan and the result, the thought and symbol, and also the action which these sustain. As in Bidney's view of culture, Durkheim's definition of religion includes both theory and practice. We deal with religion whenever we find people determining their actions, setting their goals, modifying their interests or their judgments, or explaining their raw impressions of the phenomenal world with conscious regard to the miraculous or the superhuman. An act taken or avoided out of fear of divine sanction, a belief in a preternatural cause for, say the changing configurations of the stars, must be classed with more obviously religious events such as public prayer or sacrifice.

Although Durkheim's definition is useful for classifying cultural behavior, it ignores another significant attribute of religion—its universality. According to Trammel (1984), religion exists in response to the "horrendous and nonmanipulable" attributes of the human condition. These attributes are inherent in the structure of the material world—or more accurately—in the nature of human ecological relations to the world. Human beings, in common with all living things, are destined to die. This basic attribute of existence is nonmanipulable; it cannot be altered. Unlike all, or at least most, other creatures, human beings are aware of their inevitable death. It is this human consciousness of the fact of death that renders it horrendous. Of course, the limited nature of human powers, the disparity between hope and reality, the inevitability of diminished capacities with age, disease, fear, frustration, conflict, and cruelty are other horrendous and nonmanipulable attributes of the human condition.

If human beings are to live in the world, they must face the ultimate circumstances of life without giving over to despair and capitulation. At its essence, religion is humankind's primary emotional and intellectual means of struggling with the ultimate circumstances of the human condition (Yinger 1970: 7). Feuerbach (1957: xxxvi) claims this struggle is joined through the worship of gods endowed with the very human qualities we value above all others: power, knowledge, and love. Niebuhr asserts that the means is found in the transmutation of "the basic trust of childhood, based on obvious security, to a faith which transcends all the incoherences, incongruities and ills of life" (1968: x). But whatever the specific mechanism or strategy, the abiding need to cope with the human condition leads to the emergence of religion throughout human history.

## THE ROLE OF RELIGION IN SOCIOCULTURAL SYSTEMS

Let us now turn our discussion from what religion is to an interpretation of what religion does in the sociocultural system. In discussing the problem of cultural interpretation generally, Lévi-Strauss notes that two extreme positions are commonly occupied. One, the view of Malinowski, naively attributes a practical purpose or function to every cultural pattern; the other, which Lévi-Strauss identifies with Sir James Frazer, assumes that such practices and beliefs are arbitrary and irrational. Of course, this polar opposition does not exhaust the possibilities and neither view should detain us for long because "between the basic absurdity Frazer attributed to primitive practices and beliefs and the specious validation of them in terms of a supposed common sense invoked by Malinowski, there is scope for a whole science and a whole philosophy" (1966: 74). For Lévi-Strauss, that "whole science" and "whole philosophy" centers on the idea that it is meaning and coherence that humankind seeks foremost in culture. This position has an attractive moderation about it. Surely it is wise to steer a course between Malinowskian functionalism and Frazerian absurdity in any analysis of religion. Attractive also is the view that humankind craves intelligibility in the world. Let us recall, however, that in order to obtain intelligibility, humankind must also engineer its survival in the stream of history and material force. Sociocultural systems must provide coherence for their members, but they must also supply the extrasomatic means of adapting to their environment. Religion occupies a large and important place in sociocultural systems and presumably must bear some of each of these responsibilities. Thus, while I would agree that practical consequences— even rational interpretations—cannot be found for much religious belief and practice, they can for some. In fact, a great deal of decidedly nonspecious anthropological attention has been directed towards unraveling the useful or instrumental effects on society at large of religious theory and practice. What follows is an examination of some examples of the manner in which the sacred sphere provides intelligibility and is enlisted in the performance of practical social "tasks" in society. These examples have been selected both to illustrate the anthropological approach to religion in general and to aid in the interpretation of religion in the Upper Paleolithic period in particular.

Tasks implemented in the symbolic or theoretical sphere are listed first; those in the sphere of action or practice second. The performance of these tasks is critical to the maintenance of any society, and perhaps precisely because of this importance, their accomplishment has often been affected by organizing them around the sacred in the form of supernatural agency, sanction, or explanation. When we find the concept of the sacred to be present in an institution or phenomenon under investigation, we have entered into the province of religion and will find that our analysis can profitably be framed in such terms.

For the purposes of this book, I have reduced the province of religion in society to nine major offices. Four of these are in the theoretical sphere of culture, five in the practical sphere. The major offices of religion in the theoretical sphere are as follows:

1. The worldview, or characteristic manner in which a people look outward on the universe, is commonly sanctioned by religious means.

2. The ethos, or moral and evaluative standards of a given sociocultural system, is also generally sanctioned by religious means.

3. The religion of a given sociocultural system is generally responsible for demonstrating that its worldview and ethos are complementary (Geertz 1973: 126–27). That is, (a) congruence must be maintained between the worldview and ethos held by the members of a sociocultural system and (b) the glue that welds worldview and ethos together is most commonly religious in nature.

4. Religion renders history and human experience intelligible by investing it with sacred explanation and meaning.

The five major offices of religion in the sphere of action or the practical sphere of culture are as follows:

1. Religions commonly provide, sanction, or support a variety of mechanisms of social control.

2. In addition to, and in concert with the foregoing, religious systems commonly support a variety of mechanisms or services designed

to reduce tension or provide explanation or psychological support for the members of society.

3. Religions commonly provide for integrating the individual into the larger collectivities of which he or she is part family, community, tribe, or state.

4. Religions provide the organization, ideological buttressing, and supernatural sanction for a wide variety of systemic operations in society as diverse as economic production, distribution and exchange, military conflict, reproduction, and so forth.

5. In the face of societal stress, distortion or disintegration, religious movements often emerge to revitalize and transform the sociocultural system to allow it to accommodate itself to new circumstances.

While I would not pretend that this list is exhaustive, it does contain the offices of religion which are of greatest interest to the anthropologist, and therefore to the prehistorian. It would be absurd to assert that these tasks can be performed only by religious institutions or with religious sanction; they can be found cast wholly or in part in secular form in various societies throughout the world. However, supernatural agency has commonly been employed for all of these purposes throughout history—and one presumes throughout prehistory as well—and continues to be so employed in our own times.

**Religion and Sociocultural Complexity.** The "offices" of religion cannot be considered without specific reference to variations in the general level of sociocultural complexity that occurs between societies. It is important to note, however, that differences in the complexity of religious practice among societies may be correlated in a general way with dissimilarities in the level of their overall development. This correlation exists to a lesser extent for religious theory as well.

According to Dole (1973: 248), sociocultural systems increase in complexity through the operation of three interrelated processes: "(1) differentiation of structures, (2) specialization of functions, and (3) integration of both structures and functions into new levels of organization." Religious institutions are part of this process. Thus, in general the more complex the society, the more varied, differentiated, and specialized the institutional forms of religious belief and practice that characterize it (Berelson and Steiner 1964: 358). Perhaps the most useful taxonomy of the institutional differences that characterize religious organizations has been presented by Anthony F. C. Wallace (1966: 84–96). He classes religious institutions or "cults" into four types:

1. individualistic cults

2. shamanistic cults

3. communal cults

4. ecclesiastical cults

The four varieties are distinguished from one another by the nature of their organization and by the kinds of religious practitioners that characterize them. The complexity of these four different types of cults forms a scale from simple to more complex which corresponds in a broad way with the overall institutional complexity of the sociocultural systems in which they occur.

The "individualistic cult" is the simplest and most basic type of religious institution. The primary characteristic of cults of this kind is that their rituals are not performed by specialists. In effect, everyone is his own religious specialist and is able to interact directly with supernatural beings and forces without the intermediacy of shaman or priest. Much of the religious practice of the traditional hunting-and-gathering culture of the Eskimo falls in this category, but individualistic cults are found in most, if not all, human societies. However, there are no surviving examples of societies that contain this type of cult to the exclusion of all other types (Wallace 1966: 86–88).

"Shamanistic cults" are characterized by the presence of the ubiquitous part-time religious practitioner, the shaman who, "endowed by birth, training, or inspirational experience with a special power, intervenes for a fee with supernatural beings or forces on behalf of human clients" (Wallace 1966: 86). Such intervention may take the form of divination, healing, spell-casting, counseling, or the organization and management of rituals. Together with the individualistic type, shamanistic cults are the only cultic institutions found in the simpler sociocultural systems organized around the band or family cluster.

"Communal cults" are characterized by more elaborate beliefs and practices than shamanistic cults. Consequently, they are not found in the very simple, small-scale band societies which have only the shamanistic type of cult. Instead, communal cults are associated with sociocultural systems which have achieved a moderate population size and density and a more complex level of political and economic development but have not reached the point where they can support full-time religious specialists. The shaman remains important as a part-time religious specialist in communal cults, but in addition, members of age grades (hierarchical associations based on age), men's and women's societies, descent groups (corporate groups based on kinship), or other social institutions are enlisted in the performance of communal rituals. These rituals may be seasonal or triggered by events; they may foster group intensification or mark the passage of individuals through the system. What the rituals of communal cults have in common is the aim of achieving some benefit to the society as a whole.

"Ecclesiastical cults" are the most complex form of religious institutions and correspondingly are found only in the more highly developed sociocultural systems. The defining characteristic of such cults is the presence of a "clergy," that is, a cadre of full-time professional religious specialists or "priests" organized into a hierarchical bureaucracy. Societies with ecclesiastical cults are not without shamanistic and communal religious institutions. These simpler types of cults are present also, but the clergy of the ecclesiastical cults differs from their practitioners in that they

> are neither private entrepreneurs (shamans) nor lay officials (the communal religious functionaries), but rather are formally elected or appointed persons who devote all, or at least a regularly scheduled part, of their careers to the priesthood. They are not primarily responsible for supporting the church with money, labor, contributions, and so forth, these burdens being laid upon the congregation or upon sodalities of laymen. Members of the clergy are exclusively responsible for performing certain rituals on behalf of individuals, groups, or the whole community. Within certain areas of behavior—usually extending beyond ritual itself—they claim authority over laymen. (Wallace 1966: 88)

Societies with subsistence organization sufficient to support ecclesiastical cults invariably are also characterized by the presence of other specialized military, economic, political, and social institutions organized along professional bureaucratic lines. The complexity of the religious practice of ecclesiastical cults is matched by the complexity of their associated theory. Wallace notes that such cults tend to center on well-defined gods of great power. Such gods are generally regarded as difficult, even dangerous, for laymen to approach unaided. The pantheons of these cults are of either the Olympian or the monotheistic type. In the former, there are several independent deities; in the latter, a central deity is regarded as dominant (Wallace 1966: 88). Kingsley Davis, speaking in a related manner of the general developmental changes that have occurred in religious theory and practice over the last several thousand years, concludes that

> as humanity moves from small isolated societies in the direction of huge, complex, urbanized ones, the following changes can be noted: *First,* the gods tend to be gradually withdrawn from the local scene. . . . *Second,* anthropomorphism tends to diminish. . . . *Third,* religion tends to be increasingly separated from everyday affairs. . . . *Fourth,* religious homogeneity tends to diminish. . . . *Fifth,* the religious system tends to become fragmented . . . [and] the stage is set for church-state conflict. . . . All of these tendencies can be summed up under the heading of secularization. (1949: 542–43)

Thus, it would appear that the character of the religious organization in a society and the kinds of religious practitioners that are present in it are related to its overall sociocultural scale. This generalization will prove useful in our reconstruction of the Upper Paleolithic period.

## THE ARGUMENT

In *The New Science,* which first appeared in 1725, Giambattista Vico argued that we can come to know history because it has been made by people like ourselves. Through imagination we have the power to understand, to enter into the minds and the institutions of the past. As Vico himself explains:

> In the night of thick darkness enveloping the earliest antiquity, so remote from ourselves, there shines the eternal and never failing light of a truth beyond all question: that the world of civil society has certainly been made by men, and that its principals are therefore to be found within the modifications of our own human mind. Whoever reflects on this cannot but marvel that the philosophers should have bent all their energies to the study of the world of nature, which, since God made it, He alone knows; and that they should have neglected the study of the world of nations, or civil world, which since men had made it, men could come to know. (Goddard and Fisch 1968: 331)

Although rarely explicitly stated, this idea is found at the heart of all archaeological enterprise. We can know the world of the past because that world was the product of *Homo faber*—man the maker. Our affinity with, our sympathy for, these makers allow us to understand them. This is certainly true of their technology and subsistence practices and is perhaps equally true of their religion.

This work illustrates through an analysis of Upper Paleolithic archaeological data some of the ways we can use this sympathy to interpret the material remains recovered by the archaeologist and to reconstruct what appears to be farthest afield from the material. I have formulated a set of syllogisms—two major and two minor premises and a set of conclusions that follow from them. On the structure of these syllogisms I erect my reconstruction of the religion of the Upper Paleolithic. These premises are as follows:

I. All members of the species *Homo sapiens sapiens* share basically similar psychological processes and capabilities.
   1. Due in part to these shared psychological characteristics, human society is not infinitely variable but shows certain regularities throughout time and across culture.
II. Human culture is patterned.
   2. The pattern of "nonmaterial" social life is reflected to a greater or lesser degree in the material aspects of life, including art, settlement and architectural forms, debris disposal, mortuary practices, and so forth.

From these premises I conclude that it is possible to:

1. Use data drawn by anthropology from living societies to help interpret by analogy the remains of societies that have disappeared.
2. Use the patterns of ancient materials as revealed to us by archaeology to infer something about the nonmaterial behavior which produced them.
3. Discover in the external arrangement or prescribed order of prehistoric religious imagery and symbol, clues to the cosmology that once lay behind them.

These methods—inference from ethnographic analogy, material patterns, and formal analysis—cannot lead to certainty. They can, however, allow us to formulate hypotheses about a past which otherwise would be largely unknowable. Methods such as these are our best hope for translating the bones and stones of archaeology back into people. These methods are used to reconstruct the religion of ancient cultural traditions of the Upper Paleolithic period of the late Pleistocene epoch in western Europe. Since nothing of this religious system is known to us from observation or participation, it might be helpful at the outset to illustrate briefly the application of some of these methods to Christianity, a religious system with which we are generally familiar.

### THE PREHISTORY OF CHRISTIANITY—A FANCIFUL EXAMPLE

Suppose for a moment that an archaeologist far in the future is interested in reconstructing the religious system of Europe from A.D. 1 to A.D. 1990 but is confronted by the same dilemma that faces us in dealing with the Upper Paleolithic period, that is, the religious system is extinct and thus can no longer be examined in its systemic context, and written accounts and contemporary religious documents from the period no longer exist. Instead, the archaeologist must rely exclusively on archaeological remains and archaeological context in effecting his reconstruction. Those remains would consist largely of "bare ruined choirs" in Shakespeare's memorable phrase— the structural skeletons of churches, monasteries, and other religious buildings that had either fallen into decay and been forgotten or had been remodeled and used for entirely different purposes. All that would be left would be these bare structural bones, along with the remnants of their decoration and the material debris recovered in association with them. To use these remains to write the culture history of both the theoretical and the practical aspects of European religion during this period, the archaeologist would have to turn to inference from the patterns of material remains, formal analysis of their decoration, and ethnographic analogy.

**Reconstructing the Culture History of Christianity from Its Material Patterns.** Certainly the material patterns presented by Christianity would be the most reliable and useful source of information that could be obtained about the cult from the archaeological record alone. In the absence of written documentation, Christian religious architecture, art, iconography, and mortuary remains would become the primary source of data on European religious and ceremonial life. Like all archaeological remains, these would be partial, fragmentary, and dissociated from their systemic context (their original place in the sociocultural system that produced them). Such dissociation and destruction over time are due to what Rathje and Schiffer call C- and E-Transforms (1980). C-Transforms are human or cultural dissociation activities including deposition, reuse, reclamation, and disturbance.

E-Transforms refers collectively to the transformative forces of the environment including erosion, redeposition, decay, oxidation, and the effects of plants, burrowing animals, and microorganisms. These cultural and environmental transformations create the archaeological context in which the material remains of Christianity would eventually have been recovered. What survived to be discovered would largely be determined by the operation of these forces; thus what is actually discovered is in large measure determined by chance. Nonetheless, by combining chance discovery and intentional archaeological survey, followed by careful excavation of the remains of the period, the archaeologist would be able to do a number of things:

1. Recognize Christian church buildings as a class or type of ceremonial architecture distinct from other classes of public architecture or from domestic structures. This recognition would be based on the distinctive architectural orders, placement, and decoration of church buildings.

2. Develop a typology of these ceremonial buildings and arrange the various subtypes in the presumed chronological order of their appearance, change, and disappearance between A.D. 1 and A.D. 1990.

3. Plot the distribution of the various subtypes of ceremonial buildings across space.

4. Recognize regional subdivisions within the overall religious architectural tradition in Europe and note changes in the degree of variation within the various subdivisions between A.D. 1 and A.D. 1990.

5. Develop a set of inferences about the functions of the various building subtypes based on a) formal similarities and differences in their architectural orders and b) changes in those orders through time.

The recognition of churches as a separate class of building would be an essential initial step in this analysis. Religious architecture occupies an important and distinctive place in the European architectural tradition as a whole. The unique form and layout of church buildings, coupled with the symbol systems and decorative conventions which are so closely associated with these forms, would provide the foundation on which the archaeologist could construct a formal culture sequence and material culture history of Christianity from its earliest appearance in Europe until, in our imaginary example, its final dissolution and disappearance.

Of course, archaeological cultural sequences and culture histories lack the richness, the detail, and the complexity of recorded history. The archaeology of Christianity would speak of changes in form and distribution of classes of structural and material remains through time and space, but the archaeologist could only speculate about the complex doctrinal and political disputes that we know (through written records) to have loomed so large. Likewise, the archaeological record could only hint at the vivid parade of pious and powerful, sinister and heroic personalities that make the written history of the Church intelligible and meaningful to us. Much else would be missing as well: the lives of the saints, the terror of the Inquisition, the first awakenings of the Reformation. However, in the absence of other sources, a great deal *could* be inferred from the pattern of material cultural remains of Christianity.

From the very beginning of this study, the archaeologist would no doubt be aware of the extra-European origins of early Christianity. Further, by plotting the earliest dated appearance of Christian symbolism and ceremonial architecture found throughout Europe, the arrival and spread of the cult throughout the continent could be charted. Next, the growth of Christianity into a powerful economic and political institution during the Middle Ages in Europe is directly, perhaps isomorphically, reflected in the material record by the scale and centrality of the church buildings relative to secular ones in the medieval towns and countryside. For example, the physical domination of church buildings over their surroundings is still evident in the hill towns of central Italy. Viewed from a distance, the skylines of these towns—even of small cities like Siena—seem to draw up and coalesce around the silhouette of their central church buildings. Such structural centrality reflects institutional centrality in these towns, even today.

The economic role played by the Church at all levels of society is recorded materially in the progressive enrichment and elaboration of church buildings, in the cosmopolitan and international elements of their design and decoration, and in the increasing construction of different types of buildings attached to or incorporated within ecclesiastical compounds. For example, in addition to its chapels, cathedral, and chapter houses, the great monastic establishments such as Chartreuse had attached dormitories, kitchens, barns, workshops, and storerooms. The complexity, differentiation, and specialization of the building plans of these ecclesiastical compounds reflect the complex interdependency of human organizations that formerly existed within them. This complex structural interdependency would probably lead our archaeologist to infer that the cult was characterized by well-developed mechanisms of social control and psychological tension-reduction. However, such conclusions would remain inferential since the recognition of actual material remains of religious mechanisms of these kind would be difficult indeed.

On another tack altogether, the archaeologist certainly would not fail to recognize that two great regional stylistic traditions (the Eastern and Western churches) came to exist within Christian Europe sometime around the middle of the culture sequence. Perhaps the most concise characterization of the fundamental differences between these two stylistic traditions is provided by von Simson, who states that in the art and thought of the Eastern Church,

> under the enduring inspiration of the Greek tradition, the ideal of the ultimate beauty remained a visual one; it centered in the image of man. In the West, and under the influence of Augustine, beauty was conceived in musical terms, and even ultimate bliss as the enjoyment of an eternal symphony. And as the icon is thought to partake of the sacred reality it represents, so, according to Augustinian aesthetics, the musical consonances in visual proportions created by man partake of a sacred concord that transcends them. (1956: 24)

The art and architecture of the Eastern and Western churches, organized in accord with these two different principles, contrast markedly. The distribution of the churches in these two different styles, the Greek and the "Augustinian," would provide excellent indicators of the former spatial boundaries of the independent political and social systems that created the two art and architectural traditions. Our archaeologist might be unable to place correctly the centers of these two systems in Rome and Constantinople, but he would surely deduce that the two great regional styles represented two powerful, rival Christian traditions and institutions. Further, upon plotting the shrinking distribution of its later ceremonial architecture through time, the archaeologist would surely observe the waning political fortunes of the Eastern Church in Christendom.

The interior architectural order of European churches would also provide insights into the nature of the Christian religious ceremonies that took place within them. Morgan (1980: xxxii) defines architectural order as "the disciplined relationship of elements in a composition." The basic architectural order in European Christian churches is the alignment of a large nave perpendicular to a central altar and pulpit. In its simplest form, the nave-altar composition is analogous to the architectural order found in the theater, lecture hall, or classroom. In all these arrangements, space is provided for a larger group of people (the audience, class, or congregation) to focus their attention forward to a featured, sometimes elevated, platform on which a drama is performed or from which information is transmitted.

As Brandon (1975:134) explains, church interiors are literally stages for the mass where "the faithful could witness, day after day, the ritual re-presentation of the drama of their salvation." In the first millennium A.D., Christian churches were generally built in basilica style in which the simple directness of the nave-altar architectural order is dominant. The early basilica nave-altar clearly reflects an essential social equality between congregation and celebrant. However, the architectural development of the European church during the nearly two thousand years of its history has been a complex and dynamic one; neither the social relationships nor the architectural order that reflected such relationships remained unchanged. With the development of Romanesque and Gothic church architecture, the actual distance between the nave and altar became greater and physical and visual barriers began to be built between them. New architectural elements such as a wide and empty transept, elevated choirs and sacristies, and even metal fences and altar screens appeared. These new elements impeded direct observation and interaction between congregation and celebrant characteristic of the basic nave-altar architectural order.

Thus it would perhaps be concluded that the increasing structural remoteness in medieval churches was correlated with the emergence of social and professional barriers between congregations and religious specialists. The archaeologist might further note that this process paralleled archaeological evidence of growing social complexity and class stratification in late medieval European society generally.

Later changes in the interior architectural order of European churches reflect the wrenching social and religious ferment of the Reformation. Perhaps the earliest evidence of this change can be observed in the iconoclasm and decorative impoverishment occasioned by the new reforming ideology. Colin Platt provides an excellent example of the kind of material change that would signal the existence of such a social movement to the archaeologist. According to Platt, the parish churches of sixteenth-century England were subject to striking interior structural and decorative changes as a result of the ideological current of the time. Speaking of the interior walls of such churches, he notes:

> Whitewashed out, the grisly lessons of the medieval paintings were replaced by the fundamental text: the Creed, the Lord's Prayer or the Ten Commandments, or selected sentences from the scripture. Over the chancel arch, where the great dooms of the later Middle Ages had customarily confronted the pre-Reformation congregation, there were now set the royal arms, perhaps accompanied, as at Tivetshall in Norfolk, by carefully chosen texts, reinforcing the lessons of authority in the Church, along with the essential elements of its teaching. (1978: 222–23)

The material order at Tivetshall specifically reflects the general replacement of myth and mystery with textual lessons in Protestant countries. Such replacement is apparently also reflected in the changing nature of the nave-altar architectural order. Our archaeologist would note that the formal altar of the late Middle Ages—with its elaborate reredo or altar screen, its niches for the bones of martyrs—is transformed into the simple communion table of the latter-day Protestant churches. At the same time, the pulpit, formerly placed to one side of the nave, moves to the front of it to overshadow the scaled-down altar communion table.

As in the case of the whitewashed walls of the English parish churches, the newly featured speaking platform and the diminished altar reflect the elevation of exhortation above ritual in the emerging Protestant Christianity. At roughly the same time, an impoverishment or simplification of Christian imagery seems to have begun in other portions of Europe. This impoverishment, which became especially pronounced following the close of the German baroque period in the late eighteenth century, would no doubt be interpreted as an indication of an important ideological change in Christianity.

We know from the historical record that the great monastic establishments in England and other Protestant countries were dissolved and their buildings abandoned, razed, or converted to secular purposes. This kind of stylistic and functional transformation would also be apparent in the archaeological record and would give a clear and dramatic clue. Our archaeologist would no doubt interpret this clue in light of two other important trends evident in the data: the increasingly fragmented and distinctly regional styles of religious art and architecture in post-medieval Europe and the conterminous decline in the size and centrality of ceremonial architecture in relation to secular buildings.

Finally, the patterns evident in European mortuary remains would help reconstruct Christian doctrine and practice. Even a cursory examination of the archaeological remains of Christian architecture, art, and iconography would reveal that the Christian religion was deeply and intimately concerned with death. As Brandon notes, "In the vast and diverse legacy of mankind's sepulchral art, Christianity rivals the religions of ancient Egypt in the magnitude of its contribution, though it differs profoundly from it in its inspiration and purpose" (1975: 212). The archaeologist would not be blind to the fact that one major "inspiration and purpose" of Christian sepulchral art and architecture was to demonstrate the active interest and intervention of the dead (at least certain of them) in the everyday affairs of the living. After all, the Christian churches of Europe commonly contain relics, reliquaries, tombs, tomb-shaped altars, memorial tablets, statuary, and other artifacts and structures to commemorate the dead. Some of the greatest cathedrals in Christendom, including the Church of the Holy Sepulchre in Jerusalem, Santiago de Compostela in Spain, Westminster Abbey in England, and numerous others are as much tombshrines as houses of worship. Mortuary structures of this type would suggest that interactions with certain especially honored classes of the dead were as important in Christianity as service to the godhead.

Mortuary studies also would surely reveal that the second inspiration and purpose of Christian sepulchral art and architecture was both to enjoin Christians to *memento mori* and to announce and celebrate the belief in the resurrection of the dead and their eternal afterlife. The belief in such an afterlife is clearly displayed, for example, in the many representations of souls entering heaven or receiving judgment. Negative data would also tell our archaeologist that the afterlife envisioned in Christianity differed in many fundamental ways from everyday life on earth. That is, Christian mortuary practices do not ordinarily involve the provisioning of the corpse with grave goods. The absence of grave goods such as foodstuffs, tools, and weapons or retainers suggests that the Christian afterlife was not viewed as a simple incorporeal duplication of the material world.

Despite the absence of grave furnishings, Christian burials would still reflect the differences in social identities, ranks, and classes present in European society at the time of their interment. Saxe (1970), Binford (1971), Tainter (1977), and numerous other scholars have demonstrated that the structural differentiation and complexity of a society are generally mirrored in its mortuary behavior. Certainly in the location and placement of Christian graves, in the degree of elaboration of their caskets and equipage, in the differences in their markers, the archaeologist would find powerful clues to the economic stratification, the political hierarchy, and the religious organization of European society.

**Reconstructing Christian Religious Theory by Formal Analysis.** If our archaeologist were to undertake a companion study of Christian art and iconography, it would probably confirm the sequence of the development of Christianity inferred from the archaeological remains and lead to an expansion and elaboration of the social implications drawn from that sequence. More than this, however, formal studies of Christian art and symbolism would provide our archaeologist with some insight into the worldview and ethos that lay behind material remains and their social history. Of course, the elusive nature of thought and belief makes the extraction of that ideology from an artistic context perilous and painfully difficult. As Silver (1979) notes, an Australian aborigine might interpret da Vinci's *Last Supper* as merely an animated dinner party. Nevertheless, some conclusions about Christian thought could probably be reached through formal study of its art:

*Christianity is an "Olympian" religion.* Although in our folk view, Christianity is considered to be a uniquely monotheistic form of worship, formal analysis of its symbology gives just the opposite impression. It seems likely that the archaeologist would identify several Christian high gods including Christ in his several aspects and the Virgin Mary. In addition, given the presence of numerous lesser deities, such as saints, angels, devils, and apostles, the subtlety of our folk view would surely be elusive, and our archaeologist would interpret Christianity—correctly, in my view—as a pantheistic cult.

*The Christian pantheon is essentially male-centered.* The central figures in most scenes from the life of Christ are generally males, and the bulk of those on the periphery tend to be males as well. Further, only male beings are depicted as pantocrators or as judges.

*When they do appear, females tend to be depicted in nurturing roles relative to men.* The most prominent example of this tendency is found in representations of the Virgin Mary. In religious scenes in which she appears as a central figure, she generally shares this placement with the image of Christ whose nimbus marks him as a divinity. His placement near her breast (which often is exposed) would appear to suggest that the Virgin Mary has an important role to play in human fertility. While this may be true in folk practice, such a conclusion on the part of the archaeologist would be misleading and probably cloud the recognition that the central aspect of the goddess is her virginity. Perhaps the archaeologist would recognize or infer that aspects of her worship functioned as a mechanism of tension-reduction and psychological support.

*Females not shown nurturing males are generally depicted as subordinate to them.* For example, one of the most common representations of Mary Magdalene shows her as the penitent sinner anointing the feet of Christ.

*The Christian pantheon is structured and hierarchical in nature.* This would be suggested by the numerous depictions of divinities or martyrs (generally male) enthroned, crowned, or marked with a nimbus and surrounded by figures whose size, aspect, or position relative to the central figure suggests subordination to it. Further, numerous religious scenes show individuals performing acts of obedience or self-mortification before another figure. The fact that the central figure is often a child suggests that the status in this hierarchy was immanent or inherited rather than earned through personal accomplishment. Of course, the very essence of a stratified social system is that it demands respect be shown for the position or office, regardless of the individual who occupies it. While the conclusion that the Christian pantheon was rigidly hierarchical would be correct, it could also be a source of confusion or distortion. For example, what place would be assigned to such "lesser deities"—saints, angels, and the Apostles—in the hierarchy? More difficult still, what interpretation would be given to depictions of Christ washing the feet of his disciples, being arrested in the Garden of Gethsemane, judged by Pilate, beaten by the mob, crowned with thorns, and crucified? Would the archaeologist recognize these scenes as recounting events from the life of a divinity or simply stand mute and perplexed before them, certain only that their meaning lay just beyond grasp?

*A complex set of symbolic and ideological associations exists among the major figures of the Christian pantheon.* The systematic association of major figures in the pantheon with vivid natural symbols might provide the archaeologist with insight into the nature of these figures. For example, Christ's association with the lamb, St. Sebastian's with arrows, St. Peter's with keys, and the Virgin Mary's association with flowers like the rose, columbine, lily, and violet might prove helpful in this regard.

*In the Christian worldview, the world is a violent and dangerous place.* Violence and danger are common themes in Christian art. Events like Christ's flagellation, his crowning with thorns, and his crucifixion are vividly represented in a variety of sacred contexts. Likewise, scenes like the martyrdom of early Christians, the slaughter of the Innocents, or Abraham sacrificing Isaac are common. But the juxtaposition of such images with those of peace and nurturance, of lions lying down with the lambs, and kisses of peace would surely be perplexing.

*Christianity has a well-developed belief in a spiritual life after death.* Artistic representations of Christ's resurrection, the soul's release from the body, the raising of the dead at the end of the world, and a host of other images would make this conclusion inescapable. Conceivably, however, some of these images might lead to the erroneous conclusion that a doctrine of reincarnation was also present in Christianity.

*Fear of divine judgment and punishment in the afterlife is an important element in maintaining adherence to the Christian ethos.* Certainly, the meaning of the vivid depictions of the judgment of souls and of the torment of the damned so common in Christian art would not be lost on our archaeologist. From such scenes the conclusion that religious sanction was an important mechanism of social control in Europe could easily be deduced.

**Ethnographic Analogy and the Reconstruction of Christianity.** The material remains of European religious behavior of the last two millennia would provide an archaeologist with at least the broad outline of the history of Christianity: its inception and spread through Europe, its ideological and political triumph, its reformation, and its decline. The formal analysis of architectural patterns, art, iconography, and mortuary remains would yield important insights into the ceremonial patterns, and yes, even clues to the complex ideology of Christianity. What could ethnographic analogy contribute to the picture? Actually, the analysis of material patterns and of formal symbol systems both are based on analogy; both tasks proceed from Vico's assumption that, "since men had made it, men could come to know it."

More than this, however, the archaeologist might use knowledge of ethnography to posit that Christianity provided rites of passage (especially funeral rites) as well as important mechanisms of social control, psychological support, and social integration in the societies of which it was a part. Of course, recognizing those mechanisms in the archaeological record might prove to be difficult in practice. Further, the scale and duration of the material remains of Christianity, along with the pervasive nature of its symbology, would no doubt convince our scholar that strong connections existed between the theory and practice of Christianity and the material basis of life in Europe between A.D. I and A.D. 1990. While remaining uncertain of the specific nature of these connections, the archaeologist would surely be inspired to seek them out.

An uncritical use of ethnographic analogy in the interpretation of these material remains, however, might lead to a distortion in the archaeological reconstruction. Viewing the scale and pervasiveness of archaeological remains of Christianity, the religion might be interpreted as a profoundly conservative state-sponsored cult whose political and economic interconnections with society at large were designed simply to contribute to the *status quo.* While this has, of course, been true of Christianity at various times and places in its history, such an interpretation neglects the potentially revolutionary nature of its message, obscures its origins as a radical revitalization movement in the early centuries of the common era, and does not give due attention to the perpetual reuse of its millennarian message in the peasant revolts of the late Middle Ages as well as in the Protestant Reformation in the centuries that followed.

Suffice it to say that in any archaeological reconstruction of this kind, much would be missing and much would have been irretrievably lost. Yet, at the conclusion of the labors, the future archaeologist would know a great deal about Christianity between A.D. 1 and A.D. 1990. More importantly, the scholar would be able to ask the right questions of the data in future research. Similar results can be achieved in reconstructing the religious systems in the Upper Paleolithic period of southwestern Europe. Patterns are evident in the material remains of these late Pleistocene epoch cultures, their art and symbols likewise are susceptible to formal analysis, and the ethnographies of modern hunter-gatherers provide a likely source of analogic interpretation. Perhaps this fanciful example will embolden the reader to accompany us in our attempt at reconstructing religious life in the Upper Paleolithic period.

# 2. An Overview of the Pleistocene and Paleolithic

Through uranium/lead and potassium/argon age determinations, cosmogenic modeling and other means, the age of the earth has been calculated at between 4.5 and 5 billion years. Geologists divide this time span into four eras: the Precambrian or Proterozoic, the Paleozoic, the Mesozoic, and the Cenozoic. Humanity's tenure on earth—our appearance in this 4.5-billion-year time stream—is at the most recent end of the latest or Cenozoic era. The australopithecines, hominid forms apparently ancestral to modern people, appeared a mere 4 to 6 million years ago, during the late Miocene or early Pliocene epochs; fully modern *Homo sapiens sapiens* first appeared during the late Pleistocene epoch, perhaps as early as 115,000 B.P. in southern Africa and as late as 33,000 B.P. in Europe.

While the very immensity of these dates makes them elusive and difficult to comprehend, we can more easily appreciate both the magnitude of the earth's age and the recent nature of humanity's appearance on it if we model the age of the earth with a twenty-four-hour day by making each second equivalent to fifty thousand years (Wolpoff 1980: 14). On such a scale, the australopithecines—the earliest definite hominids—appeared slightly more than two minutes before midnight and fully modern people only one or perhaps two *seconds* before day's close.

## THE PLEISTOCENE GEOLOGICAL EPOCH IN THE OLD WORLD

The terms "Pleistocene epoch" and "Paleolithic period" are distinct but closely related concepts which are commonly confused. The Paleolithic period is a unit of time used by prehistorians "to organize archaeological evidence so that it can be interpreted in terms of cultural change" (Rowe 1962: 40). The Paleolithic period begins almost three million years ago with the earliest evidence of hominid cultural activity and closes at around ten thousand years before the present.

The Pleistocene epoch, on the other hand, is a geological time period defined largely on the basis of the stratigraphic analysis and chronometric dating of sediment series and on changes in the fossil record within these sediments. The term Pleistocene includes the time between the end of the Pliocene epoch nearly two million years ago and about ten thousand years before the present. These last ten thousand years are then termed the Holocene, the Recent or the Postglacial epoch. Collectively, the Holocene and the Pleistocene epochs constitute the Quaternary period. Most of the events of the Paleolithic cultural period occurred during the Pleistocene epoch.

Although the Pleistocene epoch was complex and varied, our present understanding suggests that it was characterized by at least seven major processes or phenomena. First, the epoch witnessed a global increase in explosive volcanic activity and other igneous events (Kennett and Thunell 1975). Secondly, it was characterized in the higher latitudes of the earth by great cycles of continental glacial expansion punctuated by periods of interglaciation, or the remission and disappearance of most continental ice masses. Although the Pleistocene epoch is commonly styled "the Ice Age," it is now recognized that it was not the only ice age in the earth's history (Crowel and Frakes 1970). Nonetheless, the frequency and duration of continental glaciation during the Pleistocene renders the epoch very unusual.

Third, marked changes in worldwide sea levels occurred during the Pleistocene in concert with the cycles of glaciation and interglaciation. During periods of glaciation, great quantities of water were withdrawn from the oceans and converted into ice, resulting in a lowering of worldwide sea levels by as much as 100 to 150 meters. Lower sea levels exposed large portions of the continental shelves as dry land and created land bridges connecting previously isolated land masses, such as England and the continent of Europe, Java and the Malay Peninsula, Japan with the Asian Mainland and Alaska and Siberia. Conversely, increases in sea level consequent upon the reduction of glacial ice during interglacial periods reduced the amount of land exposed on the continental shelves and once again isolated these land masses from one another. The cyclical isolation and reconnection of land areas during the Pleistocene had a powerful impact on patterns of plant and animal distribution and evolution as well as upon human cultural development and interaction.

A fourth characteristic of the Pleistocene epoch was its numerous and, in terms of geological time, its rapid climatic and environmental changes. Dramatic climatic alterations began to occur some 0.7 million years ago with the onset of the periods of major continental glaciation during the middle and late Pleistocene. According to Butzer, the mean annual temperatures in northern latitudes during these periods ranged from 15° to 18° C colder than today and 1° to 6° C cooler in the middle latitudes and tropics. In many regions of the world, periods of glacial maxima were also generally more arid than either interglacial or modern times due to reduced ocean evaporation, greater quantities of permanent ice, and greater tropical atmospheric stability (Butzer 1976: 40).

Fifth, the Pleistocene epoch was characterized by extensive changes in the distribution of plants and animals, largely in response to the cyclical periods of glacial advance and retreat and to the climatic oscillations that accompanied these cycles. Of course these extensive changes in plant and animal biogeography were facilitated by land bridges during periods of glacial advance and impeded by rising sea levels during periods of interglaciation.

The sixth attribute of the Pleistocene was the accelerated pace of worldwide mammalian evolution and extinction (Lundelius 1976: 56). For example, the Villafranchian faunal assemblage, which marks the beginning of the epoch in Europe, is characterized by the appearance of three new groups of mammals: the modern horse (genus *Equus*) and the true bovines and the true elephants (Kurten 1971: 197). The onset of the major glacial episodes in the middle and late Pleistocene is correlated with the appearance in the Northern Hemisphere of reindeer (*Rangifer*) and musk ox (*Ovibos*) and a large number of other species presumably adapted to conditions of extreme cold (Kurten 1968: 253; Lundelius 1976: 50). The faunal assemblages of the interglacial and interstadial stages which separated the various glaciations included warm-loving species such as *Hippopotamus* and *Hyaena perrieri*. It appears that each successive interglacial was somewhat cooler than the one that preceded it.

A final, and from the standpoint of this book, the most important characteristic of the Pleistocene epoch is its provision of the great setting for the evolution of the hominid line. It is near the end of the epoch that our subspecies *Homo sapiens sapiens* emerges in prehistory.

## THE EVOLUTION OF THE HOMINIDS IN THE PLIOCENE
## AND PLEISTOCENE EPOCH

The taxonomic family *Hominidae*—the hominids—includes all living and fossil forms of humankind. The family is divided into two genuses: *Australopithecus*, all of whose members are now extinct, and *Homo*, which contains both fossil and living forms. From the standpoint of our species at least, the two most significant events of the last 4 million years have been the emergence of the hominid line within the Primate order, and the evolution of the genus *Homo* within the hominid line. While these events can never be reconstructed with complete precision, recent studies in molecular biology, paleoecology, and human paleontology have begun to clarify their outline considerably (Yunis and Prakash 1982; Ciochon 1983; Pilbeam 1984a, 1984b).

Current evidence suggests that the earliest definite hominids—the small-brained but upright and bipedal australopithecines—appeared in Tanzania and Ethiopia between 3.8 and 3.5 million years ago near the end of the Pliocene epoch. Hominids referrable to this genus persisted in South and East Africa for nearly 3 million years, and disappeared in the middle of the Lower Pleistocene about 1 million years ago (Cronin, Boas, Stringer, Rak 1981: 113).

The genus appears to have been a varied one. Four, and perhaps five, separate forms of australopithecines have been recognized by various scholars. The status of these various forms remains controversial, however. Yet to be resolved is the question of whether they represent separate species, subspecies, or races, or merely sexual dimorphism and the variation to be expected within a single lineage evolving over more than 3 million years (Pilbeam 1984a: 94–95; Wolpoff 1980: 156).

Sometime between about 2.2 and 1.8 million years ago, a new, larger-brained form of hominid appears in the East and South African fossil record. This hominid is classified as an advanced australopithecine by some students and as *Homo habilis* (a separate genus and species) by others, or most recently, simply as *Homo* sp. Depending upon the characteristics one chooses to emphasize, this form either culminates the developmental history of the genus *Australopithecus* or marks the first appearance of the new genus *Homo* in the family *Hominidae* (Leakey, Tobias, Napier 1964; Robinson 1965; Tobias 1965; Cronin, Boas, Stringer, Rak 1981: 113).

Paleoanthropologists are less certain about the lineal connections between *Homo habilis* and *Homo erectus,* the next hominid form in the Pleistocene fossil record. *Homo erectus* fossils recovered at the Sangrian site in eastern Java date to 1.9 million years ago (Ninkovich and Burkle 1978), while the earliest found in the Omo region date to between 1.6 and 1.5 million years. The most recent remains of *Homo habilis* (or *Homo* sp.) are from the Lake Turkana region and date to ca. 1.3 million years ago (Leakey and Walker 1976). Thus, *Homo erectus* apparently coexisted in northeast Africa with *Homo habilis* as well as with a robust form of australopithecine, *Australopithecus boisei* (Walker and Leakey 1978). The overall size and general morphology of the *Homo erectus* post-cranial skeleton is within the range of variation found in modern people.

*Homo erectus* was apparently a stable taxon, exhibiting little morphological change throughout most of its long history. From the perspective of our species, these characteristics appear primitive. Nonetheless, *Homo erectus* was a successful evolutionary form which persisted on earth for more than 1.5 million years.

With the exception of *Homo modjokertensis,* a possible *Homo habilis* from the Djetis beds in Java, all australopithecine and habiline fossils recovered to date are from South or East Africa. If this recovery ratio is not due to sampling error, it suggests that Plio-Pleistocene hominids were limited to unforested tropical and subtropical habitats during the two to four million years of their existence. That *Homo erectus* was not so constrained is clearly reflected in the recovery of fossils of that species from sites as far afield as Algeria, Java, and China. The wide geographical distribution of these sites indicates that certainly by one million years ago, *Homo erectus* was capable of accommodating himself to a varied and demanding range of environments. With the appearance of this species, the adaptive radiation of the hominid line begins in earnest.

In Europe, scattered and fragmentary evidence of a hominid presence—presumably that of *Homo erectus* or some closely related form—has been recovered from contexts dating to the beginning of the Middle Pleistocene around 730,000 years ago. The most notable site of this age is Vertessollos in Hungary which has produced fragmentary hominid skeletal remains together with traces of fire, animal bone, and abundant stone tools. Definite evidence for the presence of hominids in Europe in the Middle Pleistocene has also been recovered from southwestern France, central Italy, Czechoslovakia, and elsewhere. Less certainly, an even earlier Lower Pleistocene occupation of Europe has been reported from the sites of Vallonet Cave and Chilhac in France and at several other localities (Bordes and Thibault 1977).

During the Middle Pleistocene sometime between 600,000 to 500,000 years ago, *Homo erectus* apparently begins to be succeeded in the Old World by the earliest intermediate or "archaic" *Homo sapiens*. Only a handful of fragmentary skeletal remains has been recovered as evidence of this succession. Notable examples come from Arago Cave and Fontechevade in southwestern France, the Swanscombe quarry near London, Steinheim and Mauer in Germany, Petralona in Greece, as well as from South Africa, Zambia, and Java. As a consequence, the presumed evolution of the *Homo sapiens* line out of *Homo erectus* is poorly documented. In any event, by about 300,000 B.P., well before the end of the Middle Pleistocene epoch, *Homo erectus* has disappeared from the fossil record (Pilbeam 1984a: 96).

The archaic *Homo sapiens* are a diverse group of hominid fossils characterized by robust cranial features but enlarged cranial capacity. As the name implies, their physical morphology and temporal position situate them intermediately between *Homo erectus*, characterized by robust features and relatively modest cranial capacity, and later forms of *Homo sapiens*, characterized by cranial capacity in the modern range and cranial architecture that evolves over time from robust to increasingly more gracile form.

The Middle Pleistocene comes to an end around 130,000 B.P. with the close of the Penultimate glacial stage and the onset of the Last Interglacial. The Upper Pleistocene period dates to between about 130,000 and 10,000 B.P. It is sometime during the first 30,000 or 40,000 years of this final period (ca. 130,000 to 90,000 B.P.) that the earliest examples of *Homo sapiens neanderthalensis* first appear in Europe and the Middle East (Trinkaus and Howells 1979: 125).

Following Trinkaus and Howells, I restrict the term *Homo sapiens neanderthalensis* to the "classic" Neanderthal of former usage. This form is characterized by a low, platycephalic skull with prominent brow ridges, sloping forehead and nose, and teeth positioned markedly forward with regard to the cranial vault. Although the robustness of the Neanderthal cranium is reminiscent of *Homo erectus*, the cranial capacity falls within—and often exceeds—the size range of modern human populations. Analysis of Neanderthal post-cranial skeletons indicates that both males and females were bulky, solidly built, heavily muscled, and had more powerful arms, shoulders and hands than modern peoples (Trinkaus and Howells 1979: 127–28).

The Neanderthal anatomical pattern is apparently limited to Europe and southwestern Asia. Of the contemporary fossils from outside this region, the earlier ones are generally best considered archaic *Homo sapiens;* the later ones, in parts of Africa and Australia at least, as *Homo sapiens sapiens* (Trinkaus and Howells 1979: 125–31; Beaumont, de Villers, and Vogel 1978: 416).

The adaptive radiation of the hominid line begun so dramatically by *Homo erectus* continues with Neanderthal. The rigorous subarctic environments of central Europe are penetrated by this hominid, sparking the contention that the classic Neanderthal pattern was a genetic response to conditions of extreme cold with the pattern becoming established in European hominid breeding populations because of their geographical isolation during the last glacial stage (Howell 1957). Others interpret the robust Neanderthal facial morphology as largely the product of cultural behavior, specifically, the extensive and heavy use of the teeth and jaws by Neanderthals in chewing tough foods and as tools for the processing of hides and the performance of other tasks. In this scenario, the hominid face began to assume its gracile modern form when improvements in technology during the Upper Paleolithic period led to a reduction in the use of the teeth and jaws as tools and a "culinary revolution" characterized by more efficient food preparation techniques (Brace 1962, 1979).

On the other hand, there are suggestions that the emergence of the modern cranial morphology reflects the evolution of the capacity for speech in our species (and its absence in *Homo sapiens neanderthalensis* and earlier hominids) (Lieberman and Crelin 1971, Lieberman 1976). However, Tobias (1981) asserts that endocasts of australopithecine crania indicate development of "Broca's area," a region in modern skeletal anatomy closely related to speech. He suggests that even these early hominids possessed a rudimentary language (also cf., Falk 1980).

The date of the transition or emergence of fully modern hominids is also uncertain. *Homo sapiens sapiens* fossils ranging from primitive or archaic appearance to a quite modern one have been recovered in early Upper Pleistocene contexts in southern Africa. Dates suggest that the transformation of archaic *Homo sapiens* populations into modern *Homo sapiens sapiens* perhaps began as early as 100,000 years ago in Africa. Radiation of anatomically modern peoples from Africa during the early Upper Pleistocene thus seems a strong possibility (Beaumont, deVillers, and Vogel 1978; Stringer and Andrews 1988).

Elsewhere in the Old World the appearance of *Homo sapiens sapiens* seems to have occurred later. Anatomically modern hominid skeletal material recovered from a Mousterian level at Jebel Qafzeh Cave in Israel may date to before 90,000 years ago (Villadas et al. 1988). Skeletal remains from Israel and Iraq indicate that the transition to anatomical modernity took place in the Near East between about 45,000 and 40,000 years ago (Trinkaus and Howells 1979: 581).

Although the precise date is still in dispute, present evidence suggests that fully modern *Homo sapiens sapiens* did not appear in Europe until sometime after 35,000 B.P. Scholars have had difficulty accounting for the Upper Paleolithic period replacement of Neanderthal by *Homo sapiens sapiens* in Europe. Three competing hypotheses have been proposed. As framed by ApSimon, these include:

1. straightforward evolutionary transformation *in situ* of Neanderthal into *sapiens*

2. immigration of *sapiens* leading to the extinction of the Neanderthals

3. *sapiens* immigration followed by interbreeding in which the distinctive characters of the Neanderthals were lost. (1980: 271)

It is now clear that substantial differences exist between *Homo sapiens neanderthalensis* and *Homo sapiens sapiens* and that the transition from one form to the other in the fossil record is marked by important changes in the hominid cranium, post-cranial skeleton, and dentition (Howell 1975; Trinkaus and Howells 1979; Stringer 1974, 1982). The emerging consensus is that *Homo sapiens sapiens* are less like classic Neanderthals than they are like certain late archaic *Homo sapiens* and, therefore, it is unlikely that the classic European Neanderthals were direct ancestors of modern people (ApSimon 1980: 271; Stringer 1982; Stringer, Hublin, and Vandermeersch 1984: 115–24). Current evidence would seem to favor the hypothesis that *Homo sapiens sapiens* evolved outside Europe from archaic *Homo*

*sapiens* stock but immigrated there, submerging Neanderthal genetic material in their breeding population in the process (cf., Smith
1984: 192–98).

As noted above, the post-cranial skeletons of modern people tend
to be lighter, more slender, and less powerful than those of Neanderthals. Along with this general decline in skeletal robustness, the
morphology of the female pelvis changes in *Homo sapiens sapiens.*
Pilbeam (1984a: 96) takes these changes as suggesting that "formerly
easy births had become harder or even that the time of gestation
was being reduced to our present nine months from perhaps eleven
months (a period in line with predictions based on general mammalian relations among maternal body size, fetal size and length of
gestation)."

Sexual dimorphism is also reduced in late Upper Pleistocene
*Homo sapiens sapiens* populations as compared with those of the
Neanderthals. And, as Frayer (1978) notes, sexual dimorphism in our
species continues to decline following the close of the Pleistocene
epoch in the subsequent Mesolithic period. He states that while late
Pleistocene males show consistently larger dimensions than their
Mesolithic descendants, females from the two periods are relatively
stable in postcranial dimensions.

Frayer relates this reduction in male robustness to changing hunting patterns. He hypothesizes that there occurred at this time climate change and extinction which led to a general reduction in the
size and aggressiveness of the game animals being hunted in Europe,
and an improvement in the effectiveness of the tools and weapons
used to hunt them. He suggests that such changes would result in the
development of new hunting strategies that placed less reliance upon
simple physical strength. Assuming that later Paleolithic peoples
divided labor by sex, such changes would reduce the selective advantage of large body size in males. Since female activities would be
unaffected by these developments, little change would be expected in
their body sizes. Frayer's model is perhaps even more plausible as an
explanation of the reduced sexual dimorphism in *Homo sapiens
sapiens* populations as compared to Neanderthals, since the technical contrasts between the cultures associated with the two forms are
even more dramatic than those between the cultures of the terminal
Pleistocene and the early Holocene epochs.

Perhaps the most important differences between Neanderthals and modern people were not directly reflected in their contrasting skeletal morphology. Rather these differences were probably mental and behavioral. The appearance of *Homo sapiens sapiens* is correlated with a series of fundamental technical changes in the hominid cultural repertoire and with evidence of increasingly complex aesthetic and religious impulses. Separated as we are from these terminal Pleistocene people by time, their culture nonetheless seems familiar in its essentials. With the appearance of *Homo sapiens sapiens*, another important intellectual watershed in evolution is surely crossed.

## THE LOWER AND MIDDLE PALEOLITHIC PERIOD
## IN THE OLD WORLD

The Paleolithic period begins with the earliest evidence of hominid cultural activity. This early evidence consists mainly of the remains of stone-tool manufacture in Africa. At present, the earliest reported occurrence of stone tools dates to between 2.9 and 2.5 million years ago from the Hadar region of Ethiopia (Lewin 1981: 806; Klein 1983: 26). However, the recovery of a possible tool from Miocene deposits dated between 9 and 10 million years ago in India (Prasad 1983) suggests that earlier industrial traditions remain to be discovered and that 3 million years ago is probably a minimum for the onset of the Paleolithic period.

Subdivisions of the Paleolithic period into Lower, Middle, and Upper portions are generally made with reference to changes in stone-tool form and technology which have occurred through time in the archaeological record (see table below). The detailed charting of these changes through time has been called by Laville, Rigaud, and Sackett (1980: 31) "archaeological systematics." Although they are referring specifically to the French Perigord, they could have been speaking of many areas of Africa and Europe when they state that the development of such systematics has

> been one of the most impressive achievements of modern prehistoric research. It has called for refined techniques of excavation to ensure that the artifact assemblages are precisely segregated in terms of individual stratigraphic units of occupation, the design of more refined typologies for classifying stone tools according to their form, and the adoption of quantitative methods whereby artifact assemblages may be compared and then classified into industries not simply in terms of the presence and absence of these artifact types but also according to their relative frequencies. (Laville, Rigaud, Sackett 1980: 31)

Plio-Pleistocene and Paleolithic Time Scales

| B.P. | Geological Time | Archaeological Time | B.P. |
|---|---|---|---|
| | | Neolithic | |
| 10,000_ | Holocene | Mesolithic | _ 10,000 |
| | Upper Pleistocene | Upper Paleolithic | _ 35,000 |
| 128,000_ | | Middle Paleolithic | _ 90,000 |
| | Middle Pleistocene | Lower Paleolithic | |
| 730,000_ | | | |
| | Lower Pleistocene | | |
| 1,720,000_ | | | |
| | Late Pliocene | | _2,900,000 |
| 3,400,000_ | | | |

It may be said that in general terms studies of archaeological systematics of the Old World Paleolithic period indicate that stone-tool technology—and hominid culture as a whole—has moved from simplicity towards increasing complexity through time. Painfully slow at first, technical development in the Paleolithic continued throughout the period and began to accelerate dramatically by its late or Upper portion.

Presumably, the first tools were little more than "naturefacts," that is, sticks, bones, or stones taken up by early hominids and used directly and without modification. Due to the difficulty of identifying naturefacts, we are forced to begin the Lower Paleolithic period with the earliest definite evidence for the modification of such natural materials into artifacts. Evidence of such modification is found in the so-called Oldowan stone-tool tradition, named after the type site at Olduvai Gorge. The Oldowan tradition is characterized by crudely made, elementary core and flake tools which show a very limited typological variability. Mary Leakey (1971) recognizes a scant six distinct tool types in the earliest Oldowan assemblages from Olduvai Gorge and only ten in the more evolved developed Oldowan there. The center piece of the industry is the so-called unifacial pebble tool, or chopper. Oldowan choppers are merely cobble-sized stones on which a cutting edge has been created through the removal or subtraction of several flakes from one face by striking the core against a stone anvil or hitting it directly with a hammerstone. In addition to unifacial choppers, Oldowan industries include a limited variety of other kinds of core artifacts including spheroids, discoids, polyhedrals, and bifacially flaked chopping tools and proto-bifaces.

Precisely who made the Oldowan tools and what they used them for remains unclear. A widespread view in paleoanthropology credits their manufacture to *Homo habilis*. However, Oldowan tools which predate the appearance of *Homo habilis* presumably were made by some form of australopithecine. Oldowan tools from the Hadar region may have been made by *Australopithecus afarensis* or a somewhat later form of australopithecine. Other East African locations yielding Oldowan assemblages date to between 2.1 and 1.6 million years ago, a time range that corresponds fairly closely with the appearance of both *Australopithecus bosei* and *Homo habilis* (Klein 1983: 26). In addition, developed Oldowan artifacts have been recovered in southern Africa. It is often asserted that these tools, and the scattered animal-bone debris associated with them at Olduvai Gorge and elsewhere, indicate that the hominids of the Lower Paleolithic period were perhaps already hunting horses, pigs, bovids, or even game animals as large as *Elephas reckii*. Beginning with Washburn and Avis (1958), it has been widely assumed that this apparent shift from the gathering of vegetal foodstuffs to a reliance on hunting is correlated with increasing hominid brain size, the use of stone tools, the development of a sexual division of labor, the disappearance of the estreus cycle, and the emergence of the nuclear family.

Recent studies of predator and scavenger behavior—and of the bone debris such behavior leaves behind—leads Brain (1981) and Binford (1981, 1983, 1987) to the conclusion that early hominids were not hunters on the African savannah-grasslands but instead probably filled a niche as scavengers around the water holes there. To these scholars, the early hominids were more likely to fall prey to larger animals than to act as predators themselves. However, based on his study of predatory animals on the Serengeti Plains of Africa,

Schaller (1972: 68) thinks it unlikely that any large species could subsist there exclusively by scavenging. Early hominids might have been able occasionally to drive predators like lions or hyenas off their kills or managed to kill newborn, young, or sick individual game animals for themselves. Schaller suggests that early hominids would also probably have had to combine such activities with gathering. In any event, unlike the teeth of the australopithecines, those of the habilines suggest such creatures were not primarily vegetarians (Pilbeam 1984a, 1984b); beyond this observation, much remains conjectural.

***Homo Erectus* and the Lower Paleolithic Period.**  Beyond the rudiments of technology, we have only the barest outlines of the nature of subsistence and social life during the later Lower Paleolithic period. Possible evidence of the intentional use of fire by hominids sometime after 500,000 B.P. has been reported from contexts as early as 1.7 million years ago in Yuanmou, China (Jia 1985) and 1.4 million years ago from Chesowanja, Kenya (Gowlett et al. 1981). In addition, possible fire hearths have been recovered at the site of Chou-k'ou-tien (or Zhoukoudian) near Beijing in northern China. Clusters of postmolds and fire hearths exposed at the Terra Amata site in Nice, France, suggest that by the end of the Lower Paleolithic period, these hominids may have put up simple shelters and warmed them artificially (de Lumley 1969). Further, archaeological remains at sites like Torralba and Ambrona in north-central Spain suggest that hominids of the Lower Paleolithic period might have begun to hunt animals as large as elephant, horse, cattle, and steppe rhinoceros by means of cooperative fire drives (Howell 1965: 85–100; Freeman 1975: 247–48; but cf., Binford 1984; Binford and Ho 1985: 428; James 1989). The importance of these changes in terms of the hominid cultural adaptation is reflected in the marked expansion in geographic distribution of the hominid line witnessed by the end of the Lower Paleolithic period. As noted above, while the australopithecines appear to have been limited to the tropical and subtropical regions of Africa, *Homo erectus* fossils and sites dating to the last million years have been reported from the arid regions of South Africa, the North China plain, Java, southern and southeast Asia, the Mediterranean basin, southwest Asia, and southern Europe. Such evidence becomes increasingly common after about 500,000 years ago.

Presumably, the combination of an increasingly efficient tool kit, the ability to create artificial "interior environments" by building shelters and warming them with fire, and the nascent ability to organize and coordinate group efforts in common tasks like hunting led to an expansion in both the population size and the range of the species. Just as modern people adapt to hostile environments like the surface of the moon or the bottom of the ocean by cultural means, so the hominids of the Lower Paleolithic period accommodated themselves to an increasingly diverse range of circumstances largely by cultural, rather than biological change.

If this in fact is the case, it suggests that, with the emergence of *Homo erectus* sometime between 1.9 and 1.5 million years ago, an important threshold in the development both of social organization and the intellect had been crossed. Measuring "intellect" is a difficult task for the archaeologist. Nonetheless, using Jean Piaget's theory of intelligence, Wynn (1979) attempts to assess the intellectual capacity of *Homo erectus.* Piaget's theory posits four kinds of "operational spatial organization" as characteristic of the thought processes of modern adults: whole-part relations, qualitative displacement, spatio-temporal substitution, and symmetry. These operational modes of thought make it possible for individuals to work toward preconceived goals. In Piaget's view, children have an "organizational repertoire of preoperational thought." That is, they do not have a clear picture of the end product in mind before they begin a creative task; consequently, they work largely by trial and error until they achieve an acceptable result. Presumably, neither did our earliest hominid ancestors.

Wynn, interested in determining at what point modern "operational thought" came to characterize hominid thinking, examined the "geometry" of the stone tools from Oldowan and developed Oldowan assemblages recovered at Olduvai Gorge in Bed I and lower Bed II respectively and from the late Acheulian site of Isimila in Tanzania in terms of Piaget's four kinds of operational spatial organization. He concludes that while the makers of these late Acheulian implements employed "operational concepts of space" identical to those of modern *Homo sapiens sapiens,* the "Oldowan artifacts . . . did not require operational intelligence for their manufacture" (Wynn 1979: 385, 388). That is, the *Homo habilis* or australopithecine fabricators of the Oldowan tool kits did not achieve standard shapes, regular cross sections, or symmetry in their implements because they were working essentially at the "preoperational level" of thought. In Wynn's (1979: 390) view, the emergence of modern operational modes of thought may have occurred a million or more years ago with the appearance of *Homo erectus.*

Significantly, it is also among *Homo erectus* that we begin to find some of the earliest evidence of what Edwards (1978: 135) calls a "concern with realities transcending mere biological needs." The evidence of this concern cited by Edwards includes the intentional collection and use of ochre or other red-colored rocks and minerals, the special treatment of human and perhaps animal skulls, the refinement of utilitarian objects beyond the simple requirements of their purpose, and the possible appearance of rudimentary symbolic or artistic engraving on bone.

Perhaps the most dramatic indication that *Homo erectus* was concerned with more than simple survival is the evidence that these hominids intentionally collected and used ochre or other red-colored rocks and minerals. In recent years a number of scholars have called attention to the presence of red ochre in early sites and have suggested that such specimens offer important insight into the development of human cognition (for example, Blanc 1961: 123; Edwards 1978: 136; Wreschner 1980; Schmandt-Besserat 1980; Marshack 1981).

The term "ochre" refers to certain common iron oxides such as hematite, goethite, and limonite which occur naturally in a wide range of colors including red, yellow, brown, black, orange, even violet. Ochres are generally soft and leave a colored streak when they are rubbed against a harder surface, make excellent stains, paints, or dyes when ground into powder and used directly or mixed with a medium such as water or animal fat, and often change color dramatically when heated.

Specimens of ochre have been reported from some of the oldest occupation or activity sites known from the Lower Paleolithic period in the Old World, including Bed II at Olduvai Gorge in Tanzania, Ambrona in Spain, Terra Amata in France, and Becov in Czechoslovakia. The use of ochre apparently increases during the Middle Paleolithic period in the Mousterian tradition and becomes common in the Upper Paleolithic period.

Ochre has no apparent practical or technological use until the development of iron metallurgy sometime in the second millennium before Christ when it becomes a principal ore for iron smelting. Nonetheless, many of the Paleolithic period ochre specimens show evidence of having been worked or utilized in some fashion. For example, the two lumps of ochre recovered at Olduvai Gorge show signs of having been struck directly by hammerstone blows (M. Leakey 1971). Howell (1965: 129) states that the ochre specimen recovered at Ambrona showed evidence of shaping and trimming, although Butzer (1980: 635) asserts this may only be natural cleavage. Still the ochre comes from the same horizon as the famous linear arrangement of elephant tusks and bones and was probably brought to the site by the hominids who are thought to have killed and butchered elephants there.

At Terra Amata, which was occupied around 300,000 B.P., de Lumley (1969: 49) reports a number of ochre specimens recovered from the two occupation layers associated with the pole structures uncovered at the site. Specimens of red, yellow, and brown were recovered and the range of color variations suggests the ochre may have been heated. De Lumley also reports that the ends of some of the specimens were worn smooth suggesting they had been used in body painting.

Clearer evidence of ochre use comes from Becov in Czechoslovakia. This cave site, occupied ca. 250,000 B.P., yielded a specimen of red ochre that was striated on two faces with marks of abrasion together with a flat rubbing stone with a granular crystalline surface that had been abraded in the center possibly during the preparation of ochre powder (Marshack 1981: 138). Whether or not the rubbing stone was actually used in the preparation of ochre powder is uncertain, but a wide area of the occupation floor from which the ochre lump had been recovered was stained with red ochre powder.

It is important to note that at least some of the specimens referred to as ochre in the archaeological literature are merely red stones that lack the special qualities of iron oxides. Despite the specific mineralogy of these specimens, however, their very presence in Paleolithic contexts is important evidence that they were collected by early hominids capable of thought and action divorced from what we would consider exclusively practical considerations. Even if the red stones may not be classed mineralogically as ochre, they had no apparent practical use and their collection is among the first signs in the archaeological record that early hominids were developing a nascent aesthetic sense.

In any event, the recovery of ochre from Paleolithic sites has generally been taken to mean that from very early times hominids needed, sought, and used pigments. Of course, we can only speculate on the purposes to which these colors were put. Marshack suggests they

> could have been used in ritual body decoration, in body decoration to mark rank, status, age, or sex, to decorate tools or symbolic artifacts, to color habitation floors or walls, to delimit symbolic spaces (ritual areas, healing grounds, graves, or altars), or simply as a marking material (1981: 190).

His list could easily be expanded, but if these ochre lumps can be taken as evidence of early body ornamentation and the use of cosmetics, they are particularly significant. Lewis Mumford (1967: 108–11) notes the human universality of what he calls "technical narcissism." By this he means body and facial decoration, the use of masks, costumes, wigs, tattooing, scarification, and so forth. He suggests that all of these are part of humankind's "effort to establish a human identity, a human significance, a human purpose. Without that, all other acts and labors would be performed in vain" (1967: 110).

Even more striking is Mumford's assertion that such technical narcissism (of which body and face painting are essential parts) indicates that:

> primitive man's first attack upon his "environment" was probably an "attack" upon his own body; and that his first efforts at magical control were visited upon himself. As if life were not hard enough under these rude conditions, he toughened himself further in such grotesque ordeals of beautification. Whether decoration or surgery was involved, none of these practices had any direct contribution to make to physical survival. They count rather as the earliest evidence of an even deeper tendency in man: to impose his own conditions, however ill-conceived, upon nature. Yet what they point to even more significantly is a conscious effort toward self-mastery and self-actualization; and even though often exhibited in perverse, irrational ways—at self-perfection. (1967: 110)

The presence of worked ochre in Bed II at Olduvai Gorge suggests that the beginning of this "attack" may even predate the appearance of *Homo erectus* and begin instead with *Homo habilis* or the australopithecines more than 1.5 million years ago.

Another form of evidence that *Homo erectus* had begun to develop concerns beyond simple survival is the special treatment thought to have been accorded human, and perhaps animal, skulls by these hominids. It is in the context of the celebrated *Homo erectus* cave site of Chou-k'ou-tien in China that we find the earliest evidence of what is referred to as the Paleolithic Cult of Skulls. The Lower Paleolithic period deposits at this site produced the fragmentary remains of some forty-four individuals, including fourteen crania (Chang 1977: 47). All fourteen of these crania show signs of what has been interpreted as systematic mutilation: the bases are broken in around the foramen magnum, the facial regions of most of the crania were damaged or missing, and the mandibles exhibit a consistent pattern of breakage. The systematic nature of this damage, coupled with the apparent absence of all but a few fragmentary hominid postcranial bones in the deposits, has lead many scholars to conclude "that these skulls were trophies of head hunters, and furthermore, that said hunters usually bashed in the bases of the skull when fresh, presumably to eat the brains therein contained. Many crania also show that their owners met their deaths as a result of skull fractures induced by heavy blows" (Hooten 1949: 304). Over the last twenty-five years, this interpretation has become enshrined in archaeological orthodoxy. However, the venerable view that head-hunting and ritual cannibalism were practiced at Chou-k'ou-tien by *Homo erectus* has been challenged by Binford and Ho (1985). The systematic breakage patterns alone, they note, are not sufficient proof that the damage to the Chou-k'ou-tien crania was inflicted by other hominids. Recent taphonomic studies indicate scavenging animals and water rolling consistently produce similar patterns of damage to crania. Since the crania were recovered in secondary contexts at the site, and since these contexts also contained bone that had been gnawed by animals, the possibility that the crania had been deposited by animals and by natural processes cannot be rejected. The third class of evidence of nascent "aesthetic" interest among Lower Paleolithic hominids is less easily dismissed (Edwards 1978: 136). Certain classes of utilitarian stone tools show refinement beyond the simple requirements of their purpose and such refinement indicate that these early hominids appreciated form and color for their own sake.

Finally, Edwards accepts Marshack's (1976: 278; 1977: 289–92) contention that the fine engraved lines on an ox rib from the Acheulian layer at the site of Pech de l'Azé in France appear to be similar to the "meander" symbol or iconographic unit of notation that becomes an important element in the cave art of the Upper Paleolithic period. If this engraving is a meander symbol, it suggests that the complex cognitive development claimed for *Homo sapiens sapiens* near the end of the Pleistocene epoch was presaged in the mental and cultural lives of *Homo erectus* sometime before 300,000 B.P.

**The Rise of the Mousterian Industrial Tradition.** In addition to the foregoing cognitive developments in the Lower Paleolithic period, growth and change is also evident in the material or industrial sphere of culture. In the context of the late Upper Acheulian industrial tradition in Africa, Europe, and the Middle East, two major technological transformations occur: the Levallois technique is developed; and, in general, the size of tools becomes reduced. The Levallois technique of "prefabricating" flakes develops in Europe and Africa about two hundred thousand years ago (Bordaz 1970: 31). This technique involves the preparation of a stone core in such a fashion that the shape and thickness of the flakes struck from it can be predetermined before their removal. No doubt, because of its greater efficiency and economy of both raw materials and human energy, the Levallois technique becomes important in the toolmaking process in the subsequent Mousterian industrial tradition. The second, apparently related, technological transformation occurs near the end of the late Acheulian tradition. Between about 150,000 and 100,000 B.P., both core and flake tools of the tradition begin to exhibit an overall reduction in size. In part, this size reduction is a by-product of the greater control and economy gained through use of the Levallois technique and its variants (McBurney 1973: 22). However, this change also probably reflects increased tool specialization during the late Acheulian tradition and the correspondingly greater tool efficiency such specialization produces. In Asia, meanwhile, archaic *Homo sapiens* appear to be associated with later assemblages of the Chopper/Chopping tool industrial tradition.

The Lower Paleolithic period comes to an end with the replacement of the Upper Acheulian tradition by the Mousterian tradition. The term Mousterian has been assigned to a varied range of Middle Paleolithic period stone-tool complexes which appear in Europe and elsewhere near the end of the last Interglacial and early in the last Glacial stage. This appearance is considered to have taken place around 90,000 B.P. A rough temporal correlation exists between the appearance of *Homo sapiens neanderthalensis* in Europe and the gradual emergence of the Mousterian industrial tradition there.

The centerpieces of the Acheulian industrial tradition are bifa-

FIGURE 2.1. An Acheulean-style hand ax from England. *Courtesy, Field Museum of Natural History, Chicago, Illinois.*

cially flaked tools like handaxes, picks, and cleavers made on cores (*see* Fig. 2.1). In the succeeding Mousterian complexes the emphasis on bifacial core tools decreases markedly relative to tools like scrapers, triangular points, denticulates, perforators, and notches made on flakes (Bordaz 1970: 38). Generally, such flakes were produced by means of the Levallois technique or one of its variants. Tools such as burins and endscrapers, which rise to prominence in the industries of the subsequent Upper Paleolithic period, first appear in the Mousterian.

In the classificatory scheme developed by François Bordes, the Mousterian industry can be divided into sixty-three separate classes of tools. Bordes recognizes six major European variants of facies of the Mousterian tradition distinguished from one another by the variation in the ratios of key tool types (Bordes 1968: 98–105). These facies do not lend themselves to an easy interpretation since they do not follow one another in a fixed successive order. Rather, at key sites like Combe Grenal in the Dordogne, they recur almost randomly from layer to layer in the stratified cave deposits. Bordes (1972: 146–49, 1973; Bordes and de Sonneville-Bordes 1970) interpret the stratigraphic alteration of these facies in southwestern Europe as evidence for the persistence of "parallel phyla" during the Middle Paleolithic period. In his view, the six Mousterian variants represent six separate cultural groups which existed contemporaneously there for 65,000 years or more without materially affecting the independence of each other's technical traditions. Alternatively, it has been argued that this is evidence of functional rather than cultural variation and that the six Mousterian facies represent distinctive tool kits used by essentially the same people to accomplish different sets of tasks at different times or under different environmental conditions (Binford and Binford 1966, 1969; Binford 1973, 1983: 95–108; Freeman 1966).

The Mousterian industrial tradition must have offered its users certain adaptive advantages over the late Upper Acheulian industries. We may infer this from the evidence that the rigorous proglacial environment of European Russia was apparently not penetrated until the Mousterian tradition developed during the last Interglacial (Klein 1969). This penetration was also made possible through the use of artificial shelters. Features uncovered at Moldova in the Ukraine indicate that mammoth bones were used to construct frameworks which probably were then covered with hides or earth. More limited structural remains have been recovered in southwestern Europe. Remnants of dry masonry walls have been found in association with Mousterian components within the French rockshelter of Pech de l'Azé and at the site of Cueva Morin in Spain. Cobble stone pavings, uncovered in the Mousterian levels at La Ferrassie and Combe Grenal in the Perigord, perhaps once floored long-vanished wood or hide structures (Freeman 1980: 84–85).

Mousterian sites have also produced some evidence of an emerging cognitive or intellectual complexity. Ochre is fairly common in European Mousterian occupations. However, only isolated instances of art or intentional engraving have been found in Mousterian context. Freeman (1980: 85) notes that an incised cross was found scratched on a fossil at Tata in Hungary, that bones with linear "tally marks" have been found in the Charente, and that the site of Cueva Morin in Spain has produced a deer bone with "regularly spaced curvilinear grooves" (but cf., Chase and Dibble 1987 for a contrary opinion). Klein concludes that this rare and scattered evidence "indicates prefigurations of the behavior of fully modern man, but their production seems to have been confined to a few isolated and perhaps unusual individuals" (1980: 85).

Yet these scattered markings are not the most significant "prefigurations" of modern behavior to appear at this time. That title must be reserved for the intentional burials that Neanderthals began to accord some of their number during the middle Paleolithic period. Intentionally buried Neanderthal remains have been reported from a number of European and Eurasian middle Paleolithic sites including: Teshik-Tash in Uzbekistan; Shanidar in Iraq; Mount Carmel in Israel; and La Chapelle-aux-Saints, Regourdou, Le Moustier, La Ferrassie, and Correze in southwestern Europe. The occasional recovery of objects such as red ochre, stone tools, and animal bones apparently associated with these remains has been taken as evidence that the deceased were sometimes buried with mortuary offerings, personal possessions, or food.

In addition to isolated burials, complexes of mortuary remains and features have been reported from La Ferrassie and the controversial site of Regourdou in France. At La Ferrassie, burials of two adults and six children are associated with a series of regularly spaced mounds and trenches. The bulk of the excavations at La Ferrassie were done by Peyrony and Capitan before World War I. However, Delporte's (1976) limited test excavation and reanalysis of the site have confirmed most of Peyrony and Capitan's findings (Stringer, Hublin, and Vandermeersch 1984: 98). At the Regourdou site, a single individual was buried along with grave goods under a low mound or cairn of rocks. In the vicinity of the mound—and perhaps associated with it—a number of trenches were found as well as stone cysts containing brown bear (*Ursus arctos*) remains. The discovery of these Neanderthal graves provides rare insight into the expansion of the mind taking place during the Paleolithic. Following the physical demands for food, sleep, and sex, no other aspect of life shapes the consciousness of our species more than the recognition of the inevitability of our death. Although we rebel against its immutability in countless ways, the utter simplicity of this horrendous fact ultimately colors all human choices. The death of others recalls our own fate to us and forces us to prepare for it in some fashion. For these—and a thousand other reasons—we cannot allow the death of those close to us to pass unmarked. Therefore, these middle Paleolithic period burials are *prima facie* evidence that, at least on this very fundamental topic, the Neanderthals thought as we think and acted as we act. As Freeman notes: "Whatever their interpretation, these burials suggest a concern for the proper treatment and well-being of members of society beyond death's frontiers and the beginnings of complex ideological and social practices like those of fully modern man" (1980).

Are these finds legitimate or were the supposed intentional burials really accidents of the taphonomic process? That is, did the excavators at these sites confuse the results of the operation of natural, environmental formation processes with intentional human activity? Robert Gargett (1989) reviewed the excavation records from key Mousterian burial sites and in fact concludes that the archaeological evidence of purposeful disposal of the dead in the middle Paleolithic period is insufficient to reject the hypothesis of accidental burial by natural process. Gargett makes a strong case for rejecting a number of skeletons reported to have been intentionally buried and is most convincing when discussing sites dug early in the 20th century by less controlled excavation techniques. He casts his net too far in rejecting all such reports, however. As Trinkaus notes, Gargett is unable to explain how a number of Neanderthal skeletons

> managed to be found in highly accessible upper Pleistocene rockshelters and caves in near-anatomical position and overall skeletal-part frequencies identical to those of recent cemetery samples. These partial skeletons retain many fragile elements largely intact, despite the ubiquitous presence of carcass-destroying carnivores . . . and rodents in the vicinities of the sites, the lack of evidence in most cases for sufficiently rapid natural sedimentation rates to shield them from scavengers, and the absence of comparably preserved nonhominid skeletons in similarly accessible upper Pleistocene locales. (Trinkaus 1989)

Thus, there is currently sufficient evidence to justify the conclusion that at least *some* Neanderthals began burying their dead in the middle Paleolithic period. Beyond this, however, the ice becomes thinner. For example, in some instances, Neanderthal graves (as well as those of later *Homo sapiens sapiens*) have been found to contain skeletal remains tightly constricted into the fetal position. It has been suggested that the corpses of the individuals must have been tied and bound before being placed in the grave. We remain forever uncertain as to whether this binding was merely to enable the survivors to fit a large corpse into a small grave pit or was meant instead to prevent the dead person from leaving his grave and returning to the land of the living. It has often been asserted that this constricted burial position was meant by the Neanderthals to represent the position of the fetus in the womb and thus to suggest that they viewed burial to presage some form of rebirth. It seems unlikely, however, that by the middle Paleolithic period people would possess any such understanding of the position of the human fetus *in utero* (James 1957: 29).

Evidence for even more complex ideological development and ritual practiced by Neanderthals was formerly thought to be present at the cave site of Drachenloch in the Swiss Alps. Early in this century, Emil Bachler reported the recovery of a series of cave bear (*Ursus spelaeus*) skulls stacked in wall niches and in what he supposed was a man-made stone cyst at the site. He interpreted these data as evidence of the worship and ritual hunting of the cave bear by Mousterian peoples. The drama of such a cult, together with its supposed survival in the bear worship of certain Siberian peoples and the Ainu of Japan, has resulted in the widespread acceptance of Bachler's interpretation. Bachler's primitive techniques of excavation and recording render it difficult to check his findings. However, recent comparative analysis of similar bone material from cave bear sites that were never occupied by hominids has lead Kurten (1976: 83–107) to the conclusion that Drachenloch was never anything but a cave-bear lair and Bachler's piles of cave-bear "trophy heads" probably accumulated naturally in it *without* human agency. Binford (1983), studying bone attrition and patterns of bone accumulation by both modern people and animals, rejects Bachler's Neanderthal cave-bear cult hypothesis for similar reasons.

Other evidence of ritual activity during the late Middle Paleolithic period has also come under suspicion. The celebrated Burial No. 1 at the cave site of Monte Circeo near Rome is often cited as evidence for the existence of a Cult of Skulls among the Neanderthals of Europe. On the floor of an inner gallery of this site a Neanderthal cranium was discovered *in situ* surrounded by a circle of stones. The skull is described by its excavator as exhibiting two mutilations:

> one caused by violent blows on the right temporal region that has caused conspicuous damage to the frontal, the temporal, and the zygoma. This mutilation points to a violent death, more probably a ritual murder. The other mutilation consists of the careful and symmetric incising of the periphery of the *foramen magnum* (which has been completely destroyed) and the consequent artificial production of a subcircular opening about 10–12 centimeters in a diameter (Blanc 1961: 125–26).

Comparisons of this second mutilation with identically incised trophy skulls collected among head-hunting peoples of Melanesia and Borneo convinced Blanc (1961: 126–28) that, after the murder of the Monte Circeo Neanderthal, the base of his skull was broken open in order to extract his brain. Blanc further speculates that the brain was eaten in a ritual feast. He even suggests that, since the skull rested *in situ* on its forehead and left parietal with its mutilated base turned upwards, it may have served as a drinking vessel or container during the grisly ceremony. However, here again the emerging understanding of taphonomy calls this interpretation into question. The possibility that the skull breakage was the result of natural, postmortem processes in its depositional history cannot be ruled out.

The Mousterian tradition begins to disappear in western Europe sometime before 35,000 B.P. Its replacement marks the end of the Middle Paleolithic period and the beginning of the final episode of the Old Stone Age. The subsequent Upper Paleolithic, conventionally dated between ca. 35,000 B.P. and the close of the Pleistocene at around 10,000 B.P., is relatively brief compared to the two earlier subdivisions of the Paleolithic period. However, the archaeological record from the Upper Paleolithic contains dramatic evidence of accelerating technical and intellectual achievement. The replacement of Neanderthal by modern *Homo sapiens sapiens* at the outset of the Upper Paleolithic period makes the effort at understanding the increasing complexity of this period particularly important.

# 3. Southwestern Europe and Franco-Cantabria

This chapter examines the archaeology and prehistory of the Upper Paleolithic period in one geographically limited portion of the Old World, the Franco-Cantabrian region of Southwestern Europe. Southwestern Europe, as the term is used here, includes all of France south of the Paris Basin and west of the Alps. It extends across the Pyrenees into Spain and Portugal and is bounded on the south by the Straits of Gibraltar.

## THE FRANCO-CANTABRIAN REGION OF SOUTHWESTERN EUROPE

The Franco-Cantabrian region is located in the center of southwestern Europe as defined here. Its northern boundary can be placed conveniently along the Charente River and the southern edge of the Limousin Plateau section of the Massif Central. It is bounded on the west by the Bay of Biscay and the Sea of Cantabria. In France, the region includes all of the Basin of Aquitaine, the great triangular plain between the Massif Central and the Pyrenees (M. Shackleton 1969: 259).

The rugged Perigord, Charente and Quercy areas are at the northern and northeastern ends of the Basin of Aquitaine. These areas are characterized by the deeply incised, flat-floored river valleys of the Lot, Isle, Vèzere, and Dordogne rivers that drain and separate limestone plateaus ranging between 200 and 600 meters in elevation. The caves and rockshelters weathered out of these limestone formations were used extensively by people during the Pleistocene. The excavation of these sites beginning in the late nineteenth century laid the groundwork for the scientific understanding of European prehistory.

The major rivers in the Basin of Aquitaine flow from the uplands on the north and east, through the rich vineyards and wheat fields of the basin, into the Atlantic Ocean on the west coast. The northern and central portions of the basin are dominated by the great Garonne-Dordogne River system; the smaller Adour River, which empties into the Bay of Biscay just north of the Pyrenees, drains the basin's southwest corner. In France, the Franco-Cantabrian region is bounded on the east by the Rhone-Soane Depression and on the southeast by the Mediterranean coast of Languedoc, known as the Midi. The modern climate along the coast of the Basin of Aquitaine is classed as oceanic and is characterized by rainfall between 150 to 180 days per year mainly in the winter and spring. Inland from the coast, the modern climate becomes progressively more sub-oceanic in character with rainfall diminishing, winter temperatures becoming progressively lower, and frost days more frequent.

Prior to the extensive deforestation of France over the last 1,000 years, the vegetation of the Basin of Aquitaine—and the Franco-Cantabrian region in general—was part of the vast mid-latitude mixed forest of Eurasia which stretched from the coast of Western Europe to the Ural Mountains in Russia and from the south of France to the south of Scandinavia. This vegetational assemblage includes some eighty tree species. Although it is predominately a deciduous tree complex, a number of coniferous and broadleaf evergreen species are important within it. In the French Midi, the mid-latitude mixed forest gives way to the Mediterranean scrub woodland which is dominated by low to moderately tall, broadleaf evergreen tree species.

The French and Spanish Pyrenees Mountains, the Basque hill country, and the Cantabrian Mountains are located in the southern portions of the Franco-Cantabrian region. The highest mountains in the chain are found in the north-central Pyrenees. The rugged terrain of the Pyrenees and the Cantabrian mountains has formed a barrier to travel and commerce between France and Spain throughout history. Presumably, these mountains were an even greater impediment in prehistoric times. The lower, more dissected relief of the Basque hill country provide easier routes than the mountain ranges on either side of it.

In Spain, the western boundary of Franco-Cantabria may be placed at the coast of Galicia, the southern boundary in the lower portions of the modern provinces of Oviedo, Santander, Vizcaya, Guipuzcoa, Navarre, Huesca, Lerida, and Gerona at the point where the southern slopes of the Cantabrian and Pyrenees mountains meet the upper edges of two key physiographic provinces of central Spain: the Duero

Map of southwestern Europe showing the major Paleolithic period sites mentioned in the text.

Basin (Northern Basin of the Meseta) and of the Ebro Depression (M. Shackleton 1969: 102, Fig. 21). The Duero Basin is a high, dry depression surrounded on three sides by mountains and characterized by a closed drainage system. The Ebro Basin is a large, triangular depression located at the foot of the Pyrenees. It is drained by the Ebro River which flows from the northwestern end of the basin into the Mediterranean at Cape Tortosa on the east coast (Embleton 1984: 302–4, 277–82). In Spain as in France, the eastern boundary of the region is the coast of the Mediterranean Sea.

Modern Spain is divisible into two climatic provinces: pluviose and arid. The pluviose regions receive more than 600 millimeters of rainfall annually; the arid regions less than that amount. The north coast of Spain together with the Pyrenees, the Basque hill country and the Cantabrian mountains are all part of the pluviose region. Rainfall in the Pyrenees, which ranges between 1,000 and 2,000 millimeters, decreases somewhat as one moves from north to south in these mountainous regions (M. Shackleton 1969: 104). However, both moisture and temperature were sufficient to sustain a rich forest biome prior to extensive cutting of the woodlands for fuel, building material, agriculture, and pasturage. Valley floors and sides that still support woodlands are dominated by the typical oak-beech assemblage of the European mid-latitude mixed forest. At higher elevations up to the tree-line varieties of coniferous species including the Scots pine, silver fir, and Norway spruce are most common. The major terrestrial mammals in the modern fauna of Cantabrian Spain include roe deer, red deer, boar, and at higher elevations, ibex and chamois.

The southern boundary of the Franco-Cantabrian region along the edge of the Ebro Depression is also the modern southern limit of the European mid-latitude mixed forest in eastern Spain. Here the moist forest species of oak, beech, hornbeam, and elm give way to the drier grasslands of the Ebro Valley.

Reconstructions of the climate and biogeography in Franco-Cantabria during the late Pleistocene and early Holocene epochs remain incomplete. Butzer (1971: 279–80) calls attention to evidence of late Pleistocene age glaciation in the higher valleys of the Massif Central, as well as an ice wedge site which suggests that periglacial conditions formerly were present in the vicinity of modern Bordeaux. He also believes that future study may reveal that, at the end of the Pleistocene, the Garonne and Rhone lowlands supported a forest-tundra biome.

The Pyrenees are cut by a series of north-south trending valleys which form deep canyons, some of which show evidence of having been glaciated during the Pleistocene epoch. In general, Pleistocene glaciation in the Pyrenees appears to have been less extensive than in the Alps. Current evidence suggests that valley glaciers descended during the late Glacial period to elevations as low as 400 to 600 meters on the north and 800 to 1000 meters on the south slopes of the range. Correspondingly, there is evidence in the Pyrenees of intense late Pleistocene periglacial conditions. Glaciers in the Cantabrian Mountains also seem to have flowed down to 1000 meters above sea level near the end of the Pleistocene (Embleton 1984: 268, 273–75, 300). Kopp (1963) concludes that stable glaciers at this elevation indicate a depression in mean annual temperature of approximately 12° C during the late glacial maxima. Such a rigorous climatic regime would have created an environment very different than the present one. Butzer, summarizing the paleoenvironmental data from the Pyrenees, concludes that the northern slope was characterized by a "(mountain) tundra vegetation with scattered stands of wood at a little distance, and of mixed deciduous woods at greater distance in lower elevations. There is little likelihood that *Quercus* and *Corylus* pollen were derived from beyond the Pyrenees, so that these species must have occurred somewhere in the lowlands of the Gascogne." [1971: 280]. Similarly, lowland areas of Franco-Cantabria were probably cold, dry, and characterized by "alpine meadows, montane steppes, cold-temperate woodlands, or forest-steppe mosaics" during full-glacial times (1971: 311).

During glacial stages of the late Pleistocene, these biomes supported a wide range of cold-tolerant mammals including red deer, elk, boar, reindeer, various species of bison or wisent (*Bison priscus* or *schoetensacki*), ibex or wild goat, chamois, horse (*Equus caballus* or *przewalskii*), and numerous predators and smaller mammals. In addition, a number of animals which are now extinct were major elements in the faunal assemblage of full-glacial Franco-Cantabria. Major extinct species formerly present there include: the giant elk, aurochs or wild cattle, woolly mammoth, and various rhinoceros species, most notably the woolly rhinoceros (Kurten 1968). Straus (1982: 77–79) lists thirteen major carnivore species in Cantabrian

Spain during the late Pleistocene epoch. These included two species of lynx, wildcat, various forms of lion and leopard, cave bear, brown bear, spotted or cave hyena, dhole, wolf, red fox, badger, and wolverine.

The milder, more temperate climatic conditions characteristic of the late Pleistocene interstadials in Franco-Cantabria favored expansion of mixed deciduous forests dominated by oak, hazel, elm, and hickory. Straus (1985: 501) notes that during interstadial periods roe deer and boar were present in increased numbers.

## THE CULTURAL SEQUENCE IN FRANCO-CANTABRIA

Often in science, initial research quickly produces a simple solution only to have it dissolve into ambiguity as subsequent work reveals the true dimensions of the problem. Early research on the Upper Paleolithic period, done mostly in southwestern France, suggested that a linear developmental sequence could be traced from the Mousterian industrial tradition through three Upper Paleolithic traditions called the Aurignacian, Solutrean, and Magdalenian. The Aurignacian was viewed as an indigenous European development; coeval cultures in Africa, including the Capsian and the Oranian, were thought to have resulted from migrations of "Aurignacian" peoples out of France during the Upper Paleolithic period.

Work in Europe over the last fifty years has revealed that the term Aurignacian as it was formerly used included a number of distinctive cultural traditions under a single heading (Peyrony 1933; Bricker 1976: 136–37). It is now widely accepted that at least three major regional cultural traditions existed, roughly contemporary with, and yet independent of, one another in Europe at various times during the early Upper Paleolithic period. These three traditions include the Perigordian in the west, the Gravettian in the center and east, and the Aurignacian across most of Europe except the extreme eastern regions.

In southwestern Europe, the Lower Perigordian tradition emerges from a final expression of the Mousterian or Acheulian tradition (Bordes 1968: 220). Slightly later the Aurignacian appears in western Europe. According to Bordes (1968: 155) the Aurignacian did not develop *in situ* but arrived in western Europe fully formed from somewhere outside; this early Aurignacian supposedly shows affinities with the Quina Mousterian tradition.

Scholars favoring a "parallel-phyla" interpretation conclude that the Perigordian and Aurignacian traditions coexisted independent of one another in Europe for some twelve thousand or more years until they both gave way to the Solutrean tradition around twenty-one thousand years ago. They see the Solutrean then being replaced by the Magdalenian about eighteen thousand years before the present (Peyrony 1933, *passim*; Sonneville-Bordes 1960, *passim*; Bordes 1968: 157). This scenario has been strongly challenged by those who find the central premise of the parallel phyla hypothesis implausible (Binford and Binford 1966; Binford 1973, 1983; but also cf., Mellars 1973: 74–89; Bordes and Sonneville-Bordes 1970; Bordes 1973: 217–26; Dunnell 1978). Opponents of such parallelism assert that contemporary human ethnic groups could not remain culturally independent of one another while together occupying the same small region for ten or more millennia. For this reason they reject the parallel phyla interpretation of the Upper Paleolithic period—along with Bordes' similar interpretation of his six Mousterian facies.

Instead, proponents of the so-called "functional" hypothesis assert that the contrastive Aurignacian and Perigordian tool assemblages interstratified during the Würm III stadial in the sites of the Perigord reflect not the ethnic differences of the sites' inhabitants, but merely the fact that these inhabitants were performing different tasks at the sites through time. These scholars assume that different tasks call for different types of tools and combinations of tools and result in different patterns of disposal and debris. They conclude that the contrastive assemblages from the sites of the Perigord are essentially different "tool kits" which reflect the particular use or function of the site at the time they were deposited. The resolution of this dispute has yet to be effected. However, the implications of the two hypotheses are radically different and the reader should keep them in mind while examining the outline of the cultural sequence of southwestern Europe that follows.

**The Lower Perigordian or Châtelperronian.** In southwestern Europe the Upper Paleolithic period cultural sequence begins sometime between about 35,000 to 34,000 B.P. with the appearance of the Lower Perigordian facies during the Cottes or Würm II/III Interstadial. The tradition, which is found largely in France, lasts between two thousand and three thousand years and then disappears from the archaeological record after ca. 32,000 B.P., shortly after the onset of the Würm III stadial. The Lower Perigordian is now commonly referred to as the Châtelperronian. Assemblages of this facies have definitely been recovered at thirty-three sites in central and southwestern France and less certainly at thirty-one others (Howell 1984: xix). Châtelperronian assemblages have been recovered in Cantabrian Spain but the tradition is apparently unknown outside of Franco-Cantabria.

Since the Mousterian industrial tradition is assumed to be the product of the Neanderthal, the transition to the Upper Paleolithic traditions is generally correlated with the emergence of *Homo sapiens sapiens* in Europe. Given the culturally transitional position of the Châtelperronian, the question of whether or not *Homo sapiens sapiens* or *Homo sapiens neanderthalensis* was responsible for its manufacture is an important one. Unfortunately, controversy surrounds the association and identity of the scattered human remains recovered in the past from such Châtelperronian sites as Roc de Combe-Capelle and Grimaldi. As a consequence, the soundest position on the question formerly was Bricker's (1976: 139–40) view that, as long as the anatomy of the Châtelperronian artificers remained unknown, the questions of anatomy and technology had to be considered separately. The discovery in 1979 of the partial skeleton of a Neanderthal female buried in the Châtelperronian level at Saint-Cesaire in the Charente-Maritime district (Leveque and Vandermeersch 1981), suggests that these questions may be on the verge of resolution. After all, as Harrold put it, "we now know of exceptions to both of the old equations of modern man with the Upper Paleolithic, and Neanderthals with the Mousterian" (1981: 38).

The Neanderthals apparently did not disappear at the end of the Middle Paleolithic, but persisted into the early Upper Paleolithic period in southwestern France. Further, their persistence was not in some thinly populated peripheral area; Saint-Cesaire is situated in a region densely occupied during the Middle and Upper Paleolithic (Stringer, Hublin, and Vandermeersch 1984: 106).

Whatever the species of its fabricators, the Châtelperronian industrial tradition developed out of the preceding Mousterian of Acheulian facies and its technology retains a number of important Mousterian elements (Delporte 1970; Bordes 1968: 147–48; Mellars 1973). For example, numerous scrapers of various types as well as Mousterian-style points and denticulates continue to be made, and the Levallois technique is still used. Handaxes, however, are absent or extremely rare in Châtelperronian assemblages (Laville, Rigaud, and Sackett 1980: 220).

Like the earlier Mousterian industries, the Châtelperronian shows a general paucity of worked bone. However, in contrast to them, Châtelperronian occupations, such as that at the Arcy-sur-Cure site east of Paris, have produced small quantities of ornamental carved bone pendants and teeth drilled or grooved for suspension (Leroi-Gourhan and Leroi-Gourhan 1965: 40). Further, according to Harrold (1981: 37), ochre appears to have been used far more "lavishly" during the Châtelperronian than it was in the Mousterian. Limited and fragmentary as it is, this is essentially the extent of the evidence of "non-utilitarian" behavior during the Châtelperronian. To date, none of the complex representational or symbolic art of the later Upper Paleolithic period has been attributed to this complex.

The Châtelperronian is characterized by a number of distinctive tool types including backed blades and "rather mediocre" burins on a retouched truncation or dihedral butt (Bordes 1968: 148; cf., Harrold 1981: 14–22). The Châtelperronian backed knife or point is generally present in large numbers and is considered the *fossile directeur* of the facies. This implement has been described as a broad, tapered blade with one side worked into a curved blunted back (Hadingham 1979: 63). The back of the blade is blunted by steep retouching. Together with the endscraper, the Châtelperronian knife typifies the lithic assemblages of this facies. Also common in the facies are end scrapers, retouched blades, perforators and becs (Harrold 1981: 17–19).

While a great deal is known about Châtelperronian tool technology, far less information has come to light concerning the development and use of structures and other facilities within the tradition. None of the structural remains recovered in southwestern Europe so far suggest much willingness on the part of Upper Paleolithic peoples to invest a great deal of time and energy in the construction of permanent stone living facilities. Presumably tents or structures built of perishable materials like wood or brush were favored instead. The portability or ease of construction of such structures would have closely suited them to subsistence schedules involving a good deal of seasonal movement.

Of course, the absence of such substantial structures in the archaeological record of southwestern Europe may simply be due to sampling error or differential preservation. On the other hand, it may indicate a marked adaptive contrast with the peoples of European Russia and Eurasia who were known to have erected large and substantial dugout houses with superstructures of mammoth bones, stone slabs, and earthen embankments from the Middle Paleolithic period onwards (Shimkin 1978: 226–27; Soffer 1985: 392–402). Probably the more rigorous climatic regime of the steppes accounts for this difference.

Although the duration of the Châtelperronian has yet to be precisely determined, it does seem to overlap with the appearance of the early Aurignacian facies in southwest France. It is supposed by Bordes (1968: 157–58) and others that the two industrial traditions existed side by side and yet independent of one another for perhaps a millennium. Bordes supposes that such isolation and insularity could exist between contemporary and proximate cultures because the artificers of the two assemblages belonged to different "tribes" or ethnicities. Such an interpretation presents a number of theoretical and practical problems that Binford (1973) and others have sought to resolve by suggesting that the formal contrasts between such assemblages are due to "functional" or "seasonal" differences between the sites.

**The Typical Aurignacian.** Some time between about 34,000 and 33,000 B.P., the mild and humid climatic conditions of the Würm II/III or Cottes interstadial began to give way to the colder and drier conditions of the subsequent Würm III stadial. With the waning of these milder conditions, southwestern Europe witnessed the appearance of a new industrial tradition, the typical Aurignacian. Current opinion divides the typical Aurignacian into five facies designated 0 to IV. The Aurignacian IV disappears sometime after 29,000 B.P. at Laugerie-Haute.

Typical Aurignacian components have been recognized over a wide area of southwestern Europe and it is often suggested that these components have genetic or historical connections with the Aurignacian traditions of central and eastern Europe and the Near East. These similarities have lead Denise de Sonneville-Bordes (1973: 48–49) to conclude that "at this period France belonged to a sort of European community of which it formed only the Atlantic province."

In the Perigord, components of the typical Aurignacian appear stratigraphically directly atop both Mousterian and Châtelperronian layers as well as on virgin bedrock in rockshelters newly formed in the altered environmental conditions of the Würm stadial. Occasionally, they are found interstratified with Châtelperronian components (Laville, Rigaud, and Sackett 1980: 220–21). Numerous sites in southwestern Europe have produced evidence of early Aurignacian occupations.

The large number of Aurignacian components reported from the southwestern and other portions of Europe leads Mellars (1973) and others to the conclusion that the Upper Paleolithic period witnessed a marked population increase in the region. It is also partly because of the ubiquitousness of Aurignacian components that most informed opinion regards it as intrusive into southwestern Europe and therefore culturally independent of the Mousterian-Châtelperronian-Perigordian *in situ* cultural developmental sequence. Laville, Rigaud, and Sackett (1980: 221) do not rule out the possibility that early typical Aurignacian facies might have emerged locally from the Quina Mousterian tradition, while Hahn (1977) derives the Aurignacian from the Mousterian through the intermediary of the Szeletian tradition of central Europe.

The tool technology of the Aurignacian is in marked contrast to that of the Châtelperronian and the later Perigordian industries. Aurignacian assemblages are characterized by high percentages of blades and fairly low percentages of burins, although through time the number of burins increases. The opposite proportions generally characterize Châtelperronian and Perigordian assemblages. The Aurignacian is also distinguished from the Châtelperronian tradition by the extensive and often elaborate use of bone, ivory, horn, and antler for tools, weapons, and jewelry.

Perhaps the most significant characteristic of the Aurignacian tradition is the appearance within it of the earliest surviving evidence yet discovered of the beginnings of art in prehistory. The Aurignacians of western and central Europe were apparently among the first people on earth to begin to express their aesthetic impulses through the drawing and carving of representational, schematic and symbolic images. The media they chose were varied: limestone and other rock, bone, ivory, and perhaps less permanent materials that have since vanished. Collins and Onians (1978: 11) conclude that Aurignacian art centered on three subjects: vulvas, human figures (generally female), and animals.

Of these three, bas relief carvings or engravings of what appear to be human vulvas on stone slabs and cavern walls seem to be among the earliest in southwestern Europe (Wymer 1982: 255). Enigmatic "cup mark" depressions and deeply incised lines are often associated with these vulva-shaped reliefs. A limited number of red and black painted vulvas, figures, and animals are also attributed to the Aurignacians there as well (Sonneville-Bordes 1973: 47). Carved figurines appear earliest in the Aurignacian components of central Europe. The Vogelherd site in Germany produced the first animal sculptures carved in the round, out of mammoth ivory. The Aurignacian components at the Hohlenstein-Stadel and Bruno II sites each produced fragmentary male statuettes (Hahn 1972: 262–63).

The Aurignacian industries of Europe developed a complex system of signs and produced large quantities of jewelry and portable art objects. The jewelry and art objects are often recovered in Aurignacian burials associated with red ochre and other evidence of an increasingly elaborate burial ritual and religious ideology emerging within the tradition (Hahn 1972: 252).

**The Middle and Upper Perigordian.**   The technical makeup of the Châtelperronian and its temporal overlap with the Aurignacian has led Sally Binford (1968), Klein (1973) and other scholars to interpret it as a final Mousterian hybrid dead-end rather than the base culture of the Perigordian. Hammond, for example, asserts that "surely the time has come to recognize the Châtelperronian as merely a scattered and backward response by Mousterians to Aurignacian innovation, and to confess that its apparent importance is solely an accident of the history of archaeological investigation" (1974: 619).

Whether or not these scholars are correct (and the recent Neanderthal burial unearthed at Saint-Cesaire certainly strengthens their position) the Lower Perigordian or Châtelperronian disappears from southwest Europe after about 32,000 B.P. early in the Würm III stadial when it is supplanted by the Typical Aurignacian tradition, which is replaced in its turn in France perhaps as early as 29,000 B.P. (Movius 1975: 12) or as late as 27,000 B.P. by a facies referred to as the Middle Perigordian. Thus a gap of at least three thousand years or more separates the Châtelperronian from its supposed cultural descendants in the Middle Perigordian (Harrold 1981: 43). The conceptual problem presented by this gap is great. Possible transitional assemblages have been identified, but their intermediary role has been disputed by some specialists (Laville, Rigaud, and Sackett 1980: 226).

Unless clear transitional industries are discovered, it is perhaps more logical to assume that the Lower and Middle Perigordian are merely technically analogous to one another and that the genetic or historic connections supposed to exist between them are spurious. Components referrable to the various stages of the Middle and Upper Perigordian have been reported from numerous sites in France and Spain.

The Middle or Perigordian IV phase apparently spanned the years from 29,000 B.P. to 28,000 B.P. in the Perigord during a climatic phase of the Würm characterized by relatively mild and humid conditions (Laville, Rigaud, and Sackett 1980: 228, 275). According to Bordes (1968: 152), it is characterized by the disappearance of virtually all the Mousterian tool forms retained during the Châtelperronian with the exception of some types of side scrapers and a great increase in the number of burins of various types, end scrapers on blades and Gravette points ranging in size from large, down to microgravette bladelets (*see* Fig. 3.1). Sonneville-Bordes (1973: 47) also notes that while the Perigordian flintworkers excelled at the various techniques for detaching blades from cores, they either neglected to retouch finished tools or did so poorly. Their bone industry was also undistinguished.

The most provocative element of the later Perigordian tradition is the appearance of the so-called "Venus" figurines within it. These figurines, formerly thought to be associated with the Aurignacian, depict nude or semi-nude females of a variety of ages and shapes. The exaggerated character of the breasts and buttocks of some of these statuettes has lead many scholars to conclude that they are fertility images. Reported dates for the Venus figurines range from 29,000 to 14,000 B.P. However, a critical review of the evidence by Gamble (1981: 97) suggests that the bulk of them date to between 25,000 and 23,000 B.P. The figurines are carved in a variety of media and are reported from western, central, and eastern Europe. That many aspects of these figurines are similar across this vast geographic area is striking and suggests that the Upper Perigordian tradition of southwestern Europe was part of the larger Gravettian cultural province. The figurines will be discussed further in the next chapter.

Different developments apparently characterize the cave art of the Perigordian period in southwestern Europe. According to Collins and Onians (1978: 4), after about 29,000 B.P. a shift away from the earlier emphasis on the female form and sexual apparatus occurs. Thereafter, the emphasis in cave art tends to be placed on the more recogniz-

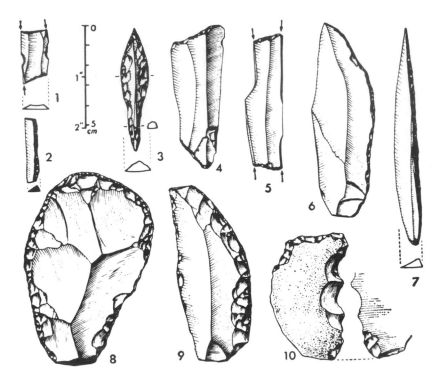

FIGURE 3.1. Perigordian tools: 1) Noailles burin; 2) backed bladelet; 3) Font-Robert point; 4) *elément tronqué*; 5) quadruple burin; 6) Châtelperron point; 7) Gravette point; 8) end scraper; 9) side scraper; 10) denticulate tool. *From Denise de Sonneville-Bordes, "Upper Paleolithic Cultures in Western Europe," Science 142:347–55. Figure courtesy of the author and the American Association for the Advancement of Science, copyright 1963 by the AAAS.*

able representations of animals. Engravings and carvings still tend to outnumber paintings at this time, according to these authors.

**The Proto-Magdalenian.** Although the components of the Upper or Perigordian VI tradition are fairly common over much of south-western Europe, the Proto-Magdalenian (or Perigordian VII) tradition, which emerges sometime after about 23,000 B.P., is known at only four sites in France.

In addition to having had a limited distribution, the Proto-Magdalenian appears also to have been relatively short-lived. Radiocarbon dates indicate that the tradition disappeared sometime after 22,000

B.P. (cf., Movius 1974: 95; Laville, Rigaud, and Sackett 1980: Fig. 8.1, 220, 277). The numerous and finely made bone tools recovered in the Proto-Magdalenian contrast with the Perigordian tradition in which the bone industry was only poorly developed. Classes of Proto-Magdalenian bone tools recovered included both grooved and un-grooved wands, points with hooked butts, small eyeless needles, and *bâtons-de-commandement* (see Fig. 3.2). The origin of the Proto-Magdalenian tradition is an important interpretive problem for pre-historians despite its brief duration, its narrow spatial compass, and the relative simplicity of its technical repertoire. Since the tradition is interposed between the final Perigordian and the Aurignacian V, the determination of both its ancestry and its descendants is crucial to the entire question of cultural interstratification in the earlier portions of the Upper Paleolithic period.

The Proto-Magdalenian tradition, first described by Peyrony at Laugerie-Haute, was so named because of its supposed foreshadow-ing of the subsequent Magdalenian tradition, both in its lithic as-semblage and in the style and decoration of its profuse bone and antler tools. Such an ancestral connection between the two tradi-tions remains plausible but undemonstrated.

**The Aurignacian V.** Even more limited in distribution than the Proto-Magdalenian is the Aurignacian V, an industrial "tradition" which has been reported only from the site of Laugerie-Haute. It has been dated to sometime after about 22,000 B.P. and is the only occupation known for the Perigord during the succeeding millennium. Sedi-ments and pollen in the layer suggest somewhat milder and more humid climatic conditions than those of the preceding Proto-Magda-lenian (Laville, Rigaud, and Sackett 1980: 272). In Cantabria, the sites of Cueva Morin and Cueva del Pendo have produced compo-nents belonging to an analogous complex called the Terminal Aurig-nacian by Freeman and Echegarcy. Like the roughly contemporary Aurignacian V in France, these two Spanish components are strati-graphically and temporally isolated from the classical Aurignacian facies that occurs there in earlier times (Butzer 1981: 168, 177). Precisely what the Aurignacian V tradition represents in the prehis-tory of southwestern Europe remains to be determined.

**The Solutrean.** Sometime after about 21,000 B.P., in the latter half of the Würm III stadial, a new cultural tradition emerges in south

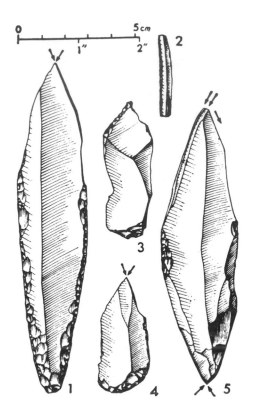

FIGURE 3.2. Proto-Magdalenian tools: 1) dihedral burin; 2) backed bladelet; 3) borer; 4) burin scraper; 5) double dihedral burin. *From Denise de Sonneville-Bordes, "Upper Paleolithic Cultures in Western Europe,"* Science *142:347–55. Figure courtesy of the author and the American Association for the Advancement of Science, copyright 1963 by the AAAS.*

western France. This industry is termed the Solutrean after Solutré, an isolated open-air site located near Lyon on a tributary of the lower Rhone River called the Saone-et-Loire. The Solutrean tradition is of relatively short duration; it disappears from the region around 17,500 B.P. after only 3,500 to 4,000 years. Its geographic distribution is also limited when compared with traditions like the Aurignacian, Perigordian, and Magdalenian. Unlike those earlier and later traditions, the classic Solutrean has been found almost entirely in southwestern

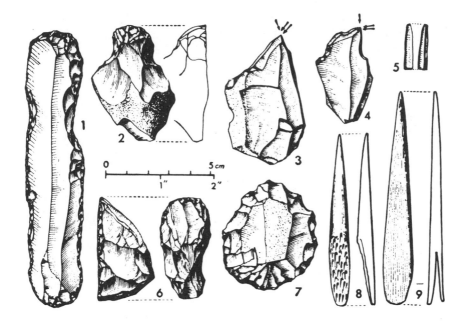

FIGURE 3.3. Aurignacian tools: 1) end scraper on an Aurignacian blade; 2) nosed scraper; 3) dihedral burin; 4) busked burin; 5) bladelet with semi-abrupt retouch; 6) carenate scraper; 7) denticulate scraper; 8) bone point with beveled base; 9) bone point with split base. *From Denise de Sonneville-Bordes, "Upper Paleolithic Cultures in Western Europe," Science 142:347–55, 1963. Figure courtesy of the author and the American Association for the Advancement of Science, copyright 1963 by the AAAS.*

France within an area bounded on the extreme southwest by the province of Asturia, in the south by the Spanish Pyrenees and the northeast coast of Spain in Catalonia, in the north by the Sarthe River in the department of the Mayenne and on the east by the lower Rhone Valley in France.

The analysis of the Solutrean component at Laugerie-Haute and other sites reveals that in general the lithic repertoire is characterized by a high proportion of specialized blade tools including end-scrapers, and the celebrated unifacial and bifacial "foliates" or leaf-shaped projectile points. These blades often exhibit characteristic flat, narrow, parallel flake scars known as "Solutrean retouch" (*see*

Stadia and Interstadials of the Würm Glacial Stage in the Late Pleistocene Epoch in Western Europe

| Beginning date (approximate) | Stadial | Interstadial |
|---|---|---|
| 10,000 B.P. | Holocene epoch | |
| 11,400 B.P. | Younger Dryas | |
| 12,200 B.P. | | Allerod |
| 15,500 B.P. | Würm IV | |
| 17,500 B.P. | | 2nd Dordogne |
| 19,000 B.P. | | 1st Dordogne |
| 34,000 B.P. | Würm III | |
| 36,000 B.P. | | Paudorf |
| 55,000 B.P. | Würm II | |
| | | Interstadial |
| | Würm I | |
| 128,000 B.P. | | |
| | Riss/Würm | Interglacial |

Fig. 3.4). Eccentric or imaginative blade forms are also common (P. Smith 1964: 53). In addition, the proportions of other scraper types, perforators, and multiple tools also are generally high in Solutrean assemblages while burins are quite rare.

Of course, the cultural traits that fated the Solutrean tradition to be the "martyr culture" of the Upper Paleolithic are the very traits which make it the most distinctive tradition in southwestern European prehistory: the spectacular leaf-shaped or foliate blades and the bravura "Solutrean retouch" flint flaking (Laville, Rigaud, and Sackett 1980: 291). The presence of these unique traits amid an otherwise rather undistinguished Upper Paleolithic tool assemblage leads Philip Smith (1965: 399) to assert that most Solutrean assemblages are a blend of rather conservative tool types and experimental, specialized artifacts.

In contrast to the stonework, Solutrean bone, horn, and ivory working remains undistinguished. For example, bone points are rare and *bâtons-de-commandement*, elaborately carved and present in great numbers in the preceding and following traditions, are absent

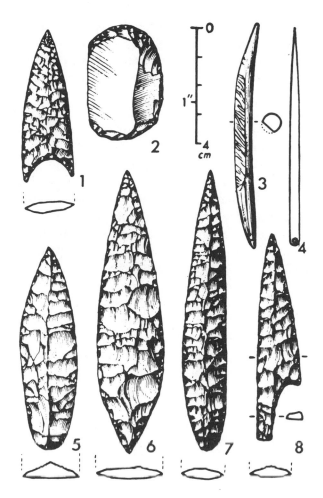

FIGURE 3.4. Solutrean tools: 1) laurel-leaf point with concave base;
2) double end scraper; 3) curved bone point; 4) needle; 5) unifacial point;
6) laurel-leaf point; 7) willow-leaf point; 8) shouldered point. *From Denise
de Sonneville-Bordes, "Upper Paleolithic Cultures in Western Europe,"*
Science *142:347–55. Figure courtesy of the author and the American Association for the Advancement of Science, copyright 1963 by the AAAS.*

in the Solutrean (P. Smith 1965: 390). Nonetheless, bracelets, pendants, and other decorative items were made, together with "spatulas." These latter objects often bear enigmatic patterns of grooves or notches which French prehistorians have traditionally referred to as *marqués-de-chasse*, or hunting tallies.

Finally, at least one major achievement in this genre must be credited to the Solutreans: eyed needles made of bone and ivory appear perhaps as early as the Middle Solutrean phase at Laugerie-Haute. For unknown reasons, their distribution in the tradition appears limited to the Dordogne (P. Smith 1965: 390). The small size of many of these needles suggests that they were used for fine stitching (P. Smith 1964). The significance of this tool can hardly be overestimated. Without it the production of weatherproof, form-fitted clothing would have been difficult. In addition, clothing could have been decorated with fancy stitchery and decorative elements like shells or ivory buttons. The elaborate shell covered cloak, of which traces were found on a burial of an apparently high status individual at the Sungir site in the Soviet Union, is but one example of the manner in which the needle could be used to produce garments capable both of keeping out the cold and at the same time marking the status of the individual who wore it.

At one time it was fashionable to speak of a Solutrean intrusion into southwestern France. Since the proto and early phases of the Solutrean have been found exclusively in southwestern France, this notion has been largely rejected (P. Smith 1964: 51). It is more consistent with current evidence to conclude that the Solutrean developed in the southwest of France and then spread outward from there later in its history. The increase through time in the number of Solutrean components suggests that the adaptive success of the tradition—combined perhaps with certain favorable climatic changes—led to population pressure in the heartland and spurred territorial expansion outward from it (cf., P. Smith 1973: 71; Jochim 1983). The type-site of Solutré on the Saone-et-Loire and the famous Spanish site of Cueva del Castillo near Santander in Cantabria were both apparently first occupied during this Middle phase outward expansion. Actually, although typologically similar to the French Middle phase, the earliest components of the Spanish Solutrean or *Solutrense iberico* may actually be more closely contemporary with the Upper and Final phases in France (P. Smith 1965: 402). Recent radiocarbon dates from

Solutré suggest that the same may be true of that site as well (Delibrias and Evin 1974; Straus 1978: 36).

In addition to appearing later there than in France, the Solutrean in Spain is characterized by a number of unique stone tool forms not found in the French heartland. Some of these forms include bifacial foliate points with concave bases or asymmetrical blades, and small barbed and tanged points. The distribution of these blades and points appears to be variable. Concave-based points are restricted in distribution to the narrow coastal zone of northern Spain between the Cantabrian Sea (Bay of Biscay) and the Cordillera, from Central Asturias to the French border (Straus 1977: 34). The small barbed and tanged points on the other hand, are generally found further east in the Pyrenees and south along the Mediterranean coast as far as Parapallo Cave in Valencia (P. Smith 1973: 68). Recent radiocarbon dating of collagen from bone samples associated with the upper Solutrean occupation at Parapallo, place the appearance of these points at around 18,000 B.P. (Davidson 1974). These have been interpreted as arrow points and compared with supposedly similar specimens from the Aterian in North Africa. The Spanish Solutrean has also produced unique bone spear points characterized by flattened middles and obliquely scored with finely incised lines (Sonneville-Bordes 1973: 50).

These stylistic differences may provide a clue to the nature of subsistence in the two regions. In recent studies, Straus (1975, 1976) compared entire assemblages of Spanish Solutrean artifacts with one another rather than merely examining limited artifact classes. In doing so, he arrived at a set of interesting conclusions about subsistence and settlement in northern Spain during the late Pleistocene. According to him (Straus 1976: 342), it is possible to isolate two basic types of Solutrean tool assemblages, which in turn can be correlated with two distinct geographic subregions in northern Spain.

The first of these "blocks" of assemblages is characterized by high percentages of endscrapers, sidescrapers, denticulate or notched pieces, and Solutrean foliate points and by low percentages of burins, truncated pieces, backed blades, and bladelets. These assemblages are found in sites in the Asturias and Santander regions. The second of these assemblage blocks is found in sites in the Basque country. The block is characterized by a reversal of the proportions of the tool classes of the first block. That is, Solutrean points, endscrapers, sidescrapers, and denticulates occur in relatively low percentages, while backed blades, burins, truncated pieces, and bladelets are relatively common.

In addition to containing distinctive artifact assemblages, the Solutrean sites of the two geographical regions have also produced distinctively different faunal collections. According to Straus (1976: 342), sites in Asturias and Santander have generally yielded large numbers of red deer, horse, and large bovines (*Bos* and/or *Bison*). Such collections are consistent with a mosaic environment of woods and grasslands. In contrast, Solutrean sites in the Basque country generally produce few of the above species but numerous alpine caprines, such as chamois and ibex, as well as fur-bearing carnivores like fox and various mustelids.

The apparent correlation between the two different types of artifact assemblages, geographical regions, and faunal collections probably indicates that, at least by the late phase, two contrastive adaptive poses had developed in northern Spain. That is, two different sets of technical and organizational solutions to the problems presented by the different environments of the two regions were in place in the Spanish Solutrean. The two artifact assemblages probably reflect differences in tool function resulting from differences in the kinds of animals being pursued.

In southwestern France, the Middle Solutrean phase comes to an end with the close of the Würm III stadial and the onset of the Würm III/IV interstadial (Bordes 1968: 159). The late or Upper phase of the Solutrean coincides with the onset of the mild Würm III/IV interstadial (also known as the first Dordogne Oscillation) which begins sometime around 19,000 B.P. Climatic conditions during this interstadial appear to have been somewhat warmer and more moist than those of the preceding Würm III stadial.

The tool assemblages from the four strata assigned to the Late Solutrean at Laugerie-Haute exhibit a number of important changes in implement types and frequencies at this time. First, the ancient unifacial point diminishes in frequency during the phase and disappears at its close. Second, the laurel leaf point continues to be finely made but diminishes in both size and frequency and, by the end of the phase, also disappears altogether. Third, the single shouldered foliate point, which first appears at the end of the middle Solutrean phase, becomes increasingly common and well made during the late

Solutrean and is generally used as one of the *fossiles directeurs* of the phase.

Late Solutrean tool assemblages are characterized by a new bifacial tool form: the willow leaf foliate point or blade. Called the willow leaf because of its thin, lanceolate shape, the blade has rounded ends and exhibits a delicate retouch on one face only (P. Smith 1964: 50). Late Solutrean assemblages also contain *micrograttoirs* or small endscrapers, backed bladelets, and occasional microburins (P. Smith 1965: 400).

However, recent archaeological and paleoclimatic work has called Philip Smith's (1966) linear temporal sequence for the Solutrean into question. According to Laville and Texier (1972) and Montet-White (1973), the Late Solutrean facies at the site of Le Malpas (only 25 kilometers away) appears to be contemporary with the *Middle* Solutrean levels at Laugerie-Haute. Correspondingly, the Upper Solutrean at Le Malpas seems also to be contemporary with the Lower Magdalenian at the latter site. If correct, these new findings reveal a profound problem in our understanding of the cultural sequence of the Perigord. Since the existing Solutrean chronology assumes that key artifact types followed one another in time, it "cannot account for the contemporaneous occurrence, in the same region, of supposedly time specific artifact types and assemblages" (R. White 1980: 85–86). But the resolution of the dilemma currently eludes us and we are forced to adhere—albeit with caution—to the linear Solutrean sequence at least for the present.

Sometime before the end of the first Dordogne Oscillation, the Late Solutrean gives way to the Final Solutrean phase at Laugerie-Haute. Philip Smith (1964: 50) notes that the occupation layers at the site become markedly thinner at this time, suggesting that human occupation at the shelter had perhaps become sporadic. He suggests that the milder climatic conditions of the oscillation had reduced the reindeer carrying capacity of the Perigord.

After 18,000 B.P. southwestern Europe experiences a brief return of cold, dry climatic conditions. It is during this short-lived cold regime that the Solutrean tradition disappears altogether. In the subsequent second Dordogne Oscillation (ca. 17,000 to 15,500 B.P.), a very different cultural tradition, the Magdalenian, comes to hold sway there.

The reason for this disappearance is unknown, although suggested causes include the climatic changes of the Dordogne Oscillations, epidemics, even wars and invasions. Whatever the cause, as Bordes notes,

> the brilliant Solutrean culture, which carried flintworking to one of its highest levels, suddenly disappeared in somewhat mysterious circumstances. The oldest Magdalenian levels often overlie the Solutrean without a break so much that it is difficult to trace the dividing line between these two levels except by the typology. But within the limits of what we know about the Paleolithic culture, it is impossible to think that the one culture might have evolved into the other. The implements are completely different; and if the Solutrean represents one of the zeniths of stone chipping, the lowest Magdalenian is certainly one of its nadirs (1968: 159–61).

The artistic achievements of the Solutreans also contrast with those of their Magdalenian successors. The Solutreans appear to have had little genius or inclination for cave painting; further they apparently did not produce the elaborately carved bone artifacts such as *bâtons-de-commandement* like those of either their successors, or for that matter, their predecessors. However, like the Upper Perigordian peoples whom they followed, the Solutrean artists seemed to have loved rotundity, solidity, and volume and sought to reproduce it in their images. For example, a number of fragmentary animal friezes carved in bas-relief have been recovered in Solutrean deposits at sites like Le Roc de Sers in the Charente and Fourneau du Diable in the Dordogne (Sonneville-Bordes 1973: 51) or Cueva Chufin in Santander (Cabrera and Bernaldo de Quiros 1977: 780) suggesting that this was a style much favored by them. However, unlike either the Aurignacians or the Perigordians, Solutrean artists seem to have avoided representing the roundest subject of all—the human female nude. If the absence is not the result of the accidents of archaeological recovery, it may indicate either a puritanical diffidence on the part of the Solutreans, or a profound change in religious ideology with the rise of their tradition.

**The Magdalenian.** The last great industrial tradition of the Upper Paleolithic period in western Europe appears in the Perigord around 17,500 to 17,000 B.P., during the brief cold interval which separates the first and second Dordogne Oscillations. The tradition disappears some six thousand to seven thousand years later with the close of the Würm IV stadial and the Pleistocene epoch between about 11,000 and 10,000 B.P.

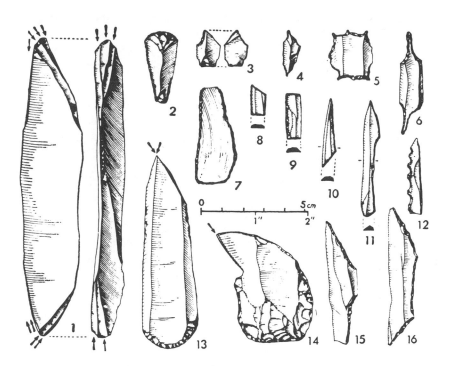

FIGURE 3.5. Magdalenian tools: 1) double dihedral burin; 2) end scraper; 3) "microburin"; 4–6) borers; 7) *raclette*; 8) trapezoid; 9) rectangle; 10) triangle; 11) shouldered point; 12) backed denticulate bladelet; 13) burin scraper; 14) parrot-beak burin; 15) shouldered point with oblique truncation; 16) trapezoid. *From Denise de Sonneville-Bordes, "Upper Pa leolithic Cultures in Western Europe," Science 142:347–55. Figure courtesy of the author and the American Association for the Advancement of Science, copyright 1963 by the AAAS.*

In its earliest two phases (Magdalenian 0, I), the distribution of the industry appears limited to south-central France north of the Garonne River and west of the Massif Central. In its later, classic phases, the Magdalenian industry spreads across the Saone and Rhone rivers as far east as Jura and the Dauphine (*see* Fig. 3.5). At about the same time it becomes established in the Pyrenees and the Cantabrian mountains and extends in Spain as far west as Asturias, as far east as Catalonia. In the north, late phase Magdalenian components occur as far as Belgium and the lower Rhine, two areas which appear to have been unoccupied during the preceding Solutrean (Sonneville-Bordes 1973: 52–53).

The Magdalenian tradition in western Europe is customarily divided into seven phases numbered from 0 to VI. The last four of the phases (Magdalenian III through VI) occur during the intensely cold climatic regime of the late Glacial or Würm IV stadial. The correlation of the classic later Magdalenian tradition with full glacial conditions is significant, as Magdalenian skeletal morphology and material culture have often been compared to that of the ethnographically known Eskimo (Stringer, Hublin, and Vandermeersch 1984: 111). In addition, the Magdalenian subsistence systems appear to have centered on large herd animals such as reindeer, bison, horse, and wild cattle; it was apparently supplemented with ibex, chamois, red deer, pig, salmon, and other fish, birds of various species, as well as bear and other fur-bearing carnivores. Similar adaptations by ethnographically known arctic and subarctic peoples have proven a rich, if often questionable, source of analogy for interpreting the Magdalenian tradition.

Certain difficulties attend the use of such modern analogies. The proglacial environment of southwestern Europe during the Pleistocene would by no means be identical with the arctic and subarctic regions of the modern world. The position of Europe on the globe means that it would not have been subject to the gloomy six months of darkness characteristic of the polar regions. Further, the angle at which the sun's radiation strikes the earth in Europe is very different than in the polar regions. This difference, coupled with the absence of the lengthy arctic night, probably means that, even under full glacial conditions, Pleistocene Europe would have supported a much larger biomass than does the modern arctic (Butzer 1971: 463). In addition to a larger overall quantity of game, Upper Paleolithic period peoples were hunting a diversity of large species that has simply not been present in northern climates since the close of the Pleistocene (Spiess 1979: 184). Philip Smith (1965: 393) also argues that the presence of rockshelters in southwestern Europe and their absence in the modern arctic and subarctic further complicates the analogy. Thus, it seems likely that neither the carrying capacity of the Pleistocene environment in Europe nor the subsistence strategies developed by Magdalenian hunters to exploit that environment has been duplicated on earth since the beginning of the Holocene epoch.

As a consequence, the precise nature of Magdalenian subsistence strategies remains a subject of some dispute among prehistorians. Bouchud (1954a, 1954b, 1966) uses a close analysis of the patterns of tooth eruptions and tooth wear evident in the reindeer mandibles from Magdalenian sites to argue that the hunters more-or-less permanently occupied the rockshelters of the Perigord and exploited nearby local reindeer herds from these base camps on a year-round basis. But research by Lewis Binford (1973: 238–44) and Spiess (1979: 186–235) suggests that the reindeer remains actually indicate a *seasonal* use of the Dordogne shelters during the Magdalenian. Bahn (1977) asserts that late Upper Paleolithic subsistence systems involved long distance transhumance by Magdalenian peoples in concert with the seasonal migration of the reindeer herds that he presumes occurred between the coasts of southwestern Europe and the interior uplands of Cantabria and France in the spring and summer. This argument can be modified on the grounds that modern arctic and subarctic caribou and reindeer hunters cannot, and do not, follow the herds. Instead, they contrive to intersect and ambush them at various points along their seasonal migration routes (R. White 1980: 100; Burch 1972).

Randall White believes that late Pleistocene hunters in western Europe operated in a similar fashion and points to the strong association between Magdalenian sites and fords and natural topographic traps in the Perigord as support of his view. White (1980: 100–101) argues that such a strategy would force the hunters to develop a heavy reliance on plant and animal species besides the reindeer during a large part of the year. The open-air Magdalenian sites of the west central Dordogne with their cobblestone pavements and dense, often highly specialized, lithic debris (Sackett and Gaussen 1976; Taranik 1977: 252–55), may represent summer settlements in such a seasonally timed subsistence strategy. The rockshelters or *abris* that line the steep cliffs of the Dordogne, Lot, and Vèzere river valleys of the Perigord were apparently utilized during the late fall, winter, and perhaps early spring seasons (Speiss 1979: 234–35).

In addition, a number of scholars have suggested that "anadromous" fish—specifically the Atlantic salmon—could plausibly have complemented a transhumant subsistence system centered on the reindeer. Anadromous fish spend the bulk of their lives in saltwater but annually swim up freshwater rivers and streams in the springtime in order to spawn. Prior to river pollution and the construction of hydroelectric power dams, many of the western European rivers that empty into the Atlantic were characterized by great spring spawning runs along hundreds of miles of their lower courses (Netboy 1968). Sieveking (1976: 586–87) notes that Magdalenian sites are clustered along rivers which had some of the richest seasonal salmon runs in Europe as late as the nineteenth century.

Jochim (1983: 215–16) also makes a strong inferential case for the importance of the Atlantic salmon in late Upper Paleolithic subsistence. He notes that modern populations of the fish are limited to waters between 2° and 18° C. The CLIMAP reconstruction of the currents and water temperatures of the eastern Atlantic indicate that during the last glaciation in western Europe, such conditions would have been met only between southern England and the Straits of Gibraltar. Presumably salmon runs at the northern end of this range would have been quite short due to seasonal freezing and the shortage of food; in the south, runs would also have been short due to the large number of predators and competing species. However, Jochim concludes that in southwestern Europe (the presumed central portion of the range) the runs probably tended to last for a much longer period of time. As a consequence, "neither intensive harvesting nor storage is necessary for these fish to become a significant part of the diet. The northern coast of Spain and the southern Atlantic watershed of France contained the potential for significant exploitation of salmon without technological elaboration" (1983: 215).

Unfortunately, actual salmon remains are only rarely reported from French Magdalenian sites, although Sieveking (1976: 586–87) suggests that this absence may be due to poor preservation and poor recovery techniques, combined with the difficulty of locating open-air Magdalenian sites. In Cantabrian Spain, abundant salmon, sea trout, and trout remains have been recovered together with marine and estuarine mollusk shells from the Solutrean and Magdalenian levels at La Riera cave site near the Bay of Biscay. However, the peoples who periodically occupied La Riera Cave during the late Upper Paleolithic combined the hunting of red deer and chamois rather than reindeer with their salmon fishing (Straus, Clark, Altuna, and Ortea 1980: 142).

Sieveking calls attention to a more indirect evidence of Magdalenian familiarity with and interest in the salmon: the occasional appearance of salmon and other aquatic animals in the art of the period. One of the most dramatic examples of such artistic evidence is Marshack's (1970; 1972a; 1972b) identification of a spawning salmon as part of the decoration of a Magdalenian *bâton-de-commandement* from the site of Montgaudier in the department of Charente in southwest France. He also recognizes engravings of a flower, sprouting plant, and other images of spring flora and fauna including snakes and a pair of seals on the *bâton.* If his identifications are correct, they suggest that the engraver was concerned with the timing of the spring salmon run and sought to represent the signs associated with its arrival. As Marshack put it, the plants and animals carved on the *bâton* were "time-factored and storied images of creatures whose comings and goings and seasonal habits were known. . . . They *represented* the birth of the 'new year,' if not calendrically and arithmetically at least observationally and probably in story (1972: 173).

The great herds of late Pleistocene herbivores in southwestern Europe certainly migrated seasonally from highlands to lowlands in response to changing temperatures. It does not seem unreasonable to suppose, therefore, that the subsistence schedule of the Magdalenians was in general synchronization with the movements of these herds. Further, hunter-gatherers wintering on the lower reaches of the west-flowing rivers of Franco-Cantabria would be ideally situated to harvest the salmon toiling upstream towards them from the Atlantic in the springtime.

Perhaps the most stimulating recent work on the Upper Cantabrian Magdalenian has been done at the site of Cuevo del Juyo in the province of Santander. Here Leslie Freeman and Gonzalez Echegaray (1981) report the discovery within the cave of an elaborate mound constructed of stone, clay, and sand. Associated with the mound are large quantities of animal bones and a large block of stone which appears to have been crudely sculpted into a feline face. The placement of the mound in the cave's interior, the central position of the stone face and other unusual features, suggests to the excavators that the site served as a shrine or sanctuary. The date of 13,920 ± 240 years B.P. from a contemporary layer in the cave's main gallery places the mound's construction near the end of the Upper Cantabrian Magdalenian phase.

According to Moure-Romanillo and Cano-Herrera (1979: 281–82), the Final Cantabrian Magdalenian phase begins about 10,600 B.P. and closes with the onset of the Holocene epoch sometime after 10,000 B.P. Its technical repertoire includes uniserial and biserial bone harpoons and varied microlithic tool types. If this time range is correct, the phase is contemporary with the next tradition to be discussed, the French Azilian. As in France, the Azilian in Cantabria seems to develop directly out of terminal Magdalenian culture. Close analysis of cave stratigraphy and radiocarbon dates from Cantabria leads Butzer (1981: 177–78) to conclude that a transition or overlap of at least two thousand years in duration exists between the final Magdalenian and the early Azilian in northern Spain.

Finally, the most significant characteristic of the Magdalenian in both Spain and France is the truly splendid aesthetic outpouring that emerged from the tradition in the form of polychrome cave paintings, engravings, sculptured friezes, modeled clay statues, and elaborately carved objects of ivory, antler, horn, bone, and wood. Upper Paleolithic period art—especially painting—reaches its apogée during the Magdalenian occupation of Altamira, Lascaux, Tito Bustillo, Isturitz, Angles-sur-l'Anglin, and numerous other sites in southwestern Europe. Yet the richness of the aesthetic impulse and the complexity of the intellectual life during the Magdalenian is reflected in other ways as well. Magdalenian burials are far more common than those of earlier periods and the ochre and grave goods often included with these burials hint at an elaborate cosmology, grave-side ritual, and mortuary cult. Further, traces of an intricate system of notation, perhaps a means of calendric reckoning, has been hypothesized by Marshack (1972a; 1972b; 1972c) from the period.

**The Azilian.** Between about 12,500 and 10,000 B.P., the magisterial terminal phase of the Magdalenian tradition disappears. In both northern Spain and southwestern France it is overlapped and gradually succeeded by the Epipaleolithic tradition known as the Azilian. The Azilian appears sometime after 12,500 B.P. and fades after 9,500 B.P. with the close of Würm IV (Butzer 1981: 177; but cf., Straus 1985: 505 who places it between 11,000 B.P. and 9,000 B.P. in Cantabrian Spain). This industry is named after the French site of Le Mas d'Azil on the Arize River in the French Pyrenees. It is also represented at a number of other sites in Franco-Cantabria. Not insignificantly, these sites also generally contain Upper Paleolithic period occupations directly beneath the Azilian.

The Azilian tradition emerges directly and gradually out of the technical complex of the final Upper Paleolithic period. The tradition thus represents a continuation of the cultural adaptation developed in the rigorous environments of the late Pleistocene into the more temperate and humid condition of the Holocene or Postglacial epoch. As Bahn and Couraud put it, "the Azilian is a localized facies of the late Magdalenian, but its chronological position is not uniform and it cannot be attached to a precise climatic phase. Nevertheless, it is useful to retain the name as a sort of shorthand to denote the transitional phase for the Magdalenian to the Mesolithic" (1984: 156).

The transitional nature of the Azilian is evident in its technical repertoire. Deer antler harpoons continue to be made—but with distinctive flat sections that become the hallmark of the Azilian. In addition, a few stone-tool forms which appear near the end of the Magdalenian persist into the Azilian. On the other hand, geometric microlithic tools, later to become standard elements in the European Mesolithic period, are present in some quantity in the Azilian. The bow-and-arrow is certainly in use at this time, the dog probably domesticated. In Cantabrian Spain, at least, the Azilian subsistence appears to emphasize a broad range of species including red and roe deer, ibex, boar, horse, bovines, birds, mollusks, and fish (Straus 1985: 505). Little can be said of the Azilian mortuary cult at present. Burials of a definite Azilian age are rare and only two of them, from the sites of Le Trou Violet (Ariege, France) and Los Azules I (Asturias, Spain) have been adequately documented (Tresguerres 1976).

Many prehistorians take the changes that occurred during the transition from the Magdalenian to the Azilian and subsequent Mesolithic as signifying progressive "cultural impoverishment." The most dramatic evidence of this supposed impoverishment in the Azilian is the disappearance of the magnificent Upper Paleolithic parietal art tradition. Azilian art, at least what has survived into our time, consists of small, smooth pebbles painted (and occasionally engraved) with red and black lines, dots, and borderings. Less common designs include simple geometric elements such as crosses and chevrons. Prehistorians have often made invidious comparisons between the magnificent polychromatic cave painting and engraving of the Magdalenians and the paltry pebble art of the Azilians (cf., Clark and Piggott 1965: 144; Sonneville-Bordes 1973: 53). Suggestions that the pebbles merely served as gaming pieces adds to the image of Azilian decline.

However, recent work by Couraud suggests that these painted pebbles with their enigmatic symbols are, in fact, the material remains of a system of counting or notation. Couraud undertook a systematic reexamination of some 1,967 Azilian pebbles. Within this corpus—which included virtually all of the artifacts available for study in Europe—he identified sixteen different signs. Potentially these sixteen signs could be combined into 246 binary combinations. However, only 41 such combinations were actually used on the pebbles. Thus, some of the symbols appear to have been mutually exclusive. Further, Couraud suspects that the meaning of a symbol is dependent in part upon the position it occupies on the pebble. It seems likely that a system of morphologic and syntactic rules, that is, a grammar, governed the combination, placement, and order of the symbols on the Azilian pebbles. Yet the meaning of the messages remains elusive. The possibility that the dots and lines were numbers has been recognized virtually since the discovery of the painted pebbles in the late nineteenth century. However, Couraud discovered an apparent pattern in these numbers. Fully 85 percent of the pebbles represented digits between one and four. Some eighty-seven pebbles contained symbols that could be read as amounts ranging from twenty-one to twenty-nine or their multiples—numbers that may correspond to lunar phases or lunations (Bahn and Couraud 1984: 157–58). The possibility that systems for recording the changing phases of the moon were developed during the Upper Paleolithic will be discussed in chapters 5 and 7.

In any event, with the northward retreat or extinction of the great herds, the attendant reforestation of southern and central Europe, and the rising worldwide sea level, the Upper Paleolithic period comes to a close in the Azilian.

## THE TRANSITION TO MODERNITY: CULTURAL CONTRASTS BETWEEN MIDDLE AND UPPER PALEOLITHIC

As noted in the earlier section on hominid evolution, important morphological differences exist between *Homo sapiens sapiens* and *Homo sapiens neanderthalensis*. However, from the perspective of this book, the real question is whether or not these contrasts in physical form indicate a corresponding difference in capacity for culture and thought between modern people and Neanderthals. That is, can we assume that the intellectual capabilities and processes of the hominids of the Upper Paleolithic period operated essentially at the modern level? If we can, then it is legitimate to make analogies between these ancient peoples and the ethnographically known hunter-gatherers described in the anthropological literature. If we cannot make this assumption, if the people of Upper Paleolithic Europe were still "paleocultural," to use Arthur Jelinek's (1977: 28) memorable term, then such analogies are unjustified.

Recent comparisons between the cultural traditions of the Upper Paleolithic and those of the preceding Middle Paleolithic period do in fact suggest that the transition between the two hominid forms associated with the periods represents an important intellectual watershed in human prehistory (cf., S. Binford 1968; David 1973; Mellars 1973; Harrold 1980; R. White 1982). Cultural changes of particular significance occur in technology, subsistence patterns, population density and distribution, trade, mortuary practices, and art. Together these changes indicate a marked increase in cultural—and presumably mental—complexity during the period. Since the nature and complexity of religious practice is related to the complexity of culture in general, the major trends in Upper Paleolithic period cultural development are reviewed briefly here. These trends include:

*An increase in the size of Upper Paleolithic sites as compared to those of the Middle Paleolithic period.* While Mellars (1973: 271–72) concludes that this increase in site size indicates an increase in population during the Upper Paleolithic period, Randall White (1982: 171–72), citing work done on contemporary !Kung Bushmen settlements by Yellen (1977), notes that an increase in site size can also result when the *same* number of individuals occupy the same location for *longer* periods of time. Both Randall White (1980, 1982: 171–72) and Conkey (1981) prefer to interpret some of these larger Upper Paleolithic sites as the result of the seasonal or occasional aggregations of people who were otherwise generally dispersed in smaller groups during most of the year. If this interpretation is correct, it suggests a more complex and cosmopolitan form of social organization had begun to emerge during the Upper Paleolithic period.

*Changes in settlement pattern and subsistence.* According to Mellars (1973: 268–70), archaeological surveys in the Perigord have turned up significantly more Upper Paleolithic period sites than any dating to previous periods. Similarly, Straus (1985: 504) reports that about three times as many Upper Paleolithic sites as Mousterian sites have been recorded in Cantabrian Spain. Both scholars take these site increases as evidence that population increased in these regions during the Upper Paleolithic period. Randall White (1982: 172), however, demurs on the grounds that Mellars's simple site tallies do not give sufficient weight to multi-component sites, that some of the temporal assignments of some of the sites have proven to be in error, and that the effects of sampling error in the surveys cannot be discounted. However, White calls attention to a possible shift in site locations from "interfluvial" placements during the Middle Paleolithic period to river valley loci during the Upper Paleolithic period. White concedes that the reality of this shift has yet to be fully demonstrated through rigorous site survey work in other parts of southwestern Europe. Straus sees a locational change between the two periods in Cantabria. According to him, before the Upper Paleolithic period, "true mountain sites are nonexistent; most Mousterian sites are located along the edge of the rolling coastal plain. There is no indication of significant exploitation of marine resources" (Straus 1985: 502). The situation changes in the subsequent period; Straus (1985: 504) contends that sites in the Upper Paleolithic are placed in more diverse mountain and coastal locations.

If such shifts in site location did occur between the Middle and Upper Paleolithic periods, they would be important indicators of subsistence changes at that time. But what was the nature of such subsistence changes? Mellars (1973: 271) and Freeman (1973, 1975: 255) contend that the diversity of game in faunal assemblages from Middle Paleolithic sites indicate that broad-spectrum hunting was characteristic of the period. In contrast, they assert that faunal remains from late Upper Paleolithic sites indicate that subsistence systems of that period tended to emphasize one or a limited number of key wild resources: red deer and shellfish in Cantabrian Spain, reindeer and salmon in southwest France. Randall White (1982: 170–71) disagrees on the grounds that such assertions are based on bone counts rather than minimum numbers of individuals or live-weight estimates. Analysis of Upper Paleolithic faunal remains using the latter techniques, he says, indicate a continuation of broad-spectrum hunting rather than the emergence of game specialization. A similar view is held by Straus (1977: 66–67; 1985: 504) who suggests that in Cantabria at least, the inclusion of animals like boar, shellfish, mustelid, fox, and various species of fish, birds, and alpine mammals in the hunters' repertoire may actually indicate a broadening of the subsistence base during the Upper Paleolithic period.

*A general predominance of blades over flakes in the stone tool inventories.* While blades are found in limited numbers in the assemblages of earlier periods and flake tools continue to be made in the Upper Paleolithic period, the blade clearly increased in popularity through time. Many of these blades were probably made through "indirect percussion" or the positioning of a punch or chisel made of relatively

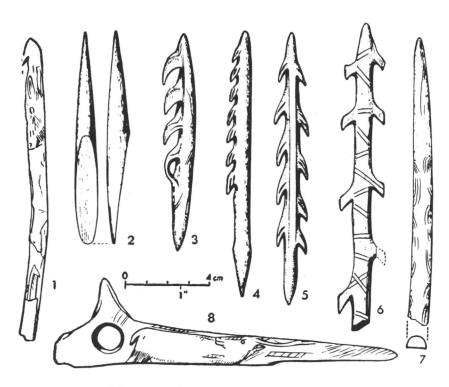

FIGURE 3.6. Magdalenian tools: 1) spearthrower or *atl-atl* throwing board; 2) bone point with beveled base; 3–6) harpoons of various styles; 7) half-cylindrical wand; 8) *bâton-de-commandement,* which perhaps actually served as an arrow shaft straightener or a wrench. *From Denise de Sonneville-Bordes, "Upper Paleolithic Cultures in Western Europe,"* Science *142:347–55. Figure courtesy of the author and the American Association for the Advancement of Science, copyright 1963 by the AAAS.*

soft material like bone, wood, or antler between the hammer and the core. Blades struck off in this manner tend to be thinner, sharper, and longer than those struck off by direct percussion (Bordaz 1970: 55). Techniques of retouch, however, remain largely unchanged during the Upper Paleolithic (Mellars 1973; R. White 1982: 169).

**The rapid appearance of new, often highly standardized, tool forms (Mellars 1973; but cf., L. Binford 1973; R. White 1982: 169).** Most commonly these new tool forms fall into three general classes: burins, backed blades, and various types of end scrapers on blades (Bordaz 1970: 57) (*see* Fig. 3.6). Of these three, the beaked burin or graver was probably the most significant since this tool enabled craftsmen to incise deep grooves in such resistant material as bone, antler, ivory, or horn and pry up and remove long strips of it by the so-called "groove and splinter method" (Bordaz 1970: 71). In this fashion, Upper Paleolithic peoples could utilize a virtually inexhaustible set of resources in a new way. In addition, Freeman notes that some of these artifact types become highly standardized for the first time during the Upper Paleolithic period. For example, "from some Solutrean levels we have laurel and willow leaf points that are almost exact duplicates in size and shapes. The same is true for some Magdalenian bone harpoons. Unprecedented control was being exerted over morphological and metrical attributes of these implements" (Freeman 1975: 253).

*Appearance of composite or multi-component tools.* The throwing stick or spearthrower is present at least by the Magdalenian period in western Europe and small, tanged projectile points—perhaps reflecting the presence of the bow-and-arrow—are found in the Levantine Solutrean assemblages. In addition, harpoons and other types of projectiles have been found with detachable foreshafts in the Magdalenian (*see* Fig. 3.7).

*An increase in the number of artifacts made of shaped bone, ivory, and antler (Mellars 1973; R. White 1989: 93).* This increase is presumably the result of the development of the burin and the groove-and-splinter method of obtaining strips of workable bone, ivory, and antler as described above. However, Freeman (1978a: 32) and Randall White (1982: 171–72) suggest that this increase may be more apparent than real due to the failure of archaeologists to recognize evidence of crude but intentional modification of bone during the excavation of Middle Paleolithic period sites. However, White goes on to note that, in contrast to the use of such material in Middle Paleolithic period contexts,

> in much of the earliest Upper Paleolithic, bone and antler working seems to be operating in a novel context which can be most conservatively described as non-utilitarian (in a technological sense). For example, in the Châtelperronian at Arcy-sur-Cure there are already a substantial number of "pendants" and decorated objects, betraying a level of formal investment not apparent in Middle Paleolithic bone and antler assemblages. The same is apparently true of the early Upper Paleolithic in Central and eastern Europe (R. White 1982: 170).

*The first appearance of artifacts that apparently served as personal ornaments (Mellars 1973; R. White 1982: 170; 1989: 93).* These new "non-

FIGURE 3.7. A photograph of three typical Upper Paleolithic tools: 1) burin from the Dordogne region; 2) borer from the French Pyrenees; 3) end scraper from Les Eyzies, France. *Courtesy, Field Museum of Natural History, Chicago.*

utilitarian" artifacts, which will be discussed in somewhat greater detail below, were made of bone, ivory, teeth, antler, shell, stone, and other materials and were often perforated for suspension.

*The first appearance of amber, flint, marine shells, ochre and other materials from exotic or non-local sources (Mellars 1973).* Randall White (1982: 172; 1989: 94–95) notes that such exotics could be obtained either through trade or transhumance across long distances. The evidence at hand indicates that neither kind of movement was previously common during the Middle Paleolithic period.

*Changes in the numbers of burials and in the nature and composition of burial populations.* Lewis Binford's (1971: 23) widely quoted dicta states that, in general, "the form and structure which characterizes the mortuary practices of any society are conditioned by the form and complexity of the organizational characteristics of the society itself." In line with this view, Sally Binford (1968), Harrold (1980),

Quechon (1976), Vandermeersch (1976), and others have sought clues to the nature of Upper Paleolithic society by comparing its burial populations with those of the preceding Middle Paleolithic period. The differences found between the two burial cohorts have interesting social implications.

First, a comparison of the raw numbers of burials reported for each period suggests that the Upper Paleolithic period witnessed a marked increase in the number of individuals who received funeral rites. Of course, this apparent increase may simply have been the result of a higher population density during the Upper Paleolithic period or their "shorter period of exposure to destructive forces before recovery" (Harrold 1980: 204).

Secondly, as compared to burials from the Middle Paleolithic, those of the Upper Paleolithic period tend to exhibit far greater quantity and diversity of grave goods such as tools, art objects, shells, and ochre (Harrold 1980: 206). Of course, this distinction cannot simply be attributed to differences in population or in the relative ages of the burials. Instead, it suggests either greater material well being in the later period or a more complex, well-developed funeral ritual and ideology, or both.

Thirdly, females buried with grave goods become common for the first time during the Upper Paleolithic. This perhaps suggests that women were allowed a greater degree of participation in the status system than had been the case in the Middle Paleolithic period. Harrold (1980: 207) concludes that "apparently at least some females in the societies represented by Upper Paleolithic burials enjoyed statuses as complex as those available to males."

Despite the willingness of Upper Paleolithic peoples occasionally to bury women with grave goods, in the burial population examined by Harrold (1980: 202), male burials outnumber females two to one. This preponderance of males could merely reflect sampling error or the well-documented tendency of researchers to class as male those specimens with intermediate characteristics. But it may indicate that males were simply more likely than females to receive this kind of burial treatment in the cultures of the Upper Paleolithic period. On the other hand, Harrold's (1980: 204–5) analysis suggests that individuals of different ages do not seem to have been treated differently from one another at death.

In contrast to those of the Middle Paleolithic, Upper Paleolithic period mortuary remains show a great deal of intra- and inter-regional variability with regard to the position of the body, associated grave goods or features, and so forth. Following Binford (1971), Harrold (1980: 204) states that mortuary customs function less to mark cultural boundaries than to symbolize status distinctions within societies. He thus interprets the variability in Upper Paleolithic mortuary remains as reflecting a greater number of social distinctions and social complexity in the societies of the period.

Finally, the occurrence of multiple burials, that is, the simultaneous interment of two or more individuals, is significantly more likely in Upper Paleolithic period contexts. Harrold (1980: 207) interprets the more common occurrence of these multiple burials as indirect evidence of greater population density and increased sociocultural complexity since, "the most likely causes of such multiple deaths, such as warfare, communicable disease, or ritual sacrifice, would seem likelier under (such) conditions."

However, Vallois's (1961) analysis of seventy-six skeletons from Upper Paleolithic period burials provides a sobering insight into the mortality rates of the period. Less than half of the individuals in his sample were older than twenty-one, and only 12 percent were older than forty years of age. The females in his sample all died before they were thirty. Butzer (1971: 482) concludes on the basis of this data that the mortality rates of the Upper Paleolithic period represented no improvement over those of the preceding Middle Paleolithic.

**The first appearance of cave and portable art and the possible development of complex notational and calendric systems.** The Upper Paleolithic period seems to have witnessed a powerful outpouring of aesthetic and intellectual energy. This outpouring is clearly mirrored in the representational cave and portable art of the period, and in the contemporary symbolic or nonrepresentational systems interpreted by some scholars as expressing sophisticated information, computation, or calendric reckoning.

The implications of these data for our understanding of Upper Paleolithic period religion is, of course, immense; here at last is a window into the mind of Ice Age humanity. Further, the window opens onto a mental universe that seems foreign to us in content but not in structure—a universe created and dwelt in, after all, by people like ourselves. The appearance of art and symbol in the Upper Paleolithic period thus represents a crucial step in what Teilhard de Chardin calls the process of "hominisation." And hominisation—the gradual emergence of thought and self-consciousness—is itself but one part of the "grand cosmic phenomenon of the vitalization of matter" (Teilhard de Chardin 1964: 208).

*A dramatic heightening in the pace of cultural and technical change.* As Butzer (1981: 178) notes, the Upper Paleolithic period in southwestern Europe lasts approximately twenty-three thousand years and is characterized (in his count) by nine or ten distinct techno-industrial traditions. These traditions for the most part succeed one another in time and persist on the average for twenty-five hundred years apiece. In contrast, the European Mousterian is characterized by six distinct facies some—perhaps most—of which are contemporary with one another rather than successive. These facies "span phenomenally long time ranges of 25 or even 70 millennia. In effect, the half-life of the Mousterian industrial variants was of an order of magnitude greater than that of the Upper Paleolithic industries" (Butzer 1981: 178).

The duration of the Mousterian is remarkable. More remarkable still is the apparent capacity of the various Mousterian facies to maintain their separate identities despite each others' contemporary presence. The human cultures known to anthropology today and in historical times simply do not operate in this manner. It would appear that the archaeological record of the transition from the Middle to the Upper Paleolithic period records a radical change in the dynamics of human culture. Compared to the earlier period, the Upper Paleolithic is a time of accelerating technical development, demographic expansion, and social change. Humankind has entered into the cultural trajectory that will carry it into the present.

# 4. Burials and Art as Ancient Hierophanies

There is archaeological evidence that hominids of the Early and Middle Paleolithic periods had begun to show a concern with realities transcending mere biological needs. What is uncertain, however, is just how much of this evidence can be interpreted as the remains of ancient hierophanies, that is, manifestations of the sacred (Eliade 1958: xiv), and therefore as evidence of early hominid religious behavior. Until quite recently, the battered, disembodied crania recovered at Chou-k'ou-tien and Monte Circeo, as well as the caches of cave bear skulls at Drachenloch, were accepted as evidence of a Lower and Middle Paleolithic "Cult of Skulls" and thus as hierophanies. However, increased understanding of bone taphonomy and of the natural processes that govern the formation of cave sediments has led to rejection of these data. The formal burial practices of the Middle Paleolithic period and the appearance of ochre in various special contexts may safely be viewed as hierophanies, but the meaning and significance of even these remains are obscure.

Fortunately, the archaeological record becomes more complete—and therefore somewhat clearer—in the ensuing Upper Paleolithic period with the development of more elaborate burial practices and the production of the earliest art objects and mural paintings. This chapter describes burials, art objects, and cave paintings in an effort to detect traces of the ancient hierophanies these documents most surely represent.

## BURIAL AS A REFLECTION OF SOCIAL STRUCTURE

Death is a primary (some would say the primary) focus of religious action and speculation. This is not surprising, given its finality, the tear in the social fabric that its occurrence usually leaves, the suffering that often accompanies it, and the unknown realm that it cloaks.

It is reasonable to assume that a people's funeral practices will convey information about their religious beliefs. In fact, Paleolithic burial remains do offer limited insights into the nature of the funerary behavior of the period, and glimpses of the hierophanies of which this behavior was a part.

First, red ochre, present only in limited quantities during the Lower and Middle Paleolithic periods, was dramatically characteristic of Upper Paleolithic period interments. For example, the so-called "Red Lady of Paviland," an Aurignacian period burial from Paviland Cave in England, had been covered with a thick layer of powdered ochre before the grave was back filled. The ochre layer was so thick over the burial that the skeleton, together with its associated animal bones, tools, and other grave goods, was stained to a deep maroon color. Numerous other examples of the use of red ochre during the Upper Paleolithic period have come to light (Wymer 1982: 250–53). Ochre was also used to coat fleshless bones interred as secondary burials, and sometimes placed alongside corpses, both as lumps and as caches of powder.

The use of red ochre in these funeral contexts is often interpreted in terms of the near universal association that exists, at least among modern peoples between the color red, human blood, and the forces of life versus death. As James observes,

> This widespread custom of coating the corpse with red ochre clearly had a ritual significance. Red is the color of living health. Therefore, as Professor Macalister has pointed out, if the dead man was to live again in his own body, of which the bones were the framework, to paint them with the ruddy coloring of life was "the nearest thing to mummification that the Paleolithic people knew; it was an attempt to make the body again serviceable for its owner's use." (James 1957: 28 partly quoting Macalister 1921: 502)

Second, human remains found in Upper Paleolithic graves are frequently wearing jewelry or ornaments made of bone, shell, horn, teeth, or ivory. Bone or stone tools such as scrapers or *bâtons-de-commandement*, perhaps once favored personal implements of the deceased, are sometimes found there as well. Animal bones recovered in the graves have generally been taken as grave offerings. Unfortunately, the poor excavation of some of these graves early in this century leaves us uncertain as to whether the animal bones were actually associated with the corpse, merely mixed with the grave fill when the pit was originally closed, or residue of funeral meals consumed by the mourners. Occasionally, quantities of perforated marine shells are recovered; presumably such shells were once sewn on the garments worn by the corpse or on a skin blanket or shroud used to cover it. Unperforated shells were apparently included as grave offerings. At the least, these careful burials bespeak cautious concern for the dead. They may also reflect belief in an afterlife, an idea which may have begun to take form as early as the Middle Paleolithic period.

## ART AS REFLECTION OF METAPHYSICS

The essence of religion is found in the distinction it draws between the sacred and the profane sphere of everyday life. Yet religion remains intimately and immediately wedded to that latter sphere. Religion focuses on crises of human existence: birth, sex, pain, good, evil, and death. It also provides humanity with a powerful syllabary used to justify, to explain, to comfort, to motivate, and to threaten in ways that have important practical implications or functions in human society. What Bidney (1953: 30) said of culture in general applies equally well to religion: it must be apprehended both at its theoretical level in its myth and cosmology and at its practical level in the ritual and material expression of its doctrine. The myth and cosmos of the Upper Paleolithic period are gone. Yet what must certainly be material fragments of the practical expression of its religious theory remain for us—if we but have the wit to interpret them.

Such religious expressions remain as magnificent traces in the period's realistic cave painting and accompanying enigmatic markings and symbols. Upper Paleolithic art, which appears in Europe sometime after about 32,000 B.P., is among the first great artistic traditions known in prehistory and still possesses the power to move us. (How many artists would dare dream that their creations would still strike responsive chords in humankind three hundred centuries after they made them?) The date of the appearance of this artistic tradition allows us to conclude that the aesthetic emotion—response to form, symmetry, color, line, and texture—had become established in our species by the late Upper Pleistocene epoch.

More than aesthetic considerations appear to have spurred the creation of this tradition. Ever since its discovery, and the recognition of its true age, scholars have seen in the art of the period those unaccustomed and extraordinary elements which are associated with religious hierophanies. Let us examine the major forms and patterns

known in Upper Paleolithic art in an effort to interpret these hierophanies and the religious theory and practice they might embody.

**Mobiliary Art.** The art of the period is generally divided into two
major categories: cave or "parietal" and portable or "mobiliary" art.
Both categories include a wide and varied range of phenomena. Mobiliary art, however, is the most heterogeneous. It includes transport-
able artifacts of wood, bone, stone, ivory, antler, horn, and even fired
clay which have been decorated in some manner. Modes of decoration include shaping, carving, engraving, painting, or any combination of these. Whatever the original or practical purpose of an artifact,
if it has been decorated it is considered an *object d'art*. Conversely, an
artifact which exhibits no modification or decoration beyond the
demands of its function or purpose is not art.

*Decorated Weapons, Tools, and Ornaments.* André Leroi-Gourhan
(1965b: 54–73) divides mobiliary art into two major categories: decorated weapons, tools, and ornaments; and objects of religious significance. The first of these categories he subdivides into: 1) expendable
weapons; 2) implements of lasting utility; 3) objects to be suspended;
and 4) miscellaneous objects. The second category consists of only
two, rather disparate, classes of objects: 1) statuettes; and 2) decorated stone slabs.

Leroi-Gourhan's typology is a useful descriptive arrangement. The
discussion of mobiliary art presented here follows the general order
of his system. The category "expendable weapons," consists of spears
and harpoons. Except to the extent that implements of this sort
exhibit engraved markings or drawings or were interred as grave
goods, they contribute little to our understanding of Upper Paleolithic period religion and will not concern us further here.

Leroi-Gourhan divides the next class, "implements of lasting utility," into four types: 1) pierced staffs (*bâtons-de-commandement*); 2)
spearthrowers; 3) spatulas; and 4) half-round rods. With the exception of the spearthrowers, the functions of these types of implements
remain unknown. Ignorance, however, is often a goad to speculation.
For example, consider the cylindrical antler shafts or bars perforated
at one end and often decorated with engravings, which he calls
"pierced staffs." Investigators early in this century, finding the objects reminiscent of the swagger sticks carried by British officers as a
symbol of their rank, called them *bâtons-de-commandement*. Alternatively, their socket-wrench shape has led others to suggest that

they might have served as dart or arrow shaft-straighteners. But, at present we do not know what function they actually performed (*see* Fig. 4.1).

Equally enigmatic are the so-called "spatulas." Like the *bâtons-de-commandement*, these objects are generally made of bone or antler. Viewed in plan, the spatulas usually form long, linear "extended ovals" (although late Magdalenian types are found in short, exaggerated "tear" or ovate shapes). They generally are flat in section and narrow to a thin edge at their distal ends. The proximal ends of the spatulas are assumed to be handles. The surfaces of the spatulas have commonly been carved or engraved with naturalistic images, symbols, patterned markings, or free-flowing spaghetti lines. Occasionally, the proximal ends of the spatulas have been carved in the shape of a salmon.

Half-round rods are strips of antler 20 or more centimeters in length. Leroi-Gourhan (1965b: 70) suggests that they were originally stuck together with a resinous glue to form a more resilient weapon, much as the Japanese do with split bamboo. Half-round rods are commonly carved with elaborate geometric and linear motifs.

Leroi-Gourhan's next category, "objects to be suspended," consists of three subdivisions: 1) pendants; 2) carved silhouettes; and 3) disks. Presumably such objects were items of personal adornment. They constitute the largest category of Upper Paleolithic mobiliary art. Ice Age peoples delighted in the use of carved and perforated shell, stone, amber, animal bone, and teeth, even fossils, as pendants, charms, amulets, or bracelets. At the Sungir site in European Russia, careful plotting of the distribution of bone beads in relation to skeletons and soil discoloration revealed that many such objects probably had been sewn to leather caps and clothing worn by the graves' occupants. Ivory pins apparently were used as buttons on the outer garments (Bricker 1976: 14–15).

During the Middle Magdalenian period in the area between the Dordogne and the Pyrenees, two particularly striking classes of "objects to be suspended" were produced: carved bone silhouettes and bone disks (Leroi-Gourhan 1965b). The silhouettes usually are carved out of hyoid bones from the skulls of horses or other herbivores. Often only the head or the neck are represented. Of the limited number of species pictured, the horse is by far the most common subject, although a number of ibex and at least one bison head have been reported. Holes, presumably designed to allow the silhouettes to be

FIGURE 4.1. Some examples of Upper Paleolithic period mobiliary art.
1) reindeer antler *bâton-de-commandement* engraved with outline of
horses; 2) harpoon; 3) bone plaquette with an incised drawing of a bovine;
4) fragment of an *atl-atl* or spearthrower throwing board of reindeer antler
carved and engraved in the shape of a bison licking an insect bite, La
Madeleine, France; 5) partially restored spearthrower throwing board made
of reindeer antler carved in the shape of a bird; 6) head of a horse carved
from mammoth ivory; 7) horse figurine carved of mammoth ivory; 8) female head with headdress carved in ivory; 9a) broken *bâton* made of reindeer antler with incised images of stags and fish. This object, now in the

strung on a necklace or sewn on a garment, have been drilled near the tops of most of these artifacts.

During the Middle Magdalenian, carved disks are generally made from horse or deer scapula, but in rare instances are carved of stone. They range in size from three to eight centimeters in diameter, are thin and flat, and generally have a hole drilled through their centers. Some are plain, but the great majority exhibit schematic or naturalistic images carved into their surfaces (Sieveking 1971: 207).

The naturalistic images used in mobiliary art include the same late Pleistocene game animals used in the parietal art of the period, although the frequency with which these species were represented sometimes varies between the two art forms. The reindeer, for example, was frequently engraved on portable artifacts but only rarely painted in the caves. Further, a number of species that have never been reported in parietal art—including chamois, frogs, snakes, insects, and even plants—appear occasionally in mobiliary art. Alexander Marshack's (1970, 1972a, 1972b, 1977) detailed examination of the images and patterns engraved on objects of this class led him to conclude that they were part of an Upper Paleolithic calendric and notational system.

*Objects of a Religious Significance.* Let us turn now to Leroi-Gourhan's second great category of mobiliary art, "objects of a religious significance," and to its subdivisions: statuettes and decorated slabs. The designation of this category is based on the questionable assumption that weapons, tools, and ornaments necessarily lack religious significance. After all, the hierophanies of Christianity should alert us to the fact that objects as mundane as goblets, unleavened bread, or crosses can, in Eliade's phrase, "manifest the sacred" under certain circumstances as dramatically as can exclusively religious objects. Context, more than nature, form, or practical function, determines

---

Musée de Antiquites Nationales in France, was recovered in the foothills of the Pyrenees at the site of Lorthet; 9b) plaster cast of a *déroulée*, on which the incised images from the Lorthet antler *bâton* are unrolled and exposed on a flat plane. Alexander Marshack interprets this scene to represent stags crossing a river at the time of the spring salmon run and thus to contain "time-factored" information; 10) the celebrated stone carving of the Venus of Willendorf from Austria. *Courtesy, American Museum of Natural History, New York.*

the religious significance of material objects. Nonetheless, both the statuettes and the carved slabs do seem set apart from the weapons, tools, and ornaments in this regard.

Although naturalistic statuettes of animals are occasionally recovered in central Europe, they are quite rare in the Franco-Cantabrian region. Animal figurines are generally carved of bone or ivory, but at Dolni Vestonice, Czechoslovakia, they were formed of baked clay, and are thus the earliest examples of ceramics know in prehistory. Common Pleistocene species are represented including horses, mammoths, bison, felines, even the rhinoceros. Animal statuettes are often interpreted as cult objects or props for rites of sympathetic magic. They may just as readily have been children's toys. Rarer still are statuettes of male human beings. Only a handful of examples of such representations have been reported, notably from Siberia and the Ukraine (Wymer 1982: 248).

**Venus of the Ice Age.** Female figurines or Venuses are far more common in the archaeological record than representations of either animals or males. In modern times at least, it is no exaggeration to say that the Venus statuettes are the most celebrated objects of Upper Paleolithic period mobiliary art.

Figurines of this type have been reported north of the Pyrenees from southwest France across Europe to the Urals. Although relatively common in France, they seem to be concentrated in central Europe (Leroi-Gourhan 1965b: 89). The Venuses were made sometime between about twenty-nine thousand and fourteen thousand years ago. Delporte (1979) identifies two major periods of intense figurine manufacture: an earlier Gravettian (or Perigordian) fluorescence and a much later Magdalenian one. As noted in chapter 3, Gamble (1981: 97) asserts that dates on the extreme ends of this range can be eliminated on a variety of archaeological grounds. When this is done, the time range of the figurines can be narrowed to between 25,000 and 23,000 B.P. in the Perigordian VI of southwestern Europe. If their time horizon can thus be abbreviated, it might be plausible to interpret Venus statuettes as the material remains of a relatively short-lived religious cult or revitalization movement that spread quickly over what is now temperate Europe during the early Upper Paleolithic period (Fagan 1983: 122).

The figurines were carved out of limestone, serpentine, hematite, or mammoth tusk ivory. A few rare examples from Dolni Vestonice were formed of baked clay tempered with pulverized bone. Generally,

FIGURE 4.2. The "Venus" of Willendorf, Austria, shown in profile here, is perhaps the most widely known Upper Paleolithic female figurine. Venus figures have been recovered in Europe from the Pyrenees to the Ural mountains in a wide variety of archaeological contexts. The Willendorf Venus is of carved stone approximately 11 centimeters in length and 6 centimeters in width. Other such female figurines were made of a number of materials including ivory, antler, and, in rare instances, fired clay. Note that despite the detailed carving of the hair-style and body features, the face remains featureless. *Courtesy, American Museum of Natural History, New York.*

the statuettes are not particularly realistic in their depictions. Artists gave little attention to facial features other than hair, and often the arms, without hands, are out of scale with the rest of the body. A large percentage of the figurines display exaggerated breasts, hips, and buttocks, and have swollen or distended lower abdomens that suggest an advanced stage of pregnancy (*see* Figs. 4.2 and 4.3). Many scholars have assumed that these features characterize all Venus statuettes and have concluded that, as a class, the fetching little

FIGURE 4.3. The "Venus" of La Mouthe, France, is a far less well-known Upper Paleolithic female figurine. It is carved in relief in a sandstone block 13 centimeters in length and 5.5 centimeters in width. In common with its more famous Austrian sister, the La Mouthe specimen exhibits ex-

objects were meant to celebrate and encourage female fertility, or to represent an ideal of female beauty that conceived of woman primarily "as a machine for giving birth and feeding efficiently" (Berenguer 1973: 51), or to symbolize a "mother goddess" that combined the previously mentioned characteristics in the person of a great, fecund deity credited with creating the earth or charged with guaranteeing its fertility.

***Decorated Slabs.*** Decorated or carved slabs, plaques, or plaquettes made of stone or bone occur virtually throughout the entire Upper Paleolithic sequence. Some specimens are small enough to hold in the hand while others are more than three feet long. They commonly are painted, carved, or engraved; some specimens exhibit all three types of decoration. Slabs carved in relief also occur.

According to Andre Leroi-Gourhan (1965b: 97), the earliest definite examples of "figurative work" or naturalistic representations are found carved crudely on decorated slabs in Aurignacian contexts at La Ferrassie, Cellier, Castanet, Isturitz, and Arcy-sur-Cure. These figures, found mixed with engraved lines and scribbles, appear to represent human females, animals, or ovals (which are often taken as vulvas or female symbols (*see* Fig. 4.4).

Through time, both the style and quality of the figures and symbols on the slabs change. According to Leroi-Gourhan, these changes closely parallel the stylistic evolution of Upper Paleolithic parietal art in general. He, therefore, sorts the slabs into the same temporal periods that he uses for parietal art. However, Denis Vialou (1984) persuasively argues that Leroi-Gourhan and other scholars have erred in according decorated blocks and slabs a minor place in their typologies. According to him, these sculpted stone objects must be regarded as a major third category of Upper Paleolithic art conceptually equal to parietal and mobiliary art—neither fully portable, nor entirely permanent—and distinguished from both media by differences in the aesthetic principles governing their decoration.

---

tremely prominent breasts and hips, a swollen abdomen, and an inattention to arms and facial features. We cannot be certain, however, whether the Venus was intended as a relief carving or was to be a full-round figurine that was never finished. *Courtesy, The Minneapolis Institute of Arts, Minneapolis.*

FIGURE 4.4. Highly stylized engravings of female figures on a stone slab from the Grotto de la Roche, a site on the Dordogne River just above its junction with the Couze near Lalinde, France. *Courtesy, Field Museum of Natural History, Chicago.*

**Parietal Art.** The term parietal art is used to refer to Upper Paleolithic period carvings or paintings on cave or rock shelter walls, on boulders, or on other permanent surfaces. In contrast to mobiliary art, some form of which is found in Upper Paleolithic period sites virtually throughout the Old World, the parietal art of the period is found primarily—but not exclusively—in southwestern Europe. It reached its greatest elaboration in France, Spain, and Italy, lands that are great modern centers of artistic endeavor (Pfeiffer 1978: 205). Evidence suggests that there were at least five major geographical centers of parietal art during the Upper Paleolithic period. The most famous of these is the Franco-Cantabrian region, defined in Chapter 3. The remaining four areas are in central Spain, along the southern

Spanish coast, in southern Italy, and on the Sicilian islands. Scattered examples of parietal art have been reported from Belgium, Germany, the Ural Mountains of Russia, and, most recently, from England. However, these examples are comparatively minor.

Rock art sites of late Pleistocene age have also been discovered beyond Europe. Apollo Cave in Namibia in southwestern Africa contains the oldest securely dated examples found thus far; painted stone tablets from this site may have been produced as many as 27,500 years ago (Butzer, Fock, Scott, and Stuckenrath 1979). Anati (1985: 54; 1986: 202) considers the celebrated rock paintings from the Kondoa and Singida districts of Tanzania in eastern Africa to be even older than those from Apollo Cave. Rock art also appears in Australia, India, and Brazil near the end of the late Pleistocene (Anati 1984: 13–54; 1986: 202; Rosenfeld, Horton, and Winter 1981: 12). However, none of these regions has ever produced parietal or mobiliary art of the quality or on the scale of southwestern Europe and a satisfactory reason for this has yet to be adduced despite the importance of such an explanation to our understanding of the evolution of *Homo sapiens sapiens* (Conkey 1983: 201–2).

More than two hundred caves containing parietal art have been reported from within the five European regions mentioned above (Conkey 1981: 20; Marshack 1976: 66). Pfeiffer (1978: 213) suggests that cave art sites tend to cluster together within the various regions. He notes, for example, the cluster of more than a dozen painted caves along the Les Eyzies River in the Dordogne. Whether this clustering reflects the former densities of Upper Paleolithic settlement, the availability of suitable caves, or both remains unclear. The density and distribution of art works within the caves are quite variable. Caves such as Tito Bustillo and Lascaux consist of huge galleries whose walls and ceilings are densely covered with paintings—in the latter cave, some images are twenty feet in length. Other caves contain only a few small and isolated examples scattered along lengthy passages.

*Chronology.* Although now recognized as definitely of Upper Paleolithic age, parietal art has proven to be much harder to date precisely than mobiliary art. Portable objects excavated from Upper Paleolithic sites can be chronologically ordered relative to one another by the superposition of the stratigraphic layers in which they were recovered. Like other classes of artifacts, mobiliary art objects also can be dated relative to one another by means of seriation. Seriational schemes can, in turn, be checked against the actual stratigraphic order in which similar material occurred in the ground. Finally, recent techniques of absolute or chronometric dating, including radiocarbon and thermoluminescence, can be used to date artifacts made of organic substances or of fired clay.

Theoretically, stratigraphy, seriation, and various chronometric techniques can be used to date parietal art as well, but their application has often proven difficult. It is the great frustration—and shame—of students of the Paleolithic that only a very small percentage of the parietal art known to science can be firmly dated. Occasionally, painted cave walls have been found covered by archaeological deposits. Since the deposits had to have accumulated after the walls were painted, the date of the deposits provides a minimum age for the parietal artwork. Examples of such coverings are reported by Breuil (1979: 37) at a number of sites including the sites of Pair-non-Pair, Isturitz, La Mouthe, and Combarelles in the Dordogne region. Even more precise dates can be obtained when parietal art is found actually incorporated within stratigraphic deposits. For example, Breuil was able to assign dates of ca. 15,000 B.C. to Solutrean wall friezes when collapsed sections were found sandwiched between two firmly dated occupation layers in Le Roc de Sers cave in the Charente Valley of the Dordogne region. Breuil also dated embedded engraved stone plaques at ca. 10,000 B.C. when they were recovered from Upper Magdalenian period deposits in the Teyat caves of the same region. Of course dates derived in this manner are the most certain— and the most exceptional. Somewhat less reliable dates are obtained through the combined use of stratigraphy and stylistic similarity. Breuil describes this technique as follows:

> It sometimes happens, as at Altamira, Castillo, Hornos de la Pena and Gargas, that levels of a definite date in the recent Paleolithic, produced small sized engravings on bone or stone of exactly the same style as those on the walls in the same localities, but not buried in a level. This allows us to attribute to the Aurignacian, Perigordian, or dawn of the local Magdalenian, the figures of the same style on the walls, whether entangled or not with figures of another style (1979: 37).

After establishing the general dates of various stylistic traditions in this manner, students of Upper Paleolithic art have attempted to cross date them with parietal paintings of uncertain age in other sites and areas of southwestern Europe. Since cave artists commonly superimposed their work one on the other, once a drawing is assigned a relative age through cross dating, it becomes possible to work out a relative chronology for the other drawings with which it appears. Of course, such a sequence is a purely relative one. There is no way of knowing how much time actually elapsed between the various superimpositions—it could have been minutes, or it could have been millennia.

Finally, parietal art has been dated by means of seriation. According to Rowe (1961), seriation is "the arrangement of archaeological materials in a presumed chronological order on the basis of some logical principle other than superposition." The first comprehensive chronological arrangement of parietal art was proposed by the Abbé Breuil (1979: 38–40), who postulated two great cycles or traditions in cave art: the Aurignacian-Perigordian and the Solutreo-Magdalenian. Breuil envisioned both of these cycles as characterized by orderly development of stylistic change. Where possible he based his ordering of these formal changes on stratigraphic evidence and the superpositions of various drawing styles on the cave walls. Of course, this was not possible in most cases and the absence of stratigraphic certainty forced Breuil to make a number of assumptions about the developmental trajectory traced by Paleolithic art. As with all seriations, the accuracy of Breuil's scheme hinges on the validity of the logical principles or assumptions upon which the arrangement is based. Breuil assumed that, in general, parietal art grew increasingly more complex during the Upper Paleolithic period, and was the product of individual artists working at separate intervals and seeking to gain magical control over the animals by reproducing their images. Breuil's assumptions still retain wide acceptance, but both have been called into question in recent years.

Breuil's scheme persisted in the scientific and popular literature on cave art until the mid-1960s, when it was largely superseded by André Leroi-Gourhan's (1965b, 1968) somewhat more complex four-period seriation. Leroi-Gourhan rejects Breuil's view that the caves were painted incrementally over countless generations by individuals seeking hunting magic. He proposes instead that they were decorated systematically, often over relatively short periods of time, as part of large-scale societal efforts. He also suggests that the caves were only gradually explored and that therefore the paintings in the deeper galleries are generally younger than those near the surface. In further contrast to Breuil, the four stylistic periods defined by Leroi-Gourhan correspond in only a general way to the archaeological subdivision of the Upper Paleolithic. His earliest period, Style I Primitive, dates from the first evidence of art in the Upper Paleolithic after ca. 32,000 B.P. until 27,000 B.P. Style I overlaps the later phases of the Typical Aurignacian and the early phases of the Upper Perigordian. According to André Leroi-Gourhan (1968), the art of Style I consists of naturalistic renderings of animals and of female genitalia as well as lines and rows of dots. The animal drawings tend to be crude and often consist only of heads or forequarters.

Style II Primitive is between 27,000 and 20,000 B.P. overlapping the later phases of the Solutrean. During the seven thousand years of the style's duration, Upper Paleolithic art achieved its maximum geographical distribution. It is to this stylistic period that André Leroi-Gourhan attributes the earliest parietal art: "paintings and engravings executed on the walls of open rockshelters or on cave walls that were illuminated by daylight" (André Leroi-Gourhan 1968: 62). He asserts that the quality of the animal drawings referrable to Style II, while improving, are still primitive and inchoate.

Style III Archaic is dated between 20,000 and 15,000 B.P. It overlaps the later Solutrean period and Magdalenian phases O, I and II. Although the character of the animal drawings in Style III retains a certain primitive quality, many such drawings are done in polychrome and reveal improved painting and sculpting technique. At the same time, the abstract rectangular or bracket-shaped signs of the period "show such a diversity of embellishment that they have been compared to heraldic coats of arms" (André Leroi-Gourhan 1968).

The final period in the scheme, Style IV Classic, dates to between 15,000 and 11,000 B.P. and is conterminous with Magdalenian phases III through IV. It was during this final stylistic period that Upper Paleolithic art achieved its technical and aesthetic zenith. Animals were rendered in polychrome with great skill and realism. The paintings of this period are no longer flat and static but convey a sense of movement and vitality through careful use of shading, texture, and line work.

Like Breuil's earlier two-cycle scheme, Leroi-Gourhan's fourfold period seriation of Upper Paleolithic art has experienced wide acceptance. But Conkey (1983: 204–5) points out that both Breuil's and Leroi-Gourhan's systems are based on the undemonstrated assumption that Upper Paleolithic art represents a unified tradition in which change was gradual and development was logical: viz., monochromatic painting evolved into polychromatic painting, techniques became more refined and sophisticated, the stiff and crude images of early times gave way to the mobile and realistic ones of the late period, and the entire tradition shared a thematic unity.

A strong case has been made by Lorblanchet (1977), Hahn (1972, 1981), and Ucko and Rosenfeld (1967) for "synchronic diversity" in Upper Paleolithic art, that is, for the contemporaneity of certain styles and techniques thought by Breuil and Leroi-Gourhan to follow one another in chronological order and therefore to be useful in establishing ages of the images relative to one another. Further, Gamble (1982), Collins and Onians (1978), and Delporte (1979) reject the notion of thematic unity during the entire Upper Paleolithic period in favor of distinct early and late artistic subtraditions characterized by distinctive themes or subjects. Once accepted as dogma, both the Breuil and the Leroi-Gourhan seriational schemes are questioned by contemporary students of Upper Paleolithic art. It would appear that the more we learn about the Paleolithic, the less certain our understanding becomes. Our inability to date precisely individual works or even to arrange them with certainty into their proper chronological order is a great impediment to the study and interpretation of Upper Paleolithic period parietal art.

**Techniques of Cave Painting.** The basic artistic techniques utilized by Upper Paleolithic artists include painting, engraving, bas-relief sculpting, sculpting in the round, and clay modeling. These techniques were often combined with one another in various ways. In addition, natural relief and other features on the cave walls were often carefully incorporated by the artist into his composition. As André Leroi-Gourhan put it:

> The expression of volume greatly preoccupied Paleolithic artists. Numerous examples show the use of natural relief in caves; a concave wall suggesting a bulging flank, the ridge used as a dorsal line or the drippings of stalactites integrated as animal feet demonstrated an interest in volume which proves the existence of true bas-reliefs in the Solutrean and Magdalenian. (1982: 9)

On the other hand, Upper Paleolithic artists seem to have taken little care to avoid covering earlier paintings that happened to be on the wall surfaces that they had chosen to decorate. In fact, the superimposition or overlapping of apparently separate compositions one atop the other is a common feature of parietal art.

The pigments used by these artists seem to have been largely mineral based. A close study of the paints used at Lascaux by Laming-

Emperaire and Coraud (cited in Arlette Leroi-Gourhan 1982: 109–10)
determined that manganese oxide was the source for blacks, while
ochre (iron oxide or ferrous oxide clay) produced reds, yellows,
browns, oranges, and violets. Porcelain clays—used directly or mixed
with powdered quartz or calcite—were used to produce whites.

Analysis of paint fragments and powdered pigment samples revealed that paints rarely consisted of a single compound. Rather,
these artists, like their modern counterparts, mixed compounds together to achieve the colors or properties they were seeking. A base of
some kind was apparently added to the mineral compounds after
they were powdered and mixed. Some scholars have suggested that
animal fat may have been used to create an oil paint. At Lascaux,
however, Arlette Leroi-Gourhan notes that, "experiments demonstrated that the pigments had been prepared by mixing the ground
mineral powders with cave water, which has a naturally high cal-
cium content that ensures good adhesion and great durability" (1982:
109–10). For the most part, these artists do not seem to have made
use of organic sources of color such as berries or charcoal. No doubt
their preference for mineral-based pigments contributed to the survival of parietal art into our day.

**Subjects and Contexts of Parietal Art.**  After the question of beauty, the
most significant aspects of any artistic tradition are, in my view, two
in number: first, the subject matter that concerned the artists and
their audience; second, the contexts in which their work appeared.
To speak of the art of Florence during the early Renaissance is to
discuss the development of themes like the Madonna enthroned, the
Annunciation, or the life of Saint Francis painted on wooden altar-
pieces or done in fresco on church walls. In contrast, to speak of
British art in the late eighteenth century is to conjure up visions of
portraits of the wealthy and well born done in oils. It is to talk of
paintings of idealized landscapes, animals, or sporting scenes hung in
private houses. Aesthetic considerations aside, the themes and contexts of these two traditions convey markedly different ideological
and sociological information. In the former tradition, works of art
were commissioned largely by ecclesiasts seeking both to glorify the
Church and to instruct the illiterate by giving tangible or objective
form to myth. In the latter tradition, works were done at the behest of
wealthy patrons seeking to affirm or announce their claim to upper-

class status, to indulge their largely secular and private interests, or to immortalize their families and their pastimes.

To speak of the art of the Upper Paleolithic period in Franco-Cantabria is also to speak of a limited range of subject matter found in a generally specifiable set of contextual circumstances. It is hoped that an examination of these themes and contexts will illuminate the ideology and society that inspired them. As noted earlier, contemporary scholars disagree on the question of the homogeneity of Upper Paleolithic art. Leroi-Gourhan (1965b) and Sieveking (1979) emphasize the unity of style and meaning in the tradition, while Conkey (1983, 1988), Vialou (1983) and others vigorously reject that position and assert that Upper Paleolithic art is remarkably diverse. Since no artistic tradition is either completely uniform or totally random in its style and imagery, we are probably safe in regarding this issue as a matter of emphasis.

***The Major Subjects and Artistic Convention.*** The most common subjects of the artist are the large mammalian game animals that inhabited Europe near the end of the Pleistocene epoch. Accurate renderings of horse, bison, auroch, or wild cattle, mammoth, ibex, or wild goat, and both stags and hinds of various species of deer are favored. Far less common are reindeer, saiga antelope, musk ox, woolly rhinoceros, bear, and lion (*see* Fig. 4.5). These naturalistic images are generally done in simple profile, but more sophisticated "bi-angular" perspectives were also used. Although depictions of game animals often occur in thick clusters, one superimposed upon another, the scale of their representation is seldom uniform.

Another frequently occurring element is a wide variety of non-naturalistic designs. These designs have been called by several names, including tectaforms, claviforms, penniforms, "W" and "M" shapes, dots, ovals, parallel lines, grids, and other terms; they may be schematic representations of natural forms or purely nonrepresentational symbols or signs. Perhaps their variety is great enough to include both schematic forms and pure symbols. Whatever their meaning, the unusual "co-existence of realistic and geometric subjects . . . is strongly characteristic of parietal art" ( André Leroi-Gourhan 1982: 62).

The second major class of apparently nonrepresentational design forms includes the enigmatic macaroni or meander lines which wind like ribbons or ivy across the ceilings and walls of many painted

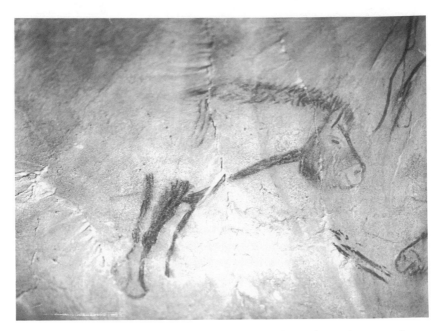

FIGURE 4.5. Outline drawing of the forepart of a horse from the cave of Niaux in the foothills of the French Pyrenees. *Courtesy, Field Museum of Natural History, Chicago.*

caves. The meanders form branching and intersecting networks 1) with single thick or thin lines; or 2) through parallel hatching with dense bundles of many thin lines; or 3) by filling the area between two thick parallel lines with cross-hatching, parallel-hatching or zigzag lines; or 4) with bands of two, three, or four distinct lines running parallel to one another. Meanders occur either as yellow, red, or black painted lines, as unpainted engravings, or simply as finger marks on the damp clay of some underground chambers. Similar networks of lines seem to have been engraved on mobiliary art objects. Animals, painted or engraved in naturalistic style, are commonly interwoven into the meander traceries. In contrast to the discrete outlines of designs like the tectaforms, penneforms or other nonrepresentational iconographic elements, meanders are rambling, inclusive, and undisciplined.

Like the subject matter, the artistic conventions of the Upper Paleolithic tradition render it distinctive. First, parietal paintings lack design fields or well-defined borders with ground or baselines for

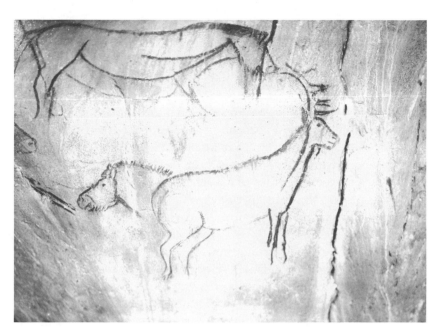

FIGURE 4.6. Outline drawings or sketches from Niaux, France. The stag in the foreground appears to have been superimposed over the horse's head and neck. *Courtesy, Field Museum of Natural History, Chicago.*

central subjects. Without clear frames or backgrounds, the individual subjects and subject groups seem to float in free space unencumbered either by earth or sky. Animals are sometimes drawn upside down relative to the floor and are often left incomplete. In such a setting, the orientation and degree of completion of the figures is apparently irrelevant. In the flickering light of a torch or tallow lamp, the unearthly qualities of the game animals on the cave walls must have been dramatically enhanced.

The floating, otherworldly quality of the parietal drawings (*see* Fig. 4.6) is enhanced by another convention commonly used by the cave artists: the superimposition of later paintings or engravings atop adjacent parts of earlier renderings. As Schapiro puts it: "The artist worked . . . on a field with no set boundaries and thought so little of the surface as a distinct ground that he often painted his animal figure over a previously painted image without erasing the latter, as if it were invisible to the viewer (1969: 223).

Early students of parietal art took these superimpositions to be random and concluded that such randomness meant the images were done at separate intervals by individual artists who, intent upon recording their own visions, disregarded the earlier work of others and painted over them. As noted above, Breuil (1979: 38) saw the cave friezes as vast palimpsests whose chronological history could be determined by carefully observing the order in which the images had been superimposed one upon the other. Leroi-Gourhan rejects the view that the superimpositions are random. He contends instead that the superimposition of the various animals was done consciously in accord with systematic rules of association or co-occurrence of species. He considers the animals to be symbols in a formal system and he attempts to specify the "grammar" governing their manipulation by the cave artist.

In addition to superimposing new images upon older ones, older representations were sometimes re-engraved or repainted after their original creation. Marshack (1972a: 253, 255; 1977: 311) refers to this process as one of "renewal or reuse" and notes that examples of it are found in both mobiliary and parietal art. His terms imply that the images were restored in order to rejuvenate them. Marshack also cites cases in which earlier images were changed slightly in the process. He concludes that in such instances new information is intentionally being conveyed or recorded by the later modification. Of course, such renewal might have been undertaken simply to retrieve the fading outline of a valued picture.

**Less Common Subjects.** In addition to the numerous straightforward representations of certain species of game animals and to the enigmatic nonrepresentational design forms, a number of other themes or subjects occur occasionally. These less common images fall into five general categories. The first category is realistic representations of fish and birds, which occur seldom in the art of the period. Although silhouettes interpreted as snow owls have been recorded at Les Trois Frères and engravings of fish have been recorded at Le Mas d'Azil (André Leroi-Gourhan 1965b: 449, 457), at El Pindal in Asturias, and elsewhere (Sieveking 1979: 173), such images are quite rare. The second group of less common subjects includes realistic images of such late Pleistocene mammals as the megaceros (the so called Irish elk), true elk, saiga antelope, wild boar, wolf, fox, and musteline or ferret (Andre Leroi-Gourhan 1982: 49).

A third class consists of imaginary or "hybrid" animal forms such as the celebrated Agnus Dei, or lamb god, from Pair-non-Pair which is an engraving of a ruminant body with the head of both an ibex and a horse. Marshack (1972c: 237) refers to these monsters as transformed story animals and assumes they illustrated complex mythological tales. Some of these images, however, may be less monstrous and apocryphal than they at first appear. Kurten (1968: 174), for example, suggests that the "Fabulous Beast" from Lascaux may in fact be a painting of a Chiru antelope (*Pantholops hodgsoni*), a central Asian ruminant not otherwise reported from Pleistocene Europe.

A fourth class includes man-animal combinations, such as the famous "Sorcerer" or "Great Magician" described by Breuil at Les Trois Frères. This upright, if hunched, bipedal creature has reindeer antlers and ears, an owlish face that ends in a human beard, bear paws instead of hands, a horse's tail and a large, flaccid human penis (*see* Fig. 4.7). Of course, the exotic qualities of the Les Trois Fréres man-animal may have been exaggerated by Breuil in the celebrated copy he made of it. In any case, the figure has been interpreted variously as a costumed dancer, a man-beast, a god, and a self-transforming sha-man. André Leroi-Gourhan (1982: 48–49) refers to these hybrid ani-mals and man-animal combinations collectively as monsters.

Fifth, naturalistic representations of the human form were only rarely done by the artists. One exception is the site of La Marche in the Lussac-les-Chateaux region of France which contains fifty or more caricature drawings of human faces shown in profile (Pales 1981). Another is the credible models of human vulvas often found carved or engraved on boulders or cave walls. Further, the image of the human hand, generally painted in black or red, appears either as negative outlines or as positive prints at sites like Abri Labatut, Tibiran, and Les Combarelles in France and the cave sites of El Castillo and El Pindal in Spain (André Leroi-Gourhan 1965a: 308). At the site of Gargas in Hautes-Pyrenees in France, hand prints occur in dense clusters. Some of these prints seem to be of deformed hands, others from hands with missing fingers. Whether disease, amputa-tion, or cheating (that is, the folding of fingers under the palm when tracing the outline of the hand) account for these missing digits has never been satisfactorily determined. Tantalizing as these hand prints are, their occurrence in Upper Paleolithic period art is really quite limited (Leroi-Gourhan 1965a: 308). Aside from these exam-ples, and a few other exceptions, the artists of the period seem to have been more comfortable rendering the human form schematically or symbolically. Rosenfeld (1977: 107), for example, interprets a large

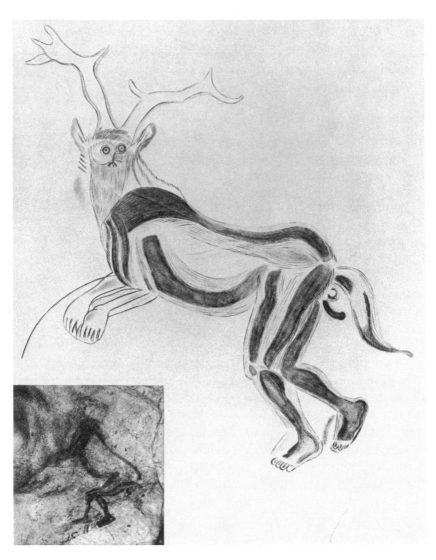

FIGURE 4.7. The celebrated copy of a man-animal combination image from the site of Les Trois Frères, France, made by the Abbé Breuil. This image, which Breuil dubbed "The Sorcerer," is some 2.55 meters long. It is located in a portion of the cave known as "The Sanctuary." This representation, which may reflect a certain artistic license on the part of the Abbé, depicts a hunched, bipedal creature with reindeer antlers and ears, an owlish face that ends in a human beard, bear paws instead of hands, a horse's tail, and a large, flaccid human penis. Both the nature and the location of this panel led Breuil (1979: 170) to the conclusion that "it is really the 'God' of Les Trois Frères." Others have interpreted it as depicting a costumed dancer, a man-beast, or a self-transforming shaman. *From Abbé Breuil's* Four Hundred Centuries of Cave Art, *courtesy of Hacker Art Books.*

number of parietal engravings and drawings as highly stylized human torsos shown headless and in profile with exaggerated hips and buttocks (*see* Fig. 4.4). He suggests that such schematic images are found throughout southwestern Europe.

Sixth, a far rarer form of human representation is compositions showing outline or stick figures of people engaged in what perhaps were hunts, fights, or shamanic seances. A prime example of this genre is the enigmatic bison-and-birdman panel discovered in the "Shaft of the Dead Man" at Lascaux (*see* Fig. 4.8). André Leroi-Gourhan (1982: 54) notes that such scenes generally depict the vanquishing of the human by his animal adversary. Works of this type are generally interpreted as narrative scenes meant to record either real events or mythical episodes, but some alternative interpretations are suggested below. In more recent rock-art traditions, like that of the San (or Bushmen) peoples of southern Africa (Lewis-Williams 1982) or the prehistoric Pueblo Indians of the American Southwest (Schaafsma 1971, 1972), narrative panels are quite common. Their rarity in the parietal art of the Upper Paleolithic period is curious.

Seventh, it is generally assumed that this period produced no naturalistic parietal paintings of landscapes and vegetation or "lesser" elements in the environment such as insects, amphibians, or reptiles. This may simply mean that their eyes were fixed elsewhere. The artists of the early Italian Renaissance, seeing only the saints and antiquity, also produced few memorable images of nature. Still, the hunting and gathering subsistence of Upper Paleolithic peoples must have been based upon a detailed knowledge of their surroundings and a profound and sustained interest in it. One would expect that such people would eventually have transformed this knowledge and interest into art. In fact, they may have done so but primarily in schematic or symbolic form and through the medium of mobiliary art rather than with realistic images on cave walls (Arlette Leroi-Gourhan 1982: 49). For example, Marshack interprets a very tiny engraved image on a *bâton-de-commandement* from Montgaudier in the Charente district of France as a

> perfectly realistic image of a spring sprout, including a careful engraving of the downward pointing branched roots and the upward spreading leaves. The image is only half an inch high and looks as though it might have been engraved with the aid of a jeweler's magnifying glass. No such specialized plant image had ever been reported for the Ice Age. (1970: 59)

FIGURE 4.8. The stick figure composition known as "The Dead Man" from the Shaft at Lascaux in Spain. The panel vividly represents a violent confrontation between a birdheaded or beaked anthropomorph and an immense bison or auroch in a charging pose. The anthropomorph has stiff legs, four-fingered hands, and an erect penis. The bison appears to have been wounded; his intestines pour out copiously just in front of his rear legs. Not shown in this photograph, but immediately adjacent to the birdman and bison figures, is a black outline drawing of a rhinoceros done in a very different artistic style. The total length of the panel, including the black rhinoceros, is 1.85 meters. *From Abbé H. Breuil's* Four Hundred Centuries of Cave Art, *courtesy of Hacker Art Books.*

Marshack goes on to suggest that images on the baton that previous scholars have taken to be barbed weapons or the feathered, distal ends of arrow shafts, are really plants in full leaf. He even identifies one small engraving as the image of a flower in bud or bloom and several others as tiny, multi-legged insects. He sees these pictures as part of a sophisticated system of symbols that in specific combinations describe or represent the changing seasons. Further, he suggests that plant images are fairly widespread and are part of a code whose meaning may be partially deciphered. More will be said of Marshack's hypotheses below. If he is correct, our present conception of the subject range of Upper Paleolithic art will have to be revised.

**The Context.** Until fairly recently, parietal art was thought to occur more or less exclusively in remote subterranean caverns. It is becoming clear that this is an over simplification. Upper Paleolithic painting now appears to have been much more ubiquitous than was first thought. For example, there is some evidence to suggest that the outer cave mouths and rock shelter areas (where the people actually lived) also may have been painted, but that the paintings have disappeared over the centuries due to exposure. As noted earlier, André Leroi-Gourhan (cited in Conkey 1981: 23) suggests that such open areas had specific themes or types of representations associated with them. According to him, vulva signs and other depictions of women or of female sexuality are more common in such daylight locales. In addition to the limited traces of parietal art at the mouths or openings of caves, some of the major underground galleries are immediately and easily accessible from the surface. Lascaux is a prime example; some of the most spectacular paintings at the site are found only a few steps from its surface entrance.

At other sites, paintings are often very difficult to reach. For example, at Niaux in the Dordogne, paintings are located some two-thirds of a mile back from the current entrance of the cave. Paintings in Montespan Cave are found at the end of an underground trail nearly a mile in length—and much of this path leads along and *in* an underground river with temperatures of 43° to 46° F. To reach the parietal art in Etcheberriko Kharbia (or Etchiberri) cave today, one must cross two underground lakes by boat and then scale a 131-foot cliff wall (Debecker 1978: 13). Wall paintings and engravings in a tiny chamber in Nerja cave in central Spain can be reached only through a life-threatening climb up a sheer rock face deep inside the cave (Lya Dams quoted in Pfeiffer 1980b: 74).

Numerous other underground parietal art sites, although less difficult to reach than those in Nerja or Etcheberriko Kharbia, are located in dark and remote underground passages which in some instances can be approached only by crawling through narrow rock cat holes or tubes, or by climbing over obstacles. André Leroi-Gourhan (1982: 75) suggests that the relative ease or difficulty of access to the paintings reflects the function of the specific caverns in which they are located. Some caves may have been temples, that is, cult places "accessible to all or at least a relatively large proportion of the community." In contrast, the more inaccessible caves, galleries, or niches might have served as sanctuaries or sacred places restricted to a minority. Of course, we cannot always be certain that we have located the entrance originally used by the cave artists. Over the millennia since the abandonment of the cave sites, former entrances may have been blocked, altered, or simply lost.

Nonetheless, in general, the placement of the paintings suggests that the subterranean context was very important to the cave artists. Of course, context is also important in contemporary religious art. Consider the images of the saints on the painted icons in a Greek Orthodox cathedral. They shimmer and seem to float above the protean sea of light created by banks of candles gleaming beneath them. The emotions such visions create are powerful and moving. In a palpable—often almost tactile—fashion they evoke faith, guilt, pain, peace, fear, or a hundred other emotions in the breast of the beholder. But, strip these icons of their semi-darkness and shimmering banks of candles; put them at eye level in a museum display case; carefully label them with crisp white cards discussing provenance, age, technique, and style in flat technical prose; observe the chipped gilding at their bases, the crudeness of their painted detail, the stilted manner of the saints' carriage . . . and their religious spell is broken.

So also with the cave art of the Upper Paleolithic period; context was surely an essential element in its appreciation and its power. The context conveys—at least to us—cold, darkness, a separation from humankind, even danger. The unease that such settings must have engendered in Paleolithic people was apparently utilized and heightened by the artists. Pfieffer suggests that the paintings and engravings were often positioned in an intentionally dramatic manner; situated, as it were,

> with malice aforethought, so that they would be encountered unexpectedly, just past a bend, under a ledge, on a high stalagmitic column, at the edge of a pit, or deep in a pit. In fact, every visit to an art cave is a series of surprises, and you get the feeling that the surprises were planned by someone with a fine sense of drama and theater, a master of illusion. (1980b: 75)

But other sorts of location also seem to have been important. Pfieffer (1978: 218) notes that parietal paintings were commonly placed in some of the most awkward and difficult positions on the cave surfaces. He concludes from such placement, and from the superimpositions of paintings atop earlier ones, that specific spots or precise locations within the caves were as important as the pictures themselves. Thus it was that such spots continued to attract artist after artist, again and again over the millennia.

In any event, the number, function, and significance of these specific locations must have changed through time as artists and engravers pushed farther into the caverns. In general, it appears that the peoples of the early Upper Paleolithic period worked near the entrances of the caves while their descendants, leaving daylight and the galleries and palimpsests of their ancestors behind, ventured deeper and deeper. Andre Leroi-Gourhan, who formulated this generalization, notes that it is not true in all instances.

> There are no low reliefs in places that do not receive daylight, perhaps for technical reasons: the execution of a sculpture by the light of lamps burning animal fat would be extremely laborious. One can only suppose that beginning at a certain epoch the Paleolithic painters and engravers moved deeper inside the caves which their ancestors had already sculptured and decorated with paint at the entrances. But there are few sanctuaries well inside caves which belong to the archaic style, such as at Gargas in the Pyrenees. At all events, it seems certain that while the first movement deeper into the caves may have occurred at an early date, the real invasion of the dark interiors was relatively late. (1965b: 51)

Thus, the interiors of the great caverns of southwestern Europe may have formed an internal frontier for the people of the Upper Paleolithic, a frontier which expanded only gradually over the generations. It would have been a frontier of space, but also one of darkness. In terms of their physical makeup, human beings are essentially creatures of the light. We function in the dark or become nocturnal chiefly by cultural means. The use of the great caverns in Franco-Cantabria must have demanded the conquest of darkness on both technical and emotional planes. Penetration of the internal cavern frontier by Upper Paleolithic peoples is thus analogous to what Melbin (1978) calls the *colonization of the night*, that is, the increasing dispersal of human activities over more and more hours of the daily twenty-four-hour cycle, which he asserts characterizes the contemporary era. In both the ancient frontier of the cavern and the modern frontier of the night, the adaptive niche of the human species has been expanded by cultural means.

Another, albeit less certain, characteristic of the context of Upper

Paleolithic parietal art has recently been noted by Bahn (1978a). He suggests that the cave art sites generally contain underground streams, lakes, or springs or are entered from mouths that are in close proximity to such water sources on the surface. He asserts that the correlation can be further qualified in the French Pyrenees and in northern Spain where the majority of the known parietal art sites are found near thermal or mineral springs. Thermal springs do not occur in the Dordogne for geological reasons, but Bahn (1978a: 132) suggests that parietal art caves may have been associated with mineral springs in that region.

Bahn (1978a: 125–26) accounts for this association between cave art and the location of what he calls "abnormal water" by reference to what he considers to be universal features of human religion: the veneration of water, the tendency of the human mind to dichotomize, and the association of caves with the human womb, with birth or maternity, with the underworld, and ultimately, with death. According to Bahn, caves worldwide tend to be viewed as points of connection between the dichotomous spheres of earth and life on one hand, and underworld and death on the other. Water that flows into, through, or out of such caverns or water that emanates from the underworld in thermal or mineral springs commonly takes on a particular significance: it seems to link or cross the boundary between these separate spheres. He suggests that this idea might have been current as early as the Upper Paleolithic period. Whether or not Bahn is correct in his interpretation, the apparent correlation that he has identified between the distribution of abnormal water sources and the location of certain caves containing parietal art is an intriguing one. This is especially so in light of Marshack's (1977: 314–15) identification of two iconographic elements of parietal art, the zigzag and the meander, as water symbols.

# 5. Interpretations of Art and Religion

Virtually since its recognition as a genuine product of Pleistocene age mankind, parietal art has stimulated and challenged scholars to interpret its cultural and religious significance. Generally, such interpretations have reflected the dominant theoretical perspectives of the day, the extent of anthropological knowledge or, at worst, the intellectual fads current in the discipline at the time (cf., Silver 1979: 267 for a similar observation about interpretations of primitive art). With a nod to Ucko and Rosenfeld (1967) who proposed this distinction, I have divided these theories into two chronological categories: classical and contemporary. Classical theories include those explanations of Upper Paleolithic art that emerged early in this century and dominated the field of prehistory for fifty years or more. The Abbé Breuil summated the classical approach in his work, just as he personified it in his life. As a watershed marking the transition from the classical to contemporary, I have chosen the publication of André Leroi-Gourhan's monumental *Prehistoire de l'art occidental* (1965a).

## CLASSICAL INTERPRETATION OF UPPER PALEOLITHIC PERIOD ART AND RELIGION

Classical theorists relied heavily on notions of primitiveness derived from the comparative work of Sir James Frazer, used concepts of social and religious life drawn from the work of Emile Durkheim and Arnold van Gennep, and drew direct analogies between the practices of contemporary peoples like Australian Aborigines and those of the Paleolithic period. The discussion of the classical theories follows in topical order and includes the views that Upper Paleolithic period art was totemic in character, was an elaborate prop for rites of passage or hunting magic or was inspired by shamanism.

**Totemism.** Parietal art had only just been recognized as dating to the Upper Paleolithic period when scholars in the early decades of the twentieth century turned to the work of Emile Durkheim and his school for its interpretation. Durkheim sought in *The Elementary Forms of the Religious Life* (1912 [1961]) to determine the function of religion in society in general by examining what he took to be its simplest form—that of the Australian Aborigines. Durkheim used the accounts of the Aborigines found in Spencer (1914) and Spencer and Gillen (1927) as the source of his ethnographic data. According to these ethnographers, the religious life of the Aborigines was organized around their totemic system.

Totemism may be defined as the symbolic association of plants, animals, or objects with individuals or classes of people, especially the use of animal species as emblems by exogamous clans. In Australia and elsewhere, peoples often name their social groups after such beings or objects and then observe a special relationship with their group's totem—for instance, by claiming it as their ancestor, refusing to eat its flesh, or carrying out rituals to increase its numbers. In other words, the Aborigines regarded their totems as sacred objects or beings and treated them accordingly. For Durkheim, the fact that the Aborigines used animals or plants as totems was not the most significant characteristic of their religious institutions. Rather, what these totems stood for was the important thing. According to Spencer and Gillen, such totems were regarded as symbols of the clans—the most important social unit among the Aborigines. Durkheim concluded that the collective worship of the symbol of the clan was in reality the worship of the clan itself. The totemic religion of the Aborigines was thus centered on the worship of their social group. According to Durkheim, what was true of totemism was true of the more complex religions as well. That is, at its core, all religion is the worship of society. Durkheim is very explicit about this conclusion. He states that society is to its members "what a god is to his worshipers . . . a being whom men think of as superior to themselves" (Durkheim 1961: 237).

Although Durkheim concedes that worshipers are not aware of the true identity of the god whom they venerate, he does not regard this as a form of deception. Instead, he sees religious belief, ritual, and worship as serving essential social functions. Specifically, such practices enhance what he terms social solidarity, that is, cohesion or integration in society, by creating a shared consciousness among its members and by aiding in the transmission of culture from generation to generation. In the absence of such social solidarity, Durkheim asserts that societies disintegrate into individual and social *anomie* or normlessness.

But are the cave paintings of Pleistocene epoch game animals depictions of totemic emblems from the Upper Paleolithic period? Some scholars have found this easy to accept, in part because the Australian Aborigines, upon whom Durkheim's work was based, used animals as totem symbols and commonly honored these creatures in ceremonies and sacrifices in which their images were drawn in the sand or painted on cave or rockshelter walls (Hadingham 1979: 201). Aside from these perhaps fortuitous parallels, no real evidence has been adduced to support the hypothesis that cave art represents the material remains of totemic rituals. However, Laming-Emperaire (1971, cited in Hadingham 1979: 203) has recently restated the view in a somewhat novel form. Using the great frieze at Lascaux as an example, she interprets the painting as complex genealogical records in which marriages, alliances, and kinship between various clans are recorded and represented through the juxtapositioning of the images of their animal totems on the cave wall.

**Rites of Passage.** The work of the French sociologist and folklorist Arnold van Gennep, a contemporary of Emile Durkheim, seems to have inspired a related explanation of at least some of the parietal art and traces of human activity of the Upper Paleolithic period. Van Gennep's influential book, *Les rites de passage* (1909 [1960]), provides a general framework for understanding the importance of ceremonies marking the transition of individuals or groups from one social position to another within society. According to van Gennep, all such rituals share in a tripartite structure defined by the necessary function of separation from one status, and reincorporation into the new one, with a marginal or liminal period in between. He emphasizes the recurring themes in marriage, initiation, and funeral rituals all over the world and suggests that there was a general structure underlying such similarities.

Van Gennep's view of the rite of passage may be diagrammed with three examples in the following way (Huntington and Metcalf 1979: 9):

| one<br>*distinction*: | adult | marriage | death |
|---|---|---|---|
| two<br>*categories*: | child/adult | single/married | alive/dead |
| three<br>*stages*: | child/initiate/adult | single/engaged/married | alive/dying/dead |

Van Gennep's work was enlisted indirectly in the interpretation of Upper Paleolithic period cave art and ritual following the discovery of the site of Tuc d'Audoubert near Ariege in France. Deep within the cave a large cluster of some fifty small heel prints were found preserved in a clay bank adjacent to two modeled clay bison (*see* Plate 3, p. xiv) (Breuil 1979: 234). Since the size of these prints suggested that they had been made by adolescents or children, it was concluded that the grotto had been used as the setting for puberty rites marking the passage from the asexual world of childhood to adult status and the assumption of one's sexual role. Ethnographic accounts of puberty rites from around the world indicate that the liminal stages in their performance often include rigorous ordeals, tests of stamina and courage, or long periods of isolation. Certainly the dark, damp, and remote inner grotto of Tuc d'Audoubert would be an ideal setting for such rites of separation and initiation. The dense clustering of the small heel prints suggests that a rather large number of young people (not more than fifteen years of age, concludes the Abbé Breuil) were brought together for the performance of a joint dance or ritual. The notion that Tuc d'Audoubert, and by implication other cave art sites in Europe, had been the location of such initiation rites of passage during the Upper Paleolithic period is a compelling one indeed. (Pfeiffer [1982a] provides a recent, forceful re-statement of this view.) Unfortunately, with the possible exception of a group of engraved human figures from the Grotta dell'Addaura, Palermo, Sicily, which some scholars have interpreted as recording an initiation scene (Sieveking 1979: 196–98), no further evidence, either of children's footprints or large group rituals, have come to light in other sites to confirm this hypothesis.

**Hunting Magic.** The most widely acknowledged interpretation of Upper Paleolithic period cave art to emerge in the early twentieth century was the view that it had been produced as part of rituals of hunting magic. This thesis was derived largely from Sir James Frazer's monumental study in comparative folklore, *The Golden Bough*, which appeared in twelve volumes between 1911 and 1915. In that work, Frazer made his famous distinction between magic and religion. Magic he defined as primitive or pseudo-science aimed at *ma-nipulating* the material world through the supernatural; religion he saw as *propitiating* the power of the supernatural. Frazer concluded that religion developed out of magic when, upon discovering that he could not, in fact, control the supernatural by magical means, man turned instead to its veneration.

In Frazer's scheme, all magic is based on a belief in two principles: homeopathy, or the notion that like produces like, and contagion, the idea that things or persons that have once been in contact can forever after influence one another. Imitative magic is defined as magic based on the principle of homeopathy; the magician attempts to produce a desired effect by imitating it. Frazer's scheme, together with the ethnographic and literary evidence he mustered to support it, inspired the classic view that Upper Paleolithic game animal paintings were done by hunters seeking to control or increase the numbers of their quarry by imitative means. Conversely, pictures of predators, such as lions, hyenas, or bears, were presumed to have been painted to bring about the magical destruction of these dangerous rivals (Breuil 1979: 21–24).

The evidence mustered to support this interpretation is quite compelling. First, the great majority of naturalistic cave paintings are of game animals. Second, the percentages of the various species represented in the cave paintings are seen, by some scholars at least, as conforming in a rather general way to the percentages of the various species represented in the faunal collections recovered from Upper Paleolithic period sites in southwestern Europe (Hammond 1974). Further, some of these game animals are associated with symbols or schematic drawings often interpreted as traps, darts, spears, or wounds and assumed by some to represent attempts at guaranteeing success in the hunt by imitative magic. In accordance with this hypothesis, the superimposition of paintings are interpreted as evidence that magical rituals had to be repeated after older pictures had lost their power.

Two classic examples of such stab-marked or wounded animal pictures are the "Fresque de la Chasse," a picture of a horse incised on a mud-coated wall at Montespan in the Ariege (Sieveking 1979: 144), and the engraved bear from Les Trois Frères, also in the Ariege, which appears to be riddled with spears and wounds and is apparently vomiting blood. Incidentally, this image is usually identified as a cave bear (*Ursus spelaeus*) but Kurten (1976: 93) concludes that it is almost certainly a brown bear (*Ursus arctos*).

A related interpretation is suggested by Leason (1939). In his view, the attitude of the bodies and position of the legs, tails, and bellies on a large percentage of the animal portraits in parietal art indicate that the subjects were *dead* rather than living creatures. By way of explanation, he suggests that the cave artists must have "made painstaking studies of dead animals" in the process of learning their craft. His idea can be enlisted in support of the hunting magic theory and taken as a further indication that cave art was an attempt at achieving hunting success by imitative or homeopathic magical principles.

Sieveking (1979: 22) notes that Upper Paleolithic period sites tend to cluster along the major river systems in southwestern Europe. She concludes from this clustering that the abundant fish life of those rivers must have figured prominently in subsistence, particularly during the seasonal spawning runs of the salmon. However, depictions of fish, waterfowl, or other aquatic creatures occur rarely in parietal art. The absence of what were no doubt important economic species might be taken as evidence that the cave drawings were not used in rituals of imitative magic concerned with the food quest. On the other hand, aquatic fishing, probably carried on with nets, weirs, perhaps even fish poisons, would essentially have been a form of food harvesting rather than a quest or sport. Compared to big-game hunting, such fish harvesting must have been relatively risk free and characterized by highly predictable results. Malinowski (1954) regarded magic as a mechanism for reducing tension and anxiety in people who find themselves confronting the uncontrollable and largely unpredictable forces of nature and circumstance. Conversely, he asserted that "where man can rely completely upon his knowledge and skill, magic does not exist" (Malinowski 1954: 31). If it could be demonstrated that fishing was an important subsistence activity in the Upper Paleolithic, the predominance of big game and the absence of fish in parietal art would conform nicely to the predictions of Malinowski's theory.

As indicated previously, Upper Paleolithic peoples may have used cave art as part of their magical attempts at increasing the numbers of game animals that they were hunting. Pictures of animals mating or apparently about to mate, such as the frieze of the bull following and nuzzling the cow at Teyat Cave in the Dordogne (André Leroi-Gourhan 1982: 42), as well as images taken as representing pregnant animals, have often been cited as evidence supporting this hypothesis. In a similar vein, Nancy Olsen (cited in Conkey 1981: 24) suggests that bison at Altamira are in the posture of females giving birth.

In this regard it may be significant, as John Pfieffer notes,

> that cave art reached a peak toward the close of the Magdalenian period when herds were becoming smaller. Most of the great polychrome paintings seem to have been done during this period, which also saw an apparent increase in depictions of slain animals, suggesting one last ritual effort to restore past abundances. Generally, ceremony and the intensity of belief tend to increase in times of crisis. (Pfieffer 1978: 218)

Yet most recent scholars find the hunting magic hypotheses unconvincing. Conkey (1981: 24) notes that modern ethnography seems to indicate that hunting and gathering peoples are not necessarily "anxiety-ridden about food and the hunt." Further she points to certain discrepancies between cave art and actual Upper Paleolithic period faunal remains and suggests,

> the frequency of certain animal depictions often contrasted sharply with the availability of those animals as well as how often they are found among excavated food debris. One conclusion, also suggested by Patricia Vinnicombe's *People of the Eland,* an elegant study of rock art of the !Kung, might be the same as Lévi-Strauss's observation that certain natural species were selected—in these cases as the subject of rock art not because they were "good to eat" but because they were "good to think." (Conkey 1981: 23)

**Cave Art and Shamanism.** In a provocative book entitled *Shamanism: The Beginnings of Art,* Andreas Lommel (1967) advances the thesis that prehistoric and primitive art is largely the outgrowth of shamanistic religious practice. As Lommel puts it, the "intellectual achievement of the early hunting culture, shamanism, is intimately connected with art, indeed both may be derived from the same basic idea" (Lommel 1967: 128). Lommel's use of wide-ranging ethnographic parallels and analogies to illustrate his thesis is reminiscent of Sir James Frazer's methods, and the conclusions which he reaches are not inconsistent with many of those of his predecessor. Both men assumed that certain universal and fundamental elements of human thought and behavior have remained constant over time. They could, therefore, extrapolate their understanding of primitive peoples derived from the ethnographic record backward into prehistory. Lommel assumed shamanic religious practice to be one such constant element.

Within the ethnographic record, the shaman is the religious figure found most commonly among simple societies whose subsistence is based on hunting and gathering, pastoral nomadism, or horticulture. The shaman has been defined by Lowie as a "ceremonial practitioner whose powers come from direct contact with the supernatural, by divine stroke; rather than from inheritance or memorized ritual" (Lowie 1948). That divine stroke and direct contact may be sought out by those wanting supernatural power (such as did young men of the Cheyenne and most Great Plains and Eastern Woodland peoples) or it may come unexpectedly, unsought and even unwanted, to individuals chosen by the spirits in some way. This spiritual election is common among the tribal peoples of Siberia where the shaman's calling is generally regarded as oppressive (cf., Levin and Potapov 1964). Lommel (1967: 9) suggests that such an unwanted calling is most often an emerging psychosis which is so strong "that the only way out open to the individual attacked by it is to escape from it into shamanistic activity." In his view, shamanic performances and artistic productivity are psychological techniques "by means of which one can subordinate 'the spirits' to oneself; that-is-to-say, bring order into one's own unconscious imagery. This seems only to be possible in an ever-repeated state of trance" (Lommel 1967: 10). In fact to Lommel, the trance is the critical element in the definition of the shaman; practitioners who do not regularly enter into trances as part of their religious and curing activities he considers to be merely "medicine men." Of course, this distinction is by no means universally accepted in the literature. Compare it for example to Norbeck's definition of the shaman as simply someone "whose acts emphasize mechanical techniques of magic [and] whose ministrations tend to be directed toward individuals rather than social groups" [Norbeck 1961: 103]. Such "mechanical techniques of magic" are carried on in shamanic performances which often involve singing, dancing, sleight-of-hand tricks, ventriloquism, narcotics, divination and fortune telling, ordeal, and sometimes, of course, trances. Individuals who practice direct contact with the supernatural by these means perform as diviners, mediums, curers, and diagnosticians.

Whether or not such activity provides relief from an emergent psychosis as Lommel would have it, shamans receive gifts and often obtain power and prestige in exchange for their service. Despite the receipt of such fees and gifts, the shaman rarely is able to support himself and his family exclusively through his practice; rather, he or she is commonly a part-time specialist—all of which makes Mircea Eliade's characterization of the shaman as a "technician of the sacred" appropriate. Like those of most technicians, the techniques of the shaman are essentially neutral in the moral sense: they can be used for good or evil.

But what leads Lommel to the conclusion that shamanism forms the major inspiration at the substratum of art? Lommel first analyzes ethnographic accounts of the shamanic experience in combination with shamanic myths and folktales. He then closely examines prehistoric and primitive art for reflections of the themes and concerns which he isolated in the shamanic accounts and myths. He concludes from this analysis and comparison that there is a certain universal "series of pictures, motifs or styles, which simply portray shamanistic myths or ideas and can be identified as such" (Lommel 1967: 128). He then discusses the following four motifs in terms of their presumed universal shamanic origin: man-animal representations, hybrid creatures, scenes depicting animals or men and animals fighting, and drawings in X-ray style.

According to him, the shaman's costume is essential to his performance and this garment is generally an animal disguise. This leads Lommel to the conclusion that depictions of men disguised as animals are very probably meant to represent shamans. As an example of this motif in Upper Paleolithic period art, he cites the celebrated man-animal picture known as "the Sorcerer" located at Les Trois Frères cave in the Ariege (*see* Fig. 4.7). In Lommel's view, this depiction is the oldest known portrayal of a shaman. As another example of this motif, he lists the engraved Magdalenian bone with its representation of a "chamois man" and the famous bird-headed man shown being charged by a wounded bull in the "Shaft of the Dead Man" at Lascaux.

As noted in chapter 5, such man-animal images are not common in Upper Paleolithic period art. As of 1960, some fifty-five man-animal representations had been formally reported from archaeological contexts (Maringer 1960: 145). However, a number of other images apparently have been discovered but not formally described or reported. For example, McCollough (1971: 32) was informed by a knowledgeable amateur archaeologist that the undescribed sites of Cueva de los Casares and Cueva de la Hoz in the province of Guadalajara in central Spain contain numerous engravings of fish-headed or bird-headed anthropomorphic figures. How many such unreported cave art sites are there? An adequate inventory of the contents of such sites might change our perception of Upper Paleolithic art—and Lommel's thesis—substantially.

Lommel also suggests that the animal skins, antlers, and masks of the shaman's costume probably symbolize the animal spirit familiars who were believed to assist the practitioner in the spirit realm and sometimes to transfer their particular qualities to him. He notes that in Siberia and elsewhere, shamans commonly decorated their costumes with pendants in the shape of humans, animals, nature spirits, the sun and moon, and other symbols, drawn from the iconography of shamanism (Lommel 1967: 125). At least some of the pendants, disks, carved animal silhouettes, and other specimens of mobiliary art might have decorated shamans' costumes.

For similar reasons, Lommel (1967: 128) suggests that drawings in which parts of animals are combined more-or-less arbitrarily to create unnatural compound or hybrid creatures also betray shamanic inspiration. Describing this motif, Lommel says "for instance a stag is given several legs or heads, a panther is decked out with a stag's antlers, parts of these antlers are in the heads and hoofs of other animals" (1967: 128). Examples of such compound creatures or "monsters" include: the famous "Agnus Dei" or ibex-and-horse-headed ruminant from Pair-non-Pair mentioned earlier; the carved relief of a bison or auroch with the head of a boar from Le Roc de Sers (Breuil 1979: 330); the bison-headed deer from Les Trois Frères in the Ariege (Sieveking 1979: 149); and the painting of a figure with a rhinoceros body and a horned head, perhaps meant to represent that of an antelope, at Lascaux (Breuil 1979: 128). Also found at Les Trois Frères was a composite animal motif associated with one of Lommel's costumed-shaman images. In this example, an engraving of an animal with the body of a hind and the head of a bison turns to stare backwards at the image of an upright, bipedal figure whose human legs support the upper body and head of the bison. One of the figure's legs is raised as if in dance. In its outstretched arms, which perhaps end in hooves, the figure cradles what Breuil (1979: 177) identifies as a musical bow.

Drawings of bison and reindeer with tightly interwoven and interconnected bodies, horns, or antlers like those described by Lommel are possibly also present at Les Trois Frères (Breuil 1979: 168–69) and other sites. However, these apparent interconnections may merely be due to the repeated superimpositions of images one atop the other, rather than to the inspiration of the shamanic vision or ideology.

Another set of motifs that Lommel relates to shamanism includes depictions of fights between animals or between men and animals. One example of such a motif is found at Pechialet in the Dordogne. Here an engraving illustrates a bear attack against women (Breuil 1952: 149). Another such scene, found at Villars, shows a man receiving the charge of a bison (André Leroi-Gourhan 1982: 54). Of course, the best example is the famous "hunting scene" painted near the bottom of the five-meter-deep "Shaft of the Dead Man" at Lascaux (*see* Fig. 4.8). This panel is nearly two meters long and consists of possibly four dramatically interrelated elements. The first is a figure of a black rhinoceros painted partially in heavy outline with six dots arranged in two parallel rows of three under its tail near its anus. Interestingly, this is the only rhinoceros image reported from Lascaux (Laming-Emperaire 1959: 93–96). The rhinoceros figure faces away from the main focus of the panel and was not done in the same style. Very likely it was not part of the main scene and was painted separately. The remaining three figures are clearly related to one another: 1) a bird-headed or beaked anthropomorph drawn in outline with stiff, straight legs, an erect penis, and wide-spread arms which end in four-fingered hands; 2) an upright staff topped with an outline drawing of a bird, whose beak—like the one on the anthropomorph—is open; and 3) an immense bison or auroch head lowered and legs drawn up in a charging pose. A pointed line, drawn in the lower foreground near the feet of the birdman and the bison, has often been interpreted as a spear or a throwing stick (Laming-Emperaire 1959: 193–94). A similar pointed staff is drawn across or through the lower hindquarters of the bison. From the animal's lower abdomen tumble forth lines of paint apparently meant to indicate that it has been disemboweled. The tumescent birdman is shown receiving the charge of this bison. The acute angle of this body suggests that he has just been or is about to be struck, or that he is already on the ground and is about to be gored.

As noted earlier, these pictures are generally taken at face value and viewed as representing real events. Whatever the original subject of the frieze at Lascaux, the artist did not choose to present it in a purely naturalistic manner. Scholars who interpret the panel as the record of an actual occurrence must explain why the artist depicted one of the central figures as a bird-headed anthropomorph capable of meeting the charge of a wounded bison with only an erect penis. Clearly, if the frieze is meant to be a historical account, it is one in which experience has been transformed into symbol or myth. For example, it has been suggested that the bird's head on the anthropomorph and the bird on the stick nearby signify the totemic identity of the victim and that the erect penis merely identifies his sex. The entire scene might also illustrate a fantastic event in the life of a mythical character.

Lommel rejects such interpretations and suggests instead that scenes such as this one actually represent struggles between shamans disguised or transformed into animals.

> The combats are, of course, not real fights but conflicts of a psychic nature, battles which the shaman fights within his own mind, in which opposing forces—of what kind we cannot tell—are seen and experienced in the form of animals, particularly bulls. (Lommel 1967: 128)

Kirchner (1952) also sees this scene as representing a shamanic seance, although not necessarily a struggle between two shamans. To him the spread-eagled position of the bird-man suggests that he is in a trance in the company of his familiar spirit, the bird perched nearby on the pole. Interestingly, the bird as spiritual helper and guardian is a common theme in Siberian and other forms of shamanism. More generally, the bird is a common symbol of "flight, disappearance and return" (Marshack 1972a: 28), whether that flight be one of seasonal change, physical movement, trance, or death and rebirth.

The final motif that Lommel (1967: 129–33) derives from shamanism is the so-called "X-ray style." In this motif, animals or men are drawn as outlines inside of which their skeletons or internal organs are either schematically represented or are sketched with varying degrees of realism. According to Lommel, this style

> is an expression of the shamanistic view current among the early hunters that animals could be brought back to life from certain vitally important parts of the body. The mere portrayal of these vitally important parts or of the life line brought about the resuscitation or increase of animals. Representations of animals were not merely pictures but contained the animals' vital substance. (1967: 122)

On the other hand, such X-ray views of men and animals may be taken as artistically representing the widespread conviction among hunting peoples that the supernatural vision of the shaman allows him to see inside the body and observe the skeleton. As Eliade notes, the shaman "is able to penetrate even into the source of animal life, the bony element. That we here have an experience fundamental for a certain type of mystic is proved, among other things, by the fact that it is still cultivated in Tibetan Buddhism" (Eliade 1978: 19). Although such pictures are not common in Upper Paleolithic period art, Lommel states that they occasionally appear engraved on bone in the Magdalenian period after 13,000 B.C. in southwestern France. In more recent times, the motif is found among hunting peoples in Norway, eastern Siberia, among certain Eskimo groups, and even in New Guinea and northwestern Australia and elsewhere (Lommel 1967: 129).

Lommel's thesis that shamanic religious practice was the inspiration for many of the motifs of Upper Paleolithic period art is an attractive one for a number of reasons. First, even a cursory glance at the literature demonstrates the ubiquity of the shaman in ethnographically known hunting and gathering societies. Again quoting Eliade,

> the existence of certain types of shamanism during the Paleolithic period seems to be certain. On the one hand, shamanism still dominates the religious ideology of hunters and pastoralists in our day. On the other hand, the ecstatic experience as such, as an original phenomenon, is a constitutive element of the human condition; it is impossible to imagine a period in which man did not have dreams or waking reveries and did not enter into "trance"—a loss of consciousness that was interpreted as the soul's traveling into the beyond. What was modified and changed with different forms of culture and religion was the interpretation and evaluation of the ecstatic experience. Since the spiritual universe of the Paleolithics was dominated by the mystical relations between man and animal, it is not difficult to divine the functions of a specialist in ecstasy. (1978: 19; also cf., 1964)

Second, among such hunter gatherers, it is not uncommon to find people seeking supernatural power and spirit familiars by fasting or practicing other austerities in isolation from their fellows. Surely, few more remote locations for such quests than the interiors of the cave art sites could be found in southwest Europe. It seems possible that at least some of the parietal art of the Upper Paleolithic period was drawn to encourage such supernatural contacts—or to record them after they occurred. Still other pictures may have served as props for shamanic rituals. The composite animals and the X-ray drawings referred to by Lommel seem likely candidates for such a role, as do the rare man-animal figures.

The fruitfulness of this approach in the interpretation of more recent rock art has been demonstrated by Lewis-Williams (1982) who convincingly connects the imagery and narratives from accounts of shamanic "trancing" among the historically known San or Bushman of South Africa with motifs found in the prehistoric rock art panels of that region. However, critics have argued that Lewis-Williams' "direct historical" methods and use of ethnographic analogy cannot be applied to the interpretation of Upper Paleolithic art because the peoples that produced that art have no known direct cultural descendants in the modern world and the sociocultural systems of which they were a part are unlike any primitive communities known to ethnography. Lewis-Williams and Dowson (1988) call this view "ethnographic despair" and respond to it by arguing that they are well aware that the association of certain images with shamanic religious practice in historic times does not guarantee a similar association in prehistory. Nonetheless, since the experience of "entoptic" phenomena, such as hallucinations and altered states of consciousness, appears to be universal in our species, it is their view that "a neurological bridge affords some access to the Upper Paleolithic" and that the depictions of the period may be approached from the perspectives of human neurology and psychology.

To test this view, Lewis-Williams and Dowson construct a general neuropsychological model of the manner in which humans apprehend entoptic phenomena and apply the model to the interpretation of the rock art traditions of two ethnographically well-documented hunting and gathering peoples: the San of southern Africa, and the Coso, a Shoshonean-speaking peoples of the North American Great Basin. The success of their model in linking the conventional representations found in the rock art of these two peoples to their shamanic imagery and traditions encouraged Lewis-Williams and Dowson to apply it to the interpretation of the meaning of the nonrepresentative or geometric signs found in Upper Paleolithic art. The parallels they found between geometric signs in Upper Paleolithic art and those of an apparent shamanic origin in their two ethnographic examples convince Lewis-Williams and Dowson that the signs in the former tradition were also associated with altered states of consciousness.

Simply because images are associated with shamanic religious practice in historic times, however, does not guarantee that they were so associated in prehistory. After all, the man-animal composites may quite as easily have been illustrations for some Stone Age Aesop's fables or have represented the continuity between human beings and the animal world (Conkey 1981: 23). Such an alternative interpretation is less likely in the case of the X-ray drawings, but we can never be certain that shamanic ideology was the source of their inspiration.

## CONTEMPORARY INTERPRETATION OF ART AND RELIGION

The foregoing "classical" hypotheses of Upper Paleolithic parietal art—that the paintings were totemic emblems, used in hunting-magic rituals, served as props in rites of passage, or were inspired by shamanic religious practice—are all plausible to some degree or another. All of these hypotheses are part of philosophical prehistory, that is, explanations of the past evaluated solely in terms of logic or internal consistency and not tested (or testable) against material evidence.

In recent years a number of attempts to account for Upper Paleolithic period art have been phrased in a form that does allow them to be tested. These contemporary explanations are falsifiable because they presume that a complex order or structure exists in various forms of Upper Paleolithic art. As a consequence, their interpretation of the tradition stands or falls on the demonstration that such order does in fact exist in the data.

In addition to their falsifiability, contemporary explanations can be distinguished from classical hypotheses on another dimension. Bailey (1983: 166) suggests that modern archaeological theories fall into two groups, which he terms "environmentalist" and "internalist." According to him,

> Environmentalist theories, exemplified by ecological and paleoeconomic schools of thought, derive their main inspiration from the natural sciences and emphasize ecological relationships and the determining or limiting effect of basic biological and environmental factors. Internalist theories, exemplified by neo-Marxist and structuralist schools of thought, derive their main inspiration from the social sciences and emphasize the inherent dynamic of social relations and structures of meaning. (Bailey 1983: 166)

Bailey's dichotomy provides a useful framework for organizing contemporary theories of Upper Paleolithic art and religion. Internalist theorists include André Leroi-Gourhan and Alexander Marshack. Both of these scholars regard this art and notation as a kind of "code" developed by ancient people whose mental processes operated similarly to our own. Their strategy for cracking this code is to seek to discover its pattern and then to develop a "grammar," or limited set of rules, that will generate such patterns. For them, the discovery of such grammars will lead to a partial reconstruction of the intellectual and religious life and facilitate readings of the "texts" preserved in mobiliary and parietal art.

Although they begin with similar premises about the human mind, the two scholars arrive at very different conclusions. Leroi-Gourhan sees a grand cosmic dichotomy, ultimately sexual, at the heart of Upper Paleolithic art and religion, while Marshack discovers lunar time-reckoning and storied notations of a basically seasonal character. In one sense, both sex and the lunar cycle are external, environmental factors. The theories of these two scholars are internalist, nonetheless, as they consider the structure of the human mind to be the source of the pattern and organization of Upper Paleolithic art. Thus, *meaning* is assigned to the external factors; the factors do not cause the pattern.

In contrast, it is precisely such *external* causation that is postulated by the environmentalist theories. Anne Sieveking proposes that stylistic similarities and differences in later Upper Paleolithic art are due to patterns of isolation and contact that developed among migratory Magdalenian reindeer hunters exploiting separate regions. In a similar vein, Michael Jochim compares the conflicting social implications of salmon harvesting with migratory reindeer hunting and suggests that parietal and mobiliary art may reflect different socio-economic and religious responses to climatic deterioration, population movement, and economic change. Clive Gamble flatly rejects the notion that Upper Paleolithic period art is due to the increasing intellectual capabilities of *Homo sapiens sapiens.* Instead, he considers it to be a mode of information exchange that developed in response to the need for more sophisticated communication due to climatic change, population growth, and other factors. Margaret Conkey adopts a similar view and sees an isomorphism among artistic style, social organization, and intercommunication during the period.

The environmentalists are less interested in art and religion as an intellectual system and more concerned with the social and economic functions of religions and art, and with the contribution these phenomena make to the articulation of societies and environments. Art is valued chiefly as a mirror of social reality and is studied for the insights it offers into the material basis of life during the period. Of course, the distinction between internalist and environmentalist takes us back to Bidney's (1953) dichotomy between cultural realists and cultural idealists and his admonition that we must apprehend culture on its real or "practical" dimension as well as on its ideal or "theoretical" one. With this in mind, let us turn to an examination of the works of these scholars, beginning with the internalists.

**André Leroi-Gourhan.** Leroi-Gourhan (1965a; 1965b; 1982) asserts that the Abbé Breuil was wrong: the decoration of the cave galleries in southwest Europe was not done on a piecemeal or random basis by independent artists seeking only hunting power or the increase of the herds by imitative magic. Rather, he hypothesizes that the major caves were decorated—consciously or unconsciously—in terms of some general principle of order or system of meaning and that in many cases this decoration took place over a limited period. He considers the cave art sites to be Paleolithic "sanctuaries" and his notion that, as Upper Paleolithic period people penetrated to greater depths in the interior of the caves, they repeated the order of the earlier sanctuaries in newer, deeper galleries. At the same time, they "annotated" and embellished the work of their predecessors in the older, shallower sanctuaries by repainting them (André Leroi-Gourhan 1965b: 196–99).

According to Geertz (1973: 890), a religion consists largely of a system of sacred symbols that "function to synthesize a people's ethos." In a sense, Leroi-Gourhan has applied such a view to the interpretation of parietal art. He claims to recognize a pattern or system of symbols and infers the meaning behind that pattern in order to understand the metaphysics of its creators. The initial formulation of his hypothesis was based on the examination of some sixty cave art sites (André Leroi-Gourhan 1968). The motifs in these sites were classified and their distributions within the caves plotted. Leroi-Gourhan concludes that the caves reveal a systematic layout, a repetition of specific themes across space and through time, and a consistent association or co-occurrence of certain motifs.

Leroi-Gourhan asserts that the interior space of the cave art sites can be divided into seven zones: 1) the place where one, upon entering the cave, encounters the first image; 2) the connecting passages between the more sizeable parts of the cave; 3) the places in the forward part of the caves where one finds crevices, bays, or niches; 4) the most remote rearward places with figures; 5) the central portions of the image-bearing parts of great cave halls and chambers; 6) the marginal portions of the zones mentioned in (5) above; 7) the places in the interior of crevices, bays, or niches in the area of the central cave parts mentioned in (5) above. Leroi-Gourhan asserts that these zones were recognized and used in a systematic manner by the cave artists themselves. In the parlance of modern anthropology, the zones are "emic" categories meaningful to the participants in Upper Paleolithic culture, rather than simply "etic" concepts created by the modern investigator.

The notion of the "central position" is perhaps the most important part of his zone concept. The central position is both the most prominent chamber within a cave and the middle of a painted panel. It is in such central positions, both in the caverns and in the individual panels, that Leroi-Gourhan asserts that 85 percent of all pictures of bison, wild oxen, or aurochs and horses are to be found. To Leroi-Gourhan, the bison, auroch, and horse are the most prominent animals in Upper Paleolithic period parietal art, and he considers it particularly significant that they also tend to occupy the "central position" in both the caves and the panels. In his view, the next most prominent animals in the parietal tradition are deer, ibex, and mammoth. He contends that these creatures tend to occur in zones other than the "central positions" in the caverns. A third group of animals, which includes rhinoceros, bear, and lion, are generally found only in the deepest zones of the cave or farthest from the "central positions" (André Leroi-Gourhan 1965).

Perhaps the most interesting and controversial aspect of André Leroi-Gourhan's thesis is his notion that representations of certain animal species are systematically associated with one another and with specific classes of abstract signs or "geometric figures." In the most recent summation of his ideas, Leroi-Gourhan (1982: 55–56) divides these signs into three types: broad signs, narrow signs, and dots. He considers the signs in his first two classes to be highly stylized depictions of human genitalia. He asserts that "female" or broad signs tend to occur with pictures of bison and aurochs. "Male" or narrow signs he finds consistently associated with horses in the central position in the caverns and panels, and with ibex and mammoth on the peripheries of the panels and in the marginal zones of the caves.

In addition, he sees distinct regional differences in the distribution of the broad signs.

> They are tectiform in the Les Eyzies region, aviform in Quercy, quadrilateral at Lascaux and in Cantabria, and there are numerous variations on the theoretical model. In several cases we find no geometric signs but female sex symbols which show progressive degrees of geometricisation and which permit the identification of the extremes of this geometricisation process. In those caves where the figures are numerous and in different styles, for example at El Castillo, we may find broad signs of several more or less realistic types. One particular category of broad signs is that of the claviform signs, derived from the profile of a female figure. For these signs, too, the morphological transformations are numerous, from the female silhouettes at Pech-Merle to the hundreds of engraved figures at Gonnersdorf. The claviform sign is found in two geographically distant zones, Ariege and Cantabro-Asturian Spain. (André Leroi-Gourhan 1982: 56)

Leroi-Gourhan finds systematic co-occurrence in mobiliary art as well. According to him,

> the bison does not appear on spears, nor is it usual on pierced staffs, whereas it is by far the most common animal on the plaquettes and the cave walls. The horse, however, is the most usual animal (in mobiliary art)—except on harpoons and half-rounds, whereas sexual signs are very rare on spearthrowers. (1965b: 80)

He goes on to note that "every species of animal and every type of sign engraved on these objects is found again on the cave walls." Not only does this prove useful in dating the parietal art, it also confirms in his mind the existence of a "syntax" in the Upper Paleolithic period that governed the manipulation of both abstract signs and figures. The consistent character of these co-occurrences and the systematic nature of their placement in the caves or their appearance on the various types of portable objects can be taken as evidence that the artists and craftsmen of the period had "conscious figurative intentions," which they derived from a shared and consistent metaphysical system. The dichotomous grouping or pairing of animals, signs, locations, and artifact types suggests to Leroi-Gourhan that the metaphysical system being expressed was organized around the male-female principle and that it sought to express both the fundamental opposition and yet complementary nature of the two sexes.

Leroi-Gourhan's scheme has elicited considerable interest and a good deal of skepticism since its initial formulation in the late 1950s. Among critics of his scheme, Ucko and Rosenfeld (1967) have proven the most systematic. Perhaps the most basic uncertainties voiced by scholars have centered on Leroi-Gourhan's methods. First, can we be sure that the caves he used to formulate the scheme are, in fact, representative of the full range of variation present in the parietal art of the Upper Paleolithic? Despite the size of his corpus of caves and the prodigious industry he has shown in studying them, these caves were not selected in terms of a statistically valid sampling design and may thus systematically exclude, under- or over-represent certain categories of data. Such distortion could prove to be critical to his thesis. Second, the criteria he uses to define the distinct zones and panels in the painted caves, as well as the precise central positions within the zones and the panels, have been called insufficiently objective to allow independent observers to replicate his classification. This is not a trivial objection; independent replicability of his results is essential if his claim to have discovered the Upper Paleolithic artistic and metaphysical syntax is to be accepted.

Third, great controversy surrounds the sexual interpretation that Leroi-Gourhan has given to the binary pattern that he identifies in Upper Paleolithic art. Even if a pattern of dichotomous opposition does exist in the art of the period—and presumably in the conscious and unconscious minds of the peoples themselves—is Leroi-Gourhan justified in reducing this opposition to sexuality? Why that polarity? Or for that matter, why only one polarity? The literature of structuralism, not to say the English language, contains a host of other possibilities. For example: human/animal; culture/nature; animate/inanimate; sacred/profane; good/evil; light/dark; right/left; young/old; taxable/nontaxable, and so on.

Fourth, an important element of the structural analysis of Lévi-Strauss (1968) and others is the convertibility of the polarities. An initial dichotomy is transformed into other dichotomies to form increasingly complex, intercommunicating matrices or "codes" of myth and symbol. Must we assume that these peoples were so lacking in subtlety as to use only one dichotomy, sex, and two transformations, male into horse, female into bovine? To limit our interpretation of their metaphysics in this way is to reject the initial premise that the minds of Upper Paleolithic peoples worked as do our own.

Evidence that such complexity is present in the art and religion of this period can probably be found in the complex array of abstract signs or geometric figures of the tradition. As noted above, Leroi-Gourhan (1982: 513–14) divides these signs into three categories: broad signs, narrow signs, and dots. In his view, the broad and narrow signs represent female and male genitalia respectively. Clearly, a number of the so-called broad signs (and I presume Professor Leroi-Gourhan intends no pun here) do appear to be stylized vulvae; likewise, some of the narrow signs have a distinctly phallic quality. However, to interpret the bulk of the signs in this way demands loyalty to the concept bordering on *une idée fixe.* In fairness to Leroi-Gourhan, it should be noted that in the final major statement on Upper Paleolithic art published shortly before his death (André Leroi-Gourhan 1982), he emphasizes and elaborates his views on the spatial relations and patterns of co-occurrence with scant reference to the male/female dichotomy.

Marshack (1970, 1972a: 108, 197–200) convincingly identifies some of Leroi-Gourhan's narrow signs as plants or trees, others as spearthrowers and projectiles, still others as signs conveying more complex messages. For example, he takes the slash lines found engraved across the heads of some of the animal drawings as indicating death, perhaps in the form of a ritual killing or sacrifice.

**Alexander Marshack.** Like the work of Leroi-Gourhan, Alexander Marshack's interpretations of Upper Paleolithic art and religion represent a profound challenge to the classical position. Rejecting the view that the thinking of Ice Age people was primitive and one-dimensional, Marshack instead asserts that

> the basic functioning of the brain was the same then and now, and that man before history and in the Ice Age was not much different from what he is now. What differed primarily were the facts, ideas, and relationships with which this brain was educated and with which it worked, not the manner of its functioning, its ability, or its capacity and intelligence. (1972c: 24)

Beginning with this premise, Marshack deduces that, like modern people, early peoples understood their activities 1) "only in a 'time-factored' and 'time-factoring' context" (Marshack 1972a: 25); 2) that such activities were symbolized; 3) that such symbols, be they "animal, dart, female, anthropomorph, tectiform or meander—can be used in a number of different ways and in varying semantic contexts, alone or in association, and that the image can be used and re-used" (Marshack 1977: 308); that 4) these symbols and symbol sets are interpreted in a "storied" fashion by their makers; and 5) that where animals or plants were used symbolically, knowledge of the actual characteristics or habits of these animals and plants can allow modern scholars to partially decipher the "story" behind the symbol.

Marshack asserts that he discovered direct evidence of "time-factoring" in the groups of linear incisions, slashes, and patterns of abstract markings including dots, crosses, zigzags, V's, and forked signs (similar to the Greek lambda) engraved on bâtons, spatulas, pallets, and other mobiliary objects recovered from Upper Paleolithic contexts. These markings, found on mobiliary objects from over a wide area in Europe, appear as early as the Aurignacian and Perigordian and persist through the Azilian into the Mesolithic period. Although such markings have long been known to prehistorians, they have generally been seen as mere decoration. Asymmetrical groupings of these marks were interpreted as *marqués-de-chasse*, that is, tallies notched by Paleolithic hunters intent, like the legendary gunfighters of the Old West, on recording the numbers of their kills.

Marshack, assuming that early people were both interested in the passage of time and needed a record of it, found upon close examination that many of these supposedly decorative markings appear to have been made with different instruments at slightly different angles and depths. Such variation suggests to Marshack that the markings were not made all at once (as would be expected if they were part of a single decorative process or artistic purpose). Rather, it indicates that the marks were made at different times or were meant to express different meanings, or perhaps both.

He paid particular attention to the asymmetrical groupings of marks. When he counted these markings by groups, he discovered that they are conformable with a system for recording the changing phases of the moon. That is, he found the number of marks in some of these groups to sum to totals between twenty-nine and thirty-one, the range of the number of days in lunar months. Tallies that were slightly greater than thirty-one or smaller than twenty-nine, were attributed by Marshack to counting or observational error on the part of the original recorder. Totals which were much smaller than twenty-nine he assumed represented counts of the days between portions of the lunar cycle.

"If these analyses and interpretations were correct," he says, "then there was a common, basic tradition of notation in all the European Upper Paleolithic cultures, and this notation was cumulative, 'time-factored,' and possibly lunar" (Marshack 1972a: 108). If such records were kept, they would have allowed these early people to calculate the passage of time in lunar months, to predict the changing seasons, and to schedule their resource procurement strategies, ritual obser-vances, and other activities in advance. Such a system, if it existed at this early date, would have been a powerful adaptive tool as well as an important intellectual achievement.

Marshack undertook a detailed examination of some mobiliary objects from museum collections in Europe. In the course of this work, he concluded that the basic "time-factored" notation that he had recognized seemed to develop increasing sophistication and complexity during the course of the Upper Paleolithic period (Mar-shack 1972a: 159). At the same time, he found apparent regional stylistic differences in those systems. For example, by the end of the Magdalenian, styles of notation used in southwestern France were different from those used in eastern Spain and Italy (Marshack 1972a: 161, 168).

Marshack also discerned a related pattern in the realistic images engraved on the mobiliary objects. This pattern involved the system-atic co-occurrence of images of certain species of mammals (such as reindeer, horse, bison, or seal) with either fish, other mammals, or a class of enigmatic signs previously taken to be arrows or male sym-bols. In what was surely an inspired leap of imagination, Marshack interpreted these enigmatic signs as plants. He then concluded that the specific co-occurrence of animals or fish with the putative plant signs could be read as a code associating specific creatures by the season of their mutual appearance. For example, in his celebrated reading of the Baton of Montgaudier, Marshack (1970, 1972a: 170–73) suggests that the engravings of a male and a female seal, an ibex, a salmon with the hooked jaw characteristic of the spawning season, a budding plant, a multi-legged insect, and intertwined grass snakes apparently about to mate, all represent the arrival of spring through the depiction of a series of events which co-occur during that season in southwestern Europe. Specifically, the various images symbolize the arrival of the spring salmon run accompanied (as it must have been) by marine seals following the migrating fish upriver in order to prey upon them. The timing of the run was such that it would be heralded by the first bloom of the spring foliage and by the reappearance of snakes, insects and other warm-weather fauna.

Other engravings that Marshack interprets as carrying a time-factored, seasonal message include bellowing or fighting stags or bulls (representing fall season rutting behavior), molting bison (a summer event), and pregnant mares (wild mares probably dropped their foals in the springtime). In addition, linear incisions or "notations" and abstract signs sometimes occur in association with animal drawings on stone and bone objects. One such object, the La Marche bone slate (*see* frontispiece), was recovered in a Magdalenian III site located north of Les Eyzies in the Dordogne. A surviving portion of the slate has two blocks of linear notations along with an engraved outline of a horse's head and neck and the complete sketch of an apparently pregnant mare. Surrounding the head and lower body of the mare are five sets of linear marks which include symbols that Marshack (1972a: 195) calls darts and angles.

Marshack's count of the individual marks grouped together in the two blocks on the slate reveal that the notation could represent 7.5 lunar months. Correspondingly, Marshack reads the engravings on the slate as a seasonal message:

> The Mare drops its foal in the spring after an eleven month gestation and so the mare may be a seasonal image. The associated darts and signs may then represent rites, sacrifices or acts of participation related to the time of foaling. The combination of naturalistic "art," sequences of darts and signs, and a lunar notation hints at a complex time-factored symbolism and mythology. (1972a: 195)

Marshack's notion of time-factored, mythological complexity reflected in Upper Paleolithic art and notation is of course derived from his view that we are dealing with the works of peoples whose cognitive processes were the equal of ours and operated in a similar manner. It is a view that leads him to interpret mobiliary and parietal "texts" as reflecting the transformation of human experience and belief into symbol and the interpretation of that symbol in a "storied" fashion.

The stories that existed behind the images and linked them to the notation in coherent narrative wholes can be hypothesized by carefully identifying the species represented and then studying the natural habits and characteristics of these animals. In instances where possible lunar notations are associated with such animals, Marshack invariably concludes that the storied relationship between the creatures and the notation concerns the passage of time. In these cases, he looks to changes in the seasonal behavior of the animals so depicted for a clue to their meaning in the context of a particular engraving or painted panel. His readings of the Montgaudier bâton and the La Marche bone slate are examples of this technique.

Marshack also uses this technique to interpret Upper Paleolithic female images and Venus figurines. He assumes that figurines showing evidence of wear were used repeatedly, perhaps for many different purposes, while specimens lacking wear were probably made for and used in a single event, say to aid a woman in a difficult delivery. He then looks for evidence of blocks of notation incised on the figurines. Where such notation occurs, he concludes that the "storied" relationship behind the figurine and the apparent lunar sequence incised on it connects the periodic process of human female physiology and the cyclical disappearance and return of the moon in its passage across the night sky and through time.

The most dramatic artistic conjunction of these two phenomena is found in the famous bas-relief of the "Venus of Laussel," which was recovered at the site of that name in the Dordogne. This bas-relief depicts a frontal view of a decidedly corpulent female, naked and gorgeously upholstered with flesh. Her huge breasts hang pendulously, her hips and thighs are rolled with fat, and the protrusion of her lower abdomen suggests that she may be pregnant. Her head is turned to her right and thus shown in profile. No details of her face are represented however, her long hair falls languidly over her left shoulder all but covering her facial profile. The most interesting aspect of this bas-relief is the positioning of the arms and hands. The woman's left hand is pressed, open and palm down, against her lower abdomen; her right arm is held upright and shoulder high. In her hand she holds a crescent- or horn-shaped object with thirteen marks on it. This object has generally been interpreted as a bison horn. The turn of the figure's head indicates that she is looking at the horn she is holding. The entire relief shows signs of having been painted with red ochre.

The most significant aspect of the Laussel bas-relief for Marshack is the fact that the bison horn, in reality smooth and seamless, is represented as marked or segmented. In his view, this suggests that the marks are "storied" rather than merely representational. The partially crescentic horn with its thirteen marks symbolizes the crescent or "horned" phases of the waxing and waning moon. He bases this observation on the fact that "the count of thirteen is the number of crescent 'horns' that may make up an observational lunar year; it is also the number of days from the birth of the first crescent to just before the days of the mature full moon" (Marshack 1972a: 355). Although he does not mention it, thirteen is also nearly one-half of the ordinary twenty-eight-day female menstruation cycle. With the placement of her left hand on her lower abdomen, the Venus of Laussel seems to suggest that a relationship exists between the periodicity of the moon and her own periodic cycle. This relationship between the crescent moon, the crescentic bison horn, and the human female is perhaps also reflected in the conjunction between bison images and "female" signs identified by Leroi-Gourhan in parietal art. Further connections are recognized by Eliade who concludes that this portion of Marshack's theory renders "more comprehensible the considerable role of the moon in archaic mythologies, and especially the fact that lunar symbolism was integrated into a single system comprising such different realities as woman, the waters, vegetation, the serpent, fertility, death, rebirth, etc. (Eliade 1978: 23).

Finally, Marshack (1977) attempts to interpret the enigmatic, apparently nonrepresentational, "macaroni" or "meander" drawings that occur in Upper Paleolithic art. Breuil calls these designs "serpentine forms" and suggests they may represent snakes; Leroi-Gourhan considers them to be essentially phallic in character and therefore referrable to his class of narrow or male signs. Marshack, for once, is uncertain. Since the calendric and storied content of such iconographic elements is not obvious, Marshack seeks clues to the meaning of the meanders by closely examining the manner in which they were produced at Parapallo Cave in Spain and at Gargas and Rouffignac caves in France.

From this examination he concludes that the meanders begin with "core units," generally painted or engraved near floor level. The image is then expanded up the wall to the ceiling and back again by adding extensions to the core unit of the meander and "branches" out from, and sometimes across, the core in the form of angles or "side parallels." The meander grows in this wrapping, and secondary or subsidiary images, such as animals or geometric symbols, become associated with it. At Gargas, Marshack found that a red ochre pigment had been wiped on top of previously engraved meander lines; he interpreted this as evidence of the image's re-use later in time.

At Rouffignac, which contains the most numerous and complex meander images in Europe, Marshack made an interesting discovery: the meanders were painted sequentially by "different persons, with fingers and print spacing of different sizes." Thus, the meander complex at Rouffignac apparently represented thousands of individual "acts of participation" by many people over an extended period of time. In contrast, the approximately two hundred naturalistic animal images in the cave seem to have been done by single individuals working over relatively short intervals (1977: 311). Marshack concludes that despite the undisciplined impression that meander drawings convey, they were produced in a systematic way, rather than a random manner (1977: 312).

Both Leroi-Gourhan and Marshack offer comprehensive, grand theories of Paleolithic art and religion. Perhaps as a consequence, both have stimulated intense critical debate among prehistorians. Part of the criticism directed at Marshack has been generated by his expansive view of the significance of his hypotheses. For example, few critics are willing to grant his assertion that a single, engraved bone specimen from Cueva de la Mina in Spain is sufficient demonstration that "the integrated beginnings of arithmetic, astronomy, writing, and abstract symbolism and notation" took place during the Upper Paleolithic period (1972a: 218). This skepticism is heightened by Marshack's apparent willingness to generalize broadly about the entire Upper Paleolithic period in Europe on the basis of the relatively small corpus of mobiliary objects found to contain notation (Rosenfeld 1971: 317). Nonetheless, Marshack is not alone in his willingness to find the "roots of civilization" in the Upper Paleolithic culture. Some go even farther. Marthe Chollot-Varagnac (1980), for example, considers the non-naturalistic or geometric signs in parietal art to constitute a system of symbolic representation governed by rules distinct and separate from those governing the contemporaneous representational art in southwestern Europe. In her view, these sign systems constitute the base out of which early writing (*graphisme symbolique*) later developed.

Scholars have also expressed reservation about Marshack's initial presumptions. Rosenfeld (1971: 318) questions whether markings so small that a microscope must be used to discern them could have served as records for peoples equipped only with the naked eye. In a sharp exchange in *Antiquity*, Marshack clarifies this point by stating that

> the marks are not visible because bone is discolored and surfaces partially deteriorated. If you look at the minute and second marks of your watch you will find them so tiny that if one were in your palm it would go unnoticed. Yet you can tell time to the minute and second by their use. Five marks on a watch or rule are indistinguishable as units, but immediately recognized within their known systems. The scale of such marks is smaller than in the mobiliary engravings. The evolved capacity for such fine distinctions belongs to the species. (1972a: 65)

But even if Marshack is working at the macroscopic rather than the microscopic level, King (1973: 1897) is uncertain how he is able to differentiate with such confidence between intentional and unintentional markings. Further, experimental work convinces White (1982) that an individual using the same burin to notch fresh bone does not produce a uniform series of engravings as Marshack assumes. Rather, such work tends to produce marks of different angles and depths. White therefore strongly questions Marshack's assumption that marks of different character on an artifact necessarily indicate that it was engraved on separate occasions—as would be the case if it was marked sequentially to record the passage of the moon through its nightly phases.

The most difficult questions that can be asked of Marshack are the following. First, has he demonstrated that the markings sometimes present on Upper Paleolithic period mobiliary art fall into formal, repetitive, nondecorative patterns? Second, if these patterns exist, are they best interpreted in terms of the "lunar model," that is, as the record of cyclical changes in the moon's phases through time?

In modern systems of notation and enumeration, a limited set of grammatical rules governs the manipulation of the symbols. Of course, Upper Paleolithic period systems may be less rigid and more ambiguous in this regard than modern ones. Nonetheless, uncertainty about the nature or existence of rules governing the notation on the mobiliary objects makes it difficult to decide, for example, where in a block of marks to start counting or, in the case of the composite marks, what value to assign to each of the component parts. Marshack is aware of these problems and explicitly states the criteria he uses in arriving at such decisions. However, the way one solves these problems can profoundly change the "reading" that emerges from the notation. Scholars working independently on the same notation would in many instances arrive at results very different from those of Marshack.

Assuming that Marshack's readings are correct, are the number series that he derives from various speciments consistent with what would be expected in records of lunar cycles? Marshack defends his choice of the lunar model to interpret the numerical series on three grounds. First, the changes in the moon are dramatic, easily observed with the naked eye, and, for hominids with modern cognitive structure, inherently interesting because of their "time-factored" nature. The changing phases of the moon would form a nightly spectacle visible from fixed platforms (such as cave mouths). Second, Marshack notes that lunar record-keeping and the use of the moon to gauge the passage of time and changes in season were widely practiced in historic times by preliterate peoples in Africa, Asia, and the New World. Such records were also an important element in the astronomies of the archaic civilizations of the ancient world such as the Sumerians, Hittites, Egyptians, and numerous other peoples.

Marshack's third and most important reason is the conformity he is convinced exists between the cycle of lunar phases and the number series engraved on the artifacts. A lunar month is the length of time that it takes for the moon to pass through all of its phases from invisibility ("the dark of the moon") to full wax. The length of such a month is generally computed at twenty-nine to thirty-one days. Therefore, artifacts with groups of marks that total from twenty-nine to thirty-one are the strongest evidence that can be adduced for interpreting the notations as lunar calendars. Although such twenty-nine to thirty-one mark groups occur in the notations, so do groups with larger and smaller—sometimes much smaller—totals. Marshack explains these departures from the expected number range by suggesting they may represent imprecise observations made during the moon's dark phase or in periods of extended heavy cloud cover. Groupings with totals much smaller than twenty-nine may represent counts made between various phases within the total lunar month, say the number of days between the half and full moon. This seems plausible enough, but the practical effect of admitting such imprecision into the model is to allow "any number between 1 and 16 and between 26 and 34 [to] be considered 'significant'" (Rosenfeld 1971:

319). Granting such latitude makes it difficult to falsify Marshack's theory by rigorously comparing its predictions against simple counts of the notation.

Prehistorians remain divided on whether formal notational systems existed in the Upper Paleolithic and, if they did, whether they recorded the changes in the moon's phases. If Marshack is correct, however, his work will have granted us one of the most profound insights into the mind of early humankind since the recognition that the painted caves of Europe date to the Ice Age.

Let us turn now to an examination of the explanations of Upper Paleolithic art and religion advanced by Sieveking, Jochim, Gamble, and Conkey, scholars whom, in contrast to the foregoing internalists, I have classed as environmentalists. They seek to explain the dynamics of society and culture in general during the period, and are interested in the art primarily for the socioeconomic information that it contains. I examine their works here because the goal of understanding the connections between religion and material and social reality is very much at the heart of the anthropological enterprise.

**Anne Sieveking.** In chapter 3, I discussed the picture of late Upper Paleolithic subsistence and settlement systems being developed by contemporary scholars using refined faunal analysis, paleoenvironmental reconstructions, and analogies drawn from studies of modern hunter-gatherer groups. In the consensus emerging from this work, subsistence during the Magdalenian period in southwestern Europe is generally thought to have been based on a mixture of intensive reindeer hunting and salmon harvesting. Since the location and availability of both of these resources varies over the year, it is assumed that Magdalenian subsistence and settlement patterns changed systematically in response to this variation and that changes were closely scheduled against the seasons.

Beginning with the above assumptions, Sieveking (1976) analyzes Magdalenian IV art in an attempt at discerning the territorial and social divisions which might have emerged in southwestern France as a consequence of such seasonally shifting settlement. She begins by noting that the mobiliary art of Phase IV in the Vèzere region is so similar to that recovered in the central Pyrenees region of France that "we must suppose that these two regions represent the north and south migratory limits of identical groups of people, or that the groups from each region were in periodic close contact" (1976: 590). She rejects the first explanation, because the two regions are close environmental analogues of one another. She suggests that seasonally migratory herd animals like the reindeer would probably have summered in the Dordogne and the central Pyrenees, but would have left both regions with the onset of winter. She concludes that peoples from the Vèzere region very likely followed the river valleys downstream and wintered on the plains of the Garonne River between Toulouse and Bordeaux. Correspondingly, peoples from the western Pyrenees may have followed tributaries of the Adour and wintered in that river's valley near its mouth on the Atlantic just above the modern border between Spain and France.

From these separate migration patterns, Sieveking concludes that during Magdalenian IV, more-or-less independent and self-contained subsistence and settlement systems must have developed in the western Pyrenees and the Adour Valley region on one hand, and the central Pyrenees-Garonne valley-Vèzere region on the other. Because of their relative isolation from one another, the independent systems eventually would have developed discernibly different regional variants of the Magdalenian artistic tradition. In fact, at least during phase IV the Magdalenian art remains remarkably homogeneous. Instead of artistic parochialism, she finds styles and motifs in mobiliary art widely shared throughout southwestern France. Sieveking is forced to conclude from this "that the geographical area of interrelated people is much larger than one might have expected and that there must have been a lot of cross traffic as well as riverine communication in southwest France during the later stages of the Magdalenian." (1976: 593)

**Clive Gamble.** Like Sieveking, Clive Gamble posits a social basis for Upper Paleolithic art. However, he views reindeer hunting to be a precarious form of subsistence specialization in which small, dispersed population groups are forced to cope with changing and uncertain patterns of reindeer migrations, seasonal availability, and population density. Plus, he does not consider art to have been a mere passive reflector of the extent or intensity of socio-economic relations. Instead, he suggests that the art of the period, by facilitating and broadening social interaction among peoples, made the late Pleistocene epoch reindeer hunting adaptation possible in Europe in the first place.

Gamble considers that the stimulus for appearance of art during the late Upper Paleolithic period was certain "changes in the amount and kind of information needed by Paleolithic societies" (1982: 522). By "information" he does not mean the conscious metaphysics or aesthetics of the Upper Paleolithic artistic tradition. Rather, he refers to information of a distinctly practical variety: viz., knowledge of the movement of animal herds or the availability of food stuffs over a wide area. Although the art of the period probably did not directly convey this information, in Gamble's view it made such transmission possible by contributing to the maintenance of a shared system of understanding and ideology. Such a shared system would have provided a kind of "grammar" or meta-language in which practical data could be transmitted among participants. In Gamble's view, other social institutions would have contributed to this system as well. Connections between scattered groups of reindeer hunters could have been maintained through widely ramifying ties of kinship, marriage partner exchange, and long-distance trade.

In addition to providing a mode of information sharing, connections of this kind might have enabled groups who were temporarily unsuccessful in the food quest to obtain aid or access to the territory of more fortunate groups within the system. Thus, a central purpose of this network of information and social ties might have been the provision of a kind of "subsistence insurance" wherein the risk of starvation faced by any single social group was reduced by distributing it throughout the system as a whole and thereby sharing it among all the groups (Gamble 1982).

Gamble uses the ubiquitous Venus figurines to illustrate his thesis. These figurines have been recovered from the Pyrenees to European Russia and are attributed to a portion of the Upper Paleolithic period, which Gamble asserts can be narrowed to between 25,000 and 23,000 B.P. Although the figurines can be sorted into at least three stylistic classes, they nonetheless are remarkably similar in style. In Gamble's view, artistic homogeneity of this kind over such a vast area indicates that these figurines are the material remains of a system of shared understanding and intercommunication which was equally widespread. In a related manner, Conkey (1978, 1980a) interprets the decorative motifs that she isolates on Spanish Magdalenian carved-bone implements as a kind of artistic grammar developed to facilitate intercommunication between reindeer hunting groups in southwest Europe.

In a provocative and original paper, Steven Mithen (1988) explores the literal implications of Gamble and Conkey's view that Upper Paleolithic art facilitated the transmission of information among hunting peoples. Mithen defines information to mean "knowledge about the location and state of potential resources." He then interprets certain of the "nonrepresentative" signs found in both mobiliary and parietal art as the tracks of various game species and demonstrates that certain of the naturalistic images of the period represent elements of animal behavior—such as rutting, bellowing, and rolling—that produces signs or clues useful to the hunter engaged in game tracking and hunting. Mithen conjoins this reading of Upper Paleolithic art with the hypothesis that the deep cave galleries of southwestern Europe were used as settings for the initiation of the young and suggests that practical information about the game animals could have been transmitted to initiates in a dramatic and memorable fashion through the medium of parietal art. The examples Mithen selects to illustrate his thesis are apt and convincing but, as he carefully notes, by no means all of the art of the period can be interpreted in this manner. Whether or not Upper Paleolithic artists sought to instruct the young with their paintings, however, Mithen's analysis of their work illustrates that these artists were deeply familiar with the characteristic behaviors of their animal subjects.

**Michael Jochim.** Michael Jochim (1983: 216–19) approaches the problem in a similar manner. Like Gamble, Jochim, too, is struck by the general homogeneity of Magdalenian art, but notes that it was not uniform during *all* phases of the tradition. Cave art in particular varies through time in the degree of its stylistic uniformity from region to region, while portable art waxes and wanes in general popularity and the extent of its geographic distribution. Jochim (1983: 216) hypothesizes that these artistic trends are ultimately related to changes in strategy and emphasis in the Magdalenian subsistence economy.

According to him, reindeer hunting and salmon fishing have profoundly different implications for human population size, settlement technology, and social organization and interaction. Based on the ethnographic record, the degree of dependence of hunter-gatherers upon reindeer appears to be inversely related to their human population density; that is, the greater the dependence a group has on reindeer, the lower the density of its population. Ethnographic evidence suggests that the converse is true of salmon exploitation; the magnitude of human population density and the degree of dependence upon the salmon are directly related. Jochim further states that salmon and reindeer share many similar characteristics: both are subject to long-term cyclical fluctuation in population size, both species can be taken either by individuals or groups, both produce storable foodstuffs, and both occur in restricted localities.

Salmon, however, use the same river for spawning year after year and are therefore far more *predictable* than reindeer, who commonly shift their migration routes depending on local conditions. To Jochim, this means that groups which increase their reliance upon salmon fishing will, over time, tend to 1) develop an increasingly sedentary settlement pattern during a part of their seasonal cycle; 2) cluster around the most suitable fishing locations; and 3) develop a territorial exclusiveness that isolates them from neighboring groups. In contrast, the essential lack of predictability of the reindeer means that groups which seek to intensify their exploitation of that species will, over time, tend to 1) maintain a mobile and flexible settlement pattern; 2) develop mechanisms for assembling large task groups on a seasonal basis; 3) develop regional means of sharing information about reindeer herd movements; and 4) develop webs of social affiliation and marriage ties with surrounding groups.

Jochim suggests that socioeconomic systems centering on salmon exploitation become closed, exclusive, and characterized by relatively limited ties to surrounding systems. Such societies should tend to emphasize intragroup conflict-resolution by, for example, mediation at centralized ceremonial sites. The closed nature of such societies should be reflected in distinct and highly regionalized artistic traditions. In contrast, socioeconomic systems emphasizing reindeer hunting, which require mobility, wide-ranging communication, periodic aggregation, social flexibility, and interconnectivity, are likely to develop open networks enabling discrete social units to interface neighboring societies. The existence of such interacting networks should be reflected artistically in continuous, rather than discrete, distributions of motifs and art objects. Compared to the parochialism of the art of closed systems, the art of reindeer hunting economies should be broadly distributed and homogeneous over many contiguous regions.

Jochim (1983: 217–19) uses this bipolar scheme to interpret Leroi-Gourhan's (1965b, 1968) four-period developmental sequence of

Upper Paleolithic art discussed earlier. Leroi-Gourhan's Style I Primitive period dates to between ca. 32,000 to 25,000 B.P. and is characterized chiefly by the appearance, explosive growth, and widespread distribution of mobiliary art objects such as Venus figurines. The homogeneity, ubiquitousness, and portability of Style I art suggests to Jochim that it is the material reflection of the open communication networks whose widely ramifying ties he hypothesizes will develop in hunting economies centered on the reindeer.

Cave art does not appear on a significant scale until Leroi-Gourhan's Style II period between ca. 25,000 and 19,000 B.P. Jochim (1983: 217) notes that the beginning of this period correlates with the onset of the final glacial maximum. He hypothesizes that settlement during this period was chiefly limited to southwestern Europe and concludes that this area began to experience population pressure as peoples from surrounding regions retreated there in the face of climatic deterioration further north. He suggests that the cave art sites that appear at this time may represent loci for group ceremonial activity directed in part at developing intra-group solidarity and mediation.

In the Style III period from ca. 19,000 to 15,000 B.P., cave art becomes increasingly abundant and elaborate and begins for the first time to exhibit a distinctly regional character in the Dordogne, the Lot Valley, the Pyrenees, and Cantabria. During the same period, portable art becomes relatively rare (Leroi-Gourhan 1965a, 1965b; Jochim 1983: 217). Jochim interprets these developments as reflective of changes in subsistence emphasis in the late Solutrean and early Magdalenian traditions. But he admits that "this decline in portable art is puzzling: it may be related to the general decrease in mobility and the declining need for maintaining widespread affiliation. This together with the regionalization of the cave art styles, might reflect the formation of more closed communication networks during the Solutrean" (1983: 217).

The economic trends in the Style IV period from ca. 15,000 to 10,000 B.P. are more complex, according to Jochim (1983: 218). The beginning of the period witnesses a great increase in the number of painted caves and a corresponding breakdown in regional stylistic diversity. This is followed somewhat later in the period by a decline in parietal art, a "tremendous proliferation of portable art," and the appearance of burials that become both more abundant and more homogeneous throughout Europe (1983: 219). Jochim finds these trends somewhat more difficult to interpret within his scheme. He notes that the period is characterized by dramatic alterations between warm and cold climatic phases, an apparent population explosion in the middle and late phases of the Magdalenian, and the expansion of the Magdalenian peoples into areas outside of southwestern Europe. He suggests further that archaeological data indicate that reindeer hunting remained important in southwestern France until the end of the Pleistocene, but that in the Pyrenees and Cantabria specialized hunting seems to have given way to more broad-spectrum hunting well before that time.

Jochim, like Sieveking, Gamble, and Conkey, concludes his analysis by emphasizing the social utility of Upper Paleolithic art and religion. Its emergence and its specific morphology is a response to the environmental conditions of the late Upper Pleistocene epoch and the social reality of the Upper Paleolithic period. Like the work of the foregoing environmentalist scholars, it should prove possible to test Jochim's thesis against existing archaeological and paleoenvironmental data. However, in order to reject his thesis, it will be necessary to show either 1) that there is no correlation between the sequence of climatic change in Europe and the alternations between uniformity and regional distinctiveness in the art of the period; or 2) that his reconstruction of the subsistence or trajectory of subsistence change during the Upper Paleolithic period is in error. In the absence of such a large-scale test, we are forced to evaluate Jochim's hypothesis against more trivial criteria. For example, the dates that he assigns to the various periods of Upper Paleolithic cave art follow those of Leroi-Gourhan but depart from them sometimes by as much as a millennium or more with no stated justification. The essential "softness" of these dates points to the difficulty of correlating them with the sequence of paleoenvironmental change in Europe at this time. Further, while mobiliary objects like Venus figurines and decorated plaquettes are *relatively* abundant in the archaeological record, we have no gauge of their former absolute abundance in the systemic context of Upper Paleolithic period society. We thus have no way of being certain that they were ever sufficiently ubiquitous to serve the intercommunicating roles assigned to them by Jochim, Gamble, or Conkey.

# 6. Society and Religious Practice

This book demonstrates that it is possible to sketch the outlines of a prehistoric religious system, of which nothing can be known from observation or from participation, using three methods: ethnographic analogy, inference from material patterns, and formal analysis. While the fanciful archaeological recovery of the cultural history and the religious theory and practice of Christianity provided in chapter 1 clearly indicates that much would be missing from a reconstruction of this kind, it also shows that archaeologists could learn a great deal about Christianity from these three sources of information alone. The same is true of the religious system of the Upper Paleolithic period in southwestern Europe. Let us turn to the first of these methods—ethnographic analogy—in the reconstruction of society and culture of the Upper Paleolithic period.

## THE BASIC MODEL OF HUNTING AND GATHERING SOCIETY

By the end of the nineteenth century, most archaeologists had concluded that the peoples of southwestern Europe were food collectors or hunter-gatherers during the Paleolithic period. Since then, it has been common for scholars to examine historically or ethnographically known hunting and gathering peoples as analogues of Paleolithic peoples. The historical and ethnographic corpus available for such purposes is quite large. It contains accounts of food collecting societies located chiefly in the subarctic and arctic (or circumpolar) zone of Eurasia and North America, the deserts and steppes of North and South America, the Congo rain forests, arid southern Africa, various heavily forested regions of southern Asia, India, and the Philippines, and the Australian continent.

For the archaeologist, this corpus provides "the only living models available for reconstructing human cultural origins" (Martin 1974:

3). Based on data drawn from some, but not all, of the societies in this corpus, a general picture of hunting and gathering life has been composed by anthropologists and prehistorians. This set of generalizations is referred to here as the "basic model" of the food collecting adaptation. The basic model which has achieved widest acceptance in Paleolithic research holds that historically and ethnographically known hunting and gathering societies are characterized by fourteen attributes.

*A simple technology.* Technology consists of three elements: 1) tools and apparatus; 2) skills, methods, and procedures; and 3) the social organization of production (Winner 1977: 11–12). The tools and apparatus of hunting and gathering peoples are often ingenious, their skills justly celebrated, and their methods subtle and discerning. Nonetheless, the level of the complexity of their tools and methods is low when measured on objective scales (cf., Oswalt 1973, 1976: 33–44; Lustig-Arecco 1975). According to Brian Hayden,

> Aside from groups that rely on specialized techniques for obtaining food, such as the sea mammal hunters in Arctic regions, and the net hunters in Central Africa, most contemporary hunter/gatherers rely on a small toolkit for their subsistence activities. . . . Implements for killing and butchering animals and digging up tubers compose a basic toolkit that has probably persisted with various additions since the time of the early hominids (1981: 383).

Further, the social organization of production among hunters and gatherers rarely involves labor specialization or the differentiation of tasks beyond those based on sex and age.

*A subsistence system capable of producing only relatively low levels of food energy.* The anthropological interpretation of hunting and gathering societies has changed profoundly in recent years. Formerly regarded as living on the brink of starvation, food collectors are now seen by many modern scholars as "the original affluent societies" (Lee 1968: 43, 1984: 55; Sahlins 1974; and others). They are seen as capable of extracting an adequate livelihood from the environment with only a modest amount of daily effort (but cf., Hayden 1981: 385–86, 413). However, while hunter-gatherers' output of food energy per *unit of labor* compares favorably with that of food producers, their output *per capita* is much lower than that of agricultural or agro-industrial socio-cultural systems. Food producers work harder but produce more in the process.

*A diet in which plants contribute a greater percentage of the calories than animals.* The view that the gathering of roots, tubers, fruits, and nuts is a more significant subsistence activity than hunting among food collectors is widely held among contemporary anthropologists and archaeologists. This idea may be traced to the works of Lee (1968) among the !Kung San of the Dobe region of Botswana. Lee (1984: 51) and others report that vegetal material gathered chiefly by women and children accounts for more than 70 percent of !Kung San diet, meat for about 30 percent. Leacock (1982: 3) has gone so far as to assert that in foraging subsistence systems located outside of the arctic, "women's work provided a share of the food equal to or greater than that of men." It is worth noting that, whatever the percent of its actual contribution to their diets, most hunters and gatherers place the highest value on meat and, where possible, focus their efforts on its procurement. Lee's (1968: 41) often quoted epigram that the !Kung San "eat as much vegetable food as they need, and as much meat as they can," has been taken by many scholars as applying to food collectors generally.

*Little emphasis on accumulation.* According to Leacock (1982: 8), for hunters and gatherers, "the land is the larder and the emphasis is on mobility and adaptability to the land rather than on accumulation. There may be storage on racks and in caches and some food may be processed to be carried, especially in northern areas where seasonal shortages can be extreme, but such accumulation is very limited."

*A low density of population per square kilometer.* The population density of hunter-gatherers has been estimated to be less than one person per square kilometer with an intrinsic rate of growth near zero (Weiss 1973 cited in Wobst 1975: 75). Presumably this low density and absence of growth relates to the carrying capacities of the environments to which these food collectors have adapted. The carrying capacity of an environment is "the theoretical maximum population total at a subsistence level which can be supported with a given technology without environmental degradation. The concept implies a measurable equilibrium relationship between population, resources and environmental quality" (Nietschmann 1972: 63). According to Hassan (1981: 22–23), human carrying capacity is a function of 1) the size of the natural biomass in the environment; 2) the "optimum yield to man," that is, the maximum amount of the biomass that can be removed for human use without damaging it; and 3) the extractive efficiency of the technology and social organization of the socio-cultural systems adapting to it.

No human population can exceed the carrying capacity of its environment for very long; however, food-producing systems can readily manipulate the biomass and alter its composition in their favor, while food-collecting systems must use what is available. Hunting and gathering societies are generally characterized by low population densities because their technologies have low levels of extractive efficiency and they cannot safely increase the food-energy output of their subsistence systems beyond the optimum yield to man of their environments. They must, therefore, contain their populations below the carrying capacity of their territories by various social or artificial means—or have it contained for them by the natural checks of starvation and disease. Just as there is an upper limit on the density of population imposed upon hunting and gathering societies by environment, Wobst (1975: 80) points out that there is also a minimum density below which populations cannot sink without losing their genetic viability. His mathematical simulations indicate that, given restrictions on mating imposed by various forms of the incest taboo, a breeding population, that is, one within which mates are exchanged, must remain above 500 individuals if it is to maintain itself through time.

*A dependence upon wild food resources that tend to be spatially dispersed and to fluctuate (often seasonally) in their availability.* Exploitable wild resources are seldom uniformly available at all times and places. As a consequence, food collectors tend to develop regular patterns of group movement, aggregation, and dispersal synchronized with the annual fluctuations of resource abundance, variety, and availability. Decisions about which resources to include within the seasonal schedule and which to ignore are based upon the desire of food collectors to guarantee a certain and continuous food supply. Resource fluctuation and dispersal operate as effective constraints on the extent to which hunting and gathering peoples can live sedentary lives.

*A population size determined by the amount of wild foodstuffs collectable during the season of minimum availability.* Liebig's Law of Minimum states that population "growth is dependent on the amount of foodstuff that is present in minimum quantity" (Boughey 1968: 2). This law applies to human food collectors as well as other organisms in the natural ecology. Since food collectors generally have little control over the output of wild foodstuffs in their environment, their population can be no larger than can be supported during the annual period of greatest scarcity of edible wild plants and animals. Although collecting groups can reduce or buffer the impact of seasonal food scarcity with storage or trade, these activities are constrained by the requirement that people remain seasonally mobile. Hunting and gathering groups, therefore, commonly limit populations by social practices, including sexual abstinence, patterns of late or delayed marriage, prolonged nursing of infants, postpartum sexual avoidance, birth control, abortion, infanticide, and geronticide. Hayden (1981) concludes that the sexual division of labor among hunters and gatherers also serves to limit their population. In their view, women of child-bearing age who perform the bulk of the gathering generally find it difficult "to cope with more than one dependent offspring at a time no matter what the degree of sedentism or the richness of the environment" (Hayden 1981: 403). Presumably, recognition of such difficulty led these women to regulate their pregnancies or to practice infanticide.

*Band organization.* The term band has been appropriated by anthropologists to designate the simplest level of human sociopolitical organization. Bands consist of small clusters of related families and generally include between 25 and 500 members (Steward 1969: 290–91; Lee and DeVore 1968: 245–48). Their social structure is classless or egalitarian (Fried 1967; Woodburn 1982b). While band organizations commonly have fixed territories, the actual personnel belonging to individual bands often change. This is because individuals and families are under no single authority or control; they are theoretically free to switch their allegiances as they wish. At the same time, individual bands are generally connected to surrounding bands by complex networks maintained through the exchange of gifts, trade goods, and mates (Wiessner 1982; Wobst 1974).

*A reliance upon kinship as the most important principle of social organization.* Actual ties of descent and marriage—or fictional ones treated as genuine—tend to form the basis of social interaction, expectation, and obligation in hunting and gathering bands. The precise nature of kinship and postmarital residence patterns in band society has been a subject of extensive scholarly debate. In his pioneering work, *The Theory of Culture Change,* Julian Steward (1955: 125) concludes that male dominance and the importance of men in the food quest would have favored the development of patrilocal residence and patrilineal forms of kinship in early hunting and gathering societies. While recognizing that the ethnographic record included examples of bands organized along matrilineal and bilateral kinship lines, Steward concludes that these were decidedly rare. In a similar manner, Service (1962: 60–66) asserted that the social structure of hunter-gatherer bands was invariably characterized by patrilocal postmarital residence and was organized around groups of agnatically related male kinsmen. In Service's view, bands known in historic times to have practiced matrilocal or composite forms of residence were actually in the process of disintegration following Western contact. Steward's and Service's opinions on these matters have received widespread acceptance by prehistorians. More will be said of them below.

*Economic distribution and exchange based on reciprocity.* Reciprocity is a mode of economic distribution based on obligatory gift giving and countergiving of goods and services between persons and groups. Generally, the parties involved are of equal status and the goods or services exchanged are roughly of equal value (Polanyi 1957: 46–47). Sahlins (1965: 147–48) distinguishes among *generalized* reciprocity, which takes place without careful accounting of the exchange balance between the parties and without the necessity of an immediate return; *balanced* reciprocity, where accounting is maintained, the goods and services exchanged are directly proportionate to one another, and the return of a commodity is often immediate; and *negative* reciprocity, in which an attempt is made to extract a gift without any return. Generalized reciprocity is equivalent to Malinowski's notion of the "pure gift," but Leacock prefers to call it a system of "total sharing." She states that such sharing among hunter-gatherers occurs

> within the camp as well as with others who come to visit or to seek help if food shortages exist in their terrain. This does not mean that each item of food is divided, nor that all eat together out of a common pot. Indeed, eating may be quite individualized much of the time. However, it does mean that no one goes hungry if there is food in camp. (1982: 8)

Hayden (1981: 373–74) interprets such reciprocal exchange systems as a means of pooling resources in the face of uncertain or irregular game capture and thereby yielding "the highest poundage per man-hour of work and ensuring fairly regular provisioning of meat for all or most group members." In his view,

> a pattern consisting of individuals dispersing from a campsite in different directions and covering large areas is probably the most work-

efficient method of procuring mobile prey. Even at this relatively efficient level, however, failure is more frequent than success. Lee (1972:
342) calculates that on the average, only one in four days is productive
for individual !Kung hunters. It makes sense to maintain groups that
can field enough hunters to make at least one kill per day highly probable. (1981: 371)

Pooling of individual kills in this manner guarantees that all will
eat and that meat will be consumed before it spoils. It also works
against the emergence of wealth differences within the group because such differences can emerge only if an individual hoards, rather
than shares, his resources. Such hoarding cannot be tolerated by
group members for as Lee (1969: 76) notes, "only if all parties are
equally wealthy or, to be more accurate—equally poor, can the economic equilibrium be maintained." Consequently, there is little in-
ducement for accumulation or even storage in reciprocal exchange
systems.

*Individual and collective ownership.* Bands as corporate groups
hold land resources in common; access to these resources by members of the band is generally unrestricted. Foodstuffs and other com-
modities extracted from land become personal property only in a
very narrow sense. Speaking of the !Kung San, Fried and Fried (1980:
96) state that what they "own" is "not meat and other consumables
but the right to their distribution." However, collective ownership
seldom extends to tools, weapons, or ornaments which, although
easily lent and borrowed, generally belong to individuals themselves
(Leacock 1982: 8–9).

*An absence of full time specializations.* Beyond the sexual division
of labor, full time specialization in any activity tends to be rare or
absent in food-collecting societies. Everyone possesses the skills to
make essential tools and tends to be engaged in food collection.
When circumstances demand it, however, individuals with particular skills, knowledge, or capabilities may be called upon to engage in
specialized labor on behalf of the group. For example, those particularly adapted at entering altered states of consciousness may be
called upon to serve as shamans and mediums. In a similar manner,
group leadership tends to be informal, even atomistic. Leaders, commonly referred to as headmen in the ethnological literature, come
forth only when the situation demands it. Headmen generally cannot
command others to obey them and lack any institutional means of
coercing them into obedience. Since decisions about group policy

or action are usually based on consensus, the headman must lead through personal diplomacy, charisma, example, humor, and the giving of advice.

*An absence of ascribed statuses and roles.* Beyond the social ascriptions based on age and sex, status and role in hunting and gathering societies tend to be achieved through individual effort or demonstrated capability rather than ascribed or inherited. As Cohen (1985: 99–100) puts it, members of such societies generally have "immediate and relatively easy access to resources . . . and relatively direct personal leverage on other individuals."

*Feuding, but no true warfare.* Koch (1976: 167) defines feuding as "a prolonged state of hostility with violence confined to intermittent attacks." Warfare, on the other hand, conjures up images of rival armies of military specialists struggling with one another in a long series of skirmishes and large-scale battles. Hunter-gatherers tend to act out their hostility in raids and ambushes motivated by revenge. Rival groups of hunter-gatherers rarely confront one another in large battles and full-time military specialists are absent among them.

## LIMITATIONS OF THE BASIC MODEL

Until quite recently, prehistorians have relied almost exclusively on analogies drawn from variants of the foregoing basic model of the hunting and gathering adaptation in their reconstructions of Paleolithic period sociocultural systems. Certainly, extrapolation from actual hunting peoples to the presumed behavior of our ancient hunting ancestors is vastly superior to the purely rationalist approach or the self-reflection of the "If I were a cave man, I would . . ." variety. However, there are a number of theoretical and practical limitations to the uncritical use of the basic model in the interpretation of Paleolithic period culture. These limitations are of two general types: 1) only a portion of the hunting and gathering societies known to science have been utilized in the formulation of the basic model; therefore, it does not accommodate all of the variation reported among known food collectors; and 2) it is derived from food collecting societies adapting to social and environmental conditions very different from those found during the Pleistocene epoch.

Let us begin with the first objection. While it is true that all known hunting and gathering societies share a number of the general features included in this basic model, important differences exist. For example, Martin (1974), relying on the comparative data in the Human Relations Area File (HRAF), notes that historic and modern food-collecting peoples may be divided into at least three distinct classes based upon differences in their primary subsistence adaptations. The three classes are: 1) pedestrian hunting and gathering; 2) fishing, supplemented with hunting and gathering; and 3) equestrian hunting and gathering.

**Pedestrian Hunting and Gathering.** This form of adaptation is also known as generalized foraging and is found primarily among inland societies. While the majority of the pedestrian foraging societies in the HRAF followed a seasonal schedule characterized by periodic nucleation and dispersal, some 18 percent of those classed under this heading in the file maintained more or less permanent, year-round settlements. Meat tends to contribute an average of 30 percent to the diet of these peoples; gathering, generally done by women, and sometimes fishing tend to be more significant in subsistence. Communities of pedestrian foragers average less than one hundred people. Of course, it is societies in this class that conform most closely to the basic model of hunting and gathering life generally used by most prehistorians. Examples of societies characterized by pedestrian foraging subsistence systems include the M'buti of the Ituri Forest of the African Congo region, the Washo of the western Great Basin of the United States, the Andaman Islanders in the Bay of Bengal, the Semang of the lower Malay peninsula, and the !Kung San of southern Africa.

*The !Kung San of the Dobe region.* The !Kung San peoples currently are concentrated in Botswana and Namibia in southern and southwestern Africa. The !Kung San of the Dobe region of Botswana have been able to retain their hunting and gathering lifeway and become perhaps "the world's best-documented foraging society" (Lee 1984: 12). The Dobe region is an arid basin rung with low hills located on the northern fringe of the great Kalahari desert. The interior of the basin is a complex mosaic of savannah grasslands, dune formations, intermittent streams, and seasonally flooded pans. Available water is the chief constraint on human settlement in the Dobe region. Correspondingly, the subsistence territories or sustaining areas of the !Kung San are centered on the limited number of permanent waterholes there. Rainfall ranges between six and ten inches annually and is concentrated in the months of November through March. The remaining seven months from April to October are generally both hot and dry (Lee 1969: 56).

The economy of the !Kung San has been characterized by Lee (1969: 49) as one in which "the relation between production and consumption of food is immediate in space and time." Food gathering is a continuous process throughout the year and no effort is directed toward the accumulation of foodstuffs for future use. Hayden relates this continuous or immediate relationship between production and consumption to the high species diversity of the Kalahari, to its fairly constant climate, and to the corresponding absence of wide fluctuations in resource availability. In his view the !Kung San "may, in fact, live in conditions close to the 'ideal' hunting and gathering environment; they are probably not atypical of prehistoric groups" (Hayden 1981: 418).

The most important and reliable resource in the Dobe region is the mongongo nut. The nut has a high protein content, grows wild in great abundance, and can be gathered and processed with only a minimum of effort. Lee (1969: 59) carefully monitored the food intake of peoples there and found that this nut provides one third or more of the !Kung diet by weight. In addition to the mongongo nuts, the !Kung recognize and utilize eighty-four other species of edible plants. Vegetal food drawn from these other wild plant species contributes to slightly less than one-third of the !Kung diet. The !Kung also consider fifty-four species of animals in their territory to be edible. Major game species include the kudu, gemsbok, wildebeeste, warthog, steenbok, duiker, antbear, and porcupine (Lee 1984: 46–47). Animals are stalked and shot with bows and arrows or guns, snared, run to earth with dogs, or dug out of their burrows. Although success in hunting is highly valued, Lee (1969: 69) contends that meat actually makes up only about one-third by weight of the food intake of the Dobe !Kung. Thus Lee's dietary study indicates that root, tuber, fruit, and nut gathering—done chiefly by women and children—is of greater dietary significance than the hunting activities of the men. This conclusion has generally been substantiated by Silberbauer (1972: 282–87, 1981: 481–87) working among the G/wi San of the central Kalahari (but cf., Hayden 1981: 418; Webster 1981: 577–78).

During Lee's tenure among them, the social life of the Dobe !Kung centered on small residence units that range in size from four to thirty individuals with a mean of about eighteen. These units are bilaterally organized, and they camp and migrate together during some portion of the year. They are economically self-sufficient and are characterized by generalized reciprocity and the pooling of subsistence resources. The composition of these groups is fluid and membership changes occur frequently. In common anthropological parlance, these groups would be called "bands," but Lee (1979: 56) finds the descriptor too restrictive. He prefers to call the very simple and flexible social organization of the Dobe !Kung "camps," a term that lacks the connotations of fixed territoriality and exogamy often associated with the word "band." Further, according to Lee (1984: 88–89), Dobe camps lack headmen of any sort. Group decisions are reached by consensus, and personal relations within and between camps are governed largely by an elaborate system of kinship and name relations, gift giving, joking relationships, and gossip. Disputes that escalate into fights and murders sometime result in short-term retaliation and feuding. However, self-help involving the participants and their immediate kinsmen tends to be the rule; the camps do not appear to become mobilized in such conflicts.

The Dobe !Kung also lack religious specialists. Confronted with illness or other crises, men and women adept at entering altered states of consciousness are called upon to "cajole, plead, argue, and, if necessary, do battle" with the hostile //gangwasi spirits that hover around the Dobe !Kung camps. These trances take place in night-long ritual dances that involve the entire camp (Lee 1984: 103).

**Fishing, with Supplementary Hunting and Gathering.** In the HRAF, the term fishing is used to include shellfish gathering and sea-mammal hunting (Martin 1974: 31). Societies in this category obtain an average of 57 percent of their diet from various forms of this activity. Typically, hunting provides an average of 25 percent, gathering the remainder. Food-collecting societies based on this type of subsistence are usually located in coastal regions either forty degrees north or fifty degrees south of the equator. Seasonal movement of these fishing peoples tends to be lower than in either the pedestrian or equestrian hunting and gathering societies. Fully 28 percent of the fifty-seven fishing societies in the HRAF sample did not move seasonally at all but inhabited permanent communities. As Martin notes, "available data on community size indicates that villages among aquatic foragers generally do not exceed 100 individuals. That is, although the subsistence base is adequate to allow consistent nucleation among community segments, density remains low" (Martin 1974: 13).

Yesner (1980: 727–50) contends that both sedentism and a relatively high density of population is generally characteristic of such maritime adaptations. Examples of societies characterized by aquatic and marine foraging subsistence systems include: the Selung of southeastern Asia; various coastal Inuit groups in the circumpolar regions such as the Sukininmiut, Point Barrow Eskimo, and the Chugachigmiut; and the Indian peoples of the Northwest Coast region of North America like the Haida, Nootka, and Tlingit.

**The Tlingit.** The economic lives of the Tlingit and other Indian peoples on the Northwest Coast of North America centered around and depended upon fishing (Krause 1956: 118). As Drucker points out,

> there are five species of Pacific salmon, some of which "run" annually in every river and stream along the coast. All of these could be taken in great quantity to be dried and stored for future use. Smelt, herring, and, in the north, the oil-rich olachen or "candlefish" also assembled in vast numbers during their spawning seasons, and were easily caught by the Indians. (1955: 35)

The Tlingit relied primarily on the red, the white, and the humpback salmon. The runs of these three species followed one another in succession from the end of July until September. During that time, vast quantities of these fish were netted, speared, caught in traps, or gaffed with hooked poles. The fish were then gutted, dried on poles, bundled together, and then stored for winter use. After the winter supplies were laid by in this manner, salmon were processed for fish oil. Generally, these stores would last well into February when the annual running of the ssag began. Ssag were generally taken in numbers sufficient to last until mid-April when the bays and inlets of the Tlingit country became filled with spawning herring. The Tlingit gathered fish of this species in great numbers (Krause 1956: 120–21).

Fish were thus the staple of the Tlingit diet throughout the year for two reasons: 1) the spawning runs of the salmon, ssag, and herring occurred in markedly different seasons rendering many types of anadromous fish available from midsummer until late spring; 2) the mean annual temperature in the circumpolar region was low enough to allow surplus fish to be stored simply by drying.

In addition to its anadromous fish resources, the Tlingit country is rich in other forms of fresh and saltwater fish, sea mammals, mollusks, and waterfowl. Deer, caribou, bear, squirrel, berries, and other forest products could be obtained a short distance inland. As a consequence both of the richness and the predictability of coastal resources, the Indian populations were concentrated in villages where fishing was best—at points where streams entered the ocean. These villages were occupied virtually year-round by populations numbering in the hundreds. Although Driver (1961: 331–32) thinks it unlikely that any territorial unit on the coast exceeded 1000 people prior to Euroamerican contact, he notes that the fourteen "triblets" or federations of villages among the Tlingit averaged about 700 people each in the nineteenth century. The triblets cooperated with one another in defense and in raiding but lacked formal chiefs and centralized political forms.

The Tlingit, as other societies of the Northwest Coast, were distinguished from food collectors in more marginal environments in other ways as well. Although their economy was based on food collecting, they invested time and energy in the construction of permanent capital goods. This willingness to make long-term investments was particularly evident in their fishing technologies. According to Drucker, "a variety of efficient devices was used by Indian fishermen. Traps, constructed like huge baskets, were set up in the rivers and sometimes at points along the coast where salmon congregate. Fencelike weirs of poles were constructed to turn the fish into these traps" (Drucker 1955: 35).

These weirs and traps were owned and controlled by different clan groups and the clan heads received tribute from those wishing to use them. The resources were also owned by corporate kin groups and the differential access to the food resources that such ownership afforded formed the basis of the system of social ranking that divided people into noble and common classes. The *anyeti*, nobles of the highest order among the Tlingit, did virtually no work. According to Oberg,

> a high-born Tlingit does little outside ceremonial activities other than
> amuse himself. He will scarcely speak to anyone but his equal. Common labor is quite impossible if he wishes to maintain his prestige. *Anyeti* women are not taught the common art of weaving but cultivate
> only mannerisms of speech and movement. In fact, girls who have never
> worked are considered special prizes to be won in marriage. (1973: 87)

Commoners or slaves did the menial tasks among the socially stratified Tlingit, a major contrast from food collectors with egalitarian social orders in less-favored environments.

The Tlingit were engaged in a wide-ranging and elaborate trading network. According to Krause, an ethnographer who worked among them in the early 1880s,

> the Tlingit devotes the greatest part of his energy to trade. Long before the coming of the Europeans this was carried on; not only did neighboring tribes exchange different products of hunting and fishing, but there is evidence that more distant coastal territory and remote interior tribes carried on an active tribe to tribe trade through the Tlingit. (1956: 126)

Aboriginal trade goods included animal skins, native leather armor, woven blankets, tools and weapons, wooden canoes, shells, native copper in both raw and finished form, various handicrafts, and, of course, human slaves. Foodstuffs, particularly candlefish oil, seem to have been widely traded as well. As Krause implies, much of the trade in foodstuffs may have involved the exchange of the products of the interior for those of the coast.

Trade was not the only means whereby goods were circulated among the Tlingit. In addition to external trade, the independent Tlingit groups were interrelated in a religiously sanctioned institution called the *potlatch* that fostered economic redistribution. The *potlatch* was a ceremonial feast given by an individual and his kin group in order to validate a claim of status or to announce a change of rank. During the feast, the hosts distributed gifts of foodstuffs, handicrafts, trade goods, even slaves to their guests in a dramatic and public manner. Guests received gifts according to their rank in a distribution governed by strict rules of protocol. Often huge quantities of goods changed hands on such occasions. Guests were expected to reciprocate on an equal or greater scale in the future. Elaborate gift-giving feasts of a similar nature were also given as rites of passage for high status individuals. In aboriginal times, the Tlingit gave ceremonial feasts in conjunction with the cremation of a chief, as an anniversary ceremony meant literally to "feed the dead," and at a ceremony which provided social recognition for high-born children (Krause 1956: 163–65). As Adams (1973: 1) puts it, the *potlatch* of the Northwest Coast was a system of "giving away . . . food and wealth in return for recognition of the giver's social status."

The *potlatch* and ceremonial feasting in general played a key role in promoting social integration within the societies of the Northwest Coast (Drucker and Heizer 1967: 8) and enabled them to cope in part with the changing social and political circumstances in the region in the era of European dominance (Codere 1950). The institution of the *potlatch* may also be seen as a kind of subsistence insurance system which buffered the independent groups against shortage. The mechanisms of reciprocal feasting and gift-giving stimulated "individuals and groups to produce continuously at a level above their subsistence needs" (Netting 1977: 33); and reallocated surplus between social groups throughout the region and thereby compensated for temporary local variations in the availability of wild foodstuffs between the micro-regions along the Northwest Coast (Suttles 1962, 1968). As Netting puts it:

> Efforts to gather extra food supplies or to manufacture wealth goods would also tend to intensify the use of local resources and restricted niches. To the extent that each group used its immediate surroundings more effectively, the total carrying capacity of the area would be increased. The long-term security of any population is based not on its average production and consumption level but on the way it is able to weather periods of scarcity. If surplus production for potlachs or other types of interchange afforded such insurance, it would have given a selective advantage to the groups practicing it. In other words, socially rewarding occasions of exchange such as the potlatch provided an important social incentive to do what was ecologically beneficial—to build a surplus of food and gather wealth that could be exchanged for food. (1977: 33)

The scheduling of ceremonial activities among these Northwest Coast peoples appears to have been closely intertwined with variations in the seasonal levels of their production and storage of wild foodstuffs. The *potlatch* was a means whereby a food collecting people could cope with abundance through long-term investment. By hosting a *potlatch*, a social group could convert its surplus of presently available goods and foodstuffs into social prestige and/or future obligation.

**Equestrian Hunting and Gathering.** All of the societies classified under this rubric in the HRAF are (or were) located in North and South America and had developed an equestrian mode of subsistence adaptation following the introduction of the horse in the wake of European contact. According to Martin (1974: 11), they fall into two categories: 1) those that specialized in large-scale hunting after they acquired the horse and consequently had diets to which meat contributed an average of 79 percent; and 2) those which continued to emphasize gathering and generalized hunting and had diets to which meat contributed an average of about 39 percent. In the first category, social groups were highly mobile and communities averaged between one hundred and four hundred individuals. In the second category, group size averaged below one hundred and mobility was much lower. The Plains Gros Ventre, the Crow, and the Cheyenne fall in the former category; the Kutenai, Flathead, and Chiricahua Apache in the latter. As might be expected, seasonal aggregations among the specialized hunters of the first category were often quite large. On the Great Plains of North America for example, the otherwise independent bands of people like the Sioux, Crow, and Cheyenne would nucleate to form temporary social groups that numbered in the thousands of people during the late spring bison hunting season (Driver 1961: 341).

*The Cheyenne.* During their heyday in the nineteenth century, specialized equestrian bison hunters of the North American Great Plains such as the Cheyenne annually achieved greater levels of population aggregation and organizational complexity than even the fisher-foragers of the Northwest Coast. The short grasses of the Western High Plains region reach their most luxuriant growth in the late spring and early summer of each year and formerly the bison herds concentrated in the greatest densities at that time. Correspondingly, this was the season of great communal bison-hunting among the Cheyenne. The ten otherwise independent bands of Cheyenne would nucleate to form a temporary social unit of approximately four thousand people. It was only during this short season that food for people and graze for their horses were concentrated on the plains in sufficient quantities to permit such an aggregation.

The diverse bands united into a tribal form of political organization with a great council. This political organization, termed the Council of Forty-Four, had members representing each of the ten Cheyenne bands and was presided over by one of five priestly chiefs. The council determined the movements of the tribal camp and scheduled the communal hunts. In addition, it served both as an adjudicative body that settled disputes among tribe members, and as a forum for the discussion of the foreign relations problems that developed between the Cheyenne and surrounding peoples. While assembled, the council charged the six pan-tribal warrior societies or sodalities with maintaining order during tribal bison hunts and camp movements.

The major public events in the religious and ceremonial life of the

Cheyenne were scheduled to coincide with this tribal gathering. Annual ceremonial events included the Sun Dance, the Renewal of the Sacred Arrows, and the *Massaum* (Contrary) or Animal Dance. The first two of these ceremonies were designed to engender the well being of the tribe as a whole and its individual members; the Animal Dance was a hunting ritual, which sought to insure the continued abundance of game (Hoebel 1978: 14–24).

The pace of military raids and horse stealing against surrounding peoples also heightened in the late spring as young men from the normally separate bands formed temporary pan-tribal war parties under the leadership of warriors renowned for their military prowess and supernatural powers (Driver 1961: 341–42). As the spring wanes into summer, "the grass dries and becomes sparser; the herds break up into widely scattered foraging units. This is the essential ecological fact controlling the Cheyenne seasonal rhythm of tribal ingathering and band dispersion" (Hoebel 1978: 63).

The declining concentration of the bison forced the tribe to break up into independent bands once again and disperse throughout the territory. The individual bands continued to pursue the bison throughout the year but on a much smaller scale than in the spring and early summer. In addition, men hunted antelope, deer, elk, mountain sheep, and bear. Although elk and antelope were often hunted by stalking, men sometimes were able to drive large numbers of them into enclosures or over cliffs. Men, women, and children cooperated to drive fish into nets (Grinnell 1962: 273, 277–79, 319).

Women figured importantly in Cheyenne subsistence through their meat-processing work and by gathering large quantities of roots, nuts, berries, and various other wild products (Hoebel 1978: 64–67). Old Cheyenne women told Grinnell that they used thirty-five to forty species of wild plants as food. Although it is often overlooked, the Cheyenne also continued to practice a limited form of corn agriculture on the Great Plains until the wars of the mid-nineteenth century forced them to abandon their fields (Grinnell 1962: 250–53).

**The Implications of the Three HRAF Categories of Hunting and Gathering Societies.** These three examples of food-collecting societies from each of the three types in the HRAF differ in degree of sedentism, population size, the degree of specialization of subsistence system, and social complexity. Further, Martin (1974: 14–16) asserts that the social and political diversity present among historic collecting societies indicates that Steward's and Service's assertions that hunting bands were invariably patrilocal and male-centered is incorrect. Her review of the HRAF data led to the conclusion that, while the majority of these societies did, in fact, practice patrilocal postmarital residence, the systems of descent commonly used both male and female parentage (bilaterality) to determine ties of blood. Patrilineal descent systems were the next most common form, but systems of double and matrilineal descent appear in the corpus of societies as well. Students of prehistory who are inclined to assume that the hunting and gathering mode of production invariably creates uniform social formations strictly along the lines of the basic model should recall this variation and proceed with caution.

**Delayed-return versus Immediate-return Subsistence Systems.** Woodburn (1980) discerns another area of dissimilarity among historic and modern hunting and gathering peoples, in that food collectors may possess either "delayed-return" or "immediate-return" subsistence systems. The members of immediate-return subsistence systems reject the notion of surplus accumulation. Citing ethnographic examples, Woodburn states that immediate-return societies are "nomadic and positively value movement. They do not accumulate property but consume it, give it away, gamble it away or throw it away. Most of them have knowledge of techniques for storing food but use them only occasionally to prevent food from going rotten rather than to save it for some future occasion" (1980: 99).

In contrast to the rapid use or consumption of resources characteristic of immediate-return systems, in delayed-return economies there is always a period of weeks, months, or even years between the initial application of labor and its productive return. Further, once obtained, "this yield, or some part of it, is then allocated in some way or other to provide for the requirements of the participant or participants" (Woodburn 1980: 97). The social organization of delayed-return systems creates a surplus which enables some of the members to pursue future long-term tasks. Of course, all agricultural societies are delayed-return systems, but Woodburn (1980: 98–99) cites examples of a variety of historic and recently studied hunting and gathering societies who also must be classed in the category. He includes such sedentary and semi-sedentary hunter-gatherers as the Haida of British Columbia; fishing or trapping societies like the Inuit (Eskimo) who invest long-term effort in dams, weirs, pens, stockades, or traps; beekeepers; certain equestrian hunters and gatherers, and, as a single category, the Australian aborigines.

Woodburn's dichotomy between delayed and immediate-return subsistence systems cuts across the better-known distinctions between societies based exclusively on technology or modes of production. Woodburn's key variables are the society's willingness or reluctance to accumulate surpluses and to invest current efforts for future returns. The relevance of Woodburn's dichotomy to the analogic understanding of Upper Paleolithic period society is this: given the ethnographic record of food collectors who practiced delayed-return forms of subsistence, we cannot simply assume that the hunters and gatherers of the Upper Paleolithic period in southwest Europe conformed to the basic model and placed little emphasis on accumulation in the manner of the !Kung San or the Shoshone. They may in fact have invested a great deal of long-term efforts in facilities for trapping salmon or reindeer, and developed apparatus and procedures for storing portions of their catch. As a consequence they may have had a much lower level of production per unit of labor, a higher level of production *per capita*, a larger population, and a more complex political economy than analogies based on the basic model would lead us to suspect. In any event, if adequate reconstructions of prehistoric societies are to be developed, the analogies upon which they are based must not assume uniformity among food-collecting societies.

The final objection to the basic model as a source of analogy—that it is based on socio-cultural systems adapting to environmental conditions very different from the Pleistocene—can be expressed in five major points:

*Upper Paleolithic period hunting and gathering peoples inhabited many environments that have no equivalent in the historic or modern world.* For example, western and central Europe seems to have supported a forest-tundra and cold loess steppe or grassland environment during late glacial times. This environment has been compared to the arctic and subarctic environments of Canada and Alaska by scholars seeking to use modern Inuit culture as a source of ethnographic analogies with the Upper Paleolithic culture in Europe. Butzer (1971: 463) contends that, due to its position on the globe, western and central Europe receive the sun's radiation at a decidedly more favorable angle than does the modern circumpolar zone. Further, the region would not have experienced the long periods of annual darkness characteristic of land located within the Arctic Circle. As a result, the late Pleistocene tundra and grasslands of the region would have been far more verdant than similar cold-adapted plant assemblages in the modern world. The astounding size of the animal biomass in Late Glacial Europe apparently was due to the wealth of plant life at that time. Further, the diversity of animal life known from that region has no equal in the modern arctic and subarctic regions of the Earth.

*Upper Paleolithic peoples in Europe hunted numerous animal species now altogether extinct, regionally extinct, or far less abundantly available to historic and modern hunting peoples.* Both the paleontological and archaeological records indicate that the Northern Hemisphere was a hunter's paradise during the late Pleistocene epoch. This must have been particularly true of the great expanses of tundra and grasslands in both Europe and Eurasia. Herds of herbivorous big-game species, which included the horse, reindeer, woolly mammoth, woolly rhinoceros, bison or wisent, deer, elk, giant elk, and auroch or wild cow, inhabited these regions in great numbers. However, at the close of the Pleistocene both regions experienced a remarkable wave of animal extinctions that created the new and relatively impoverished animal assemblages of the Holocene epoch. Given the richness of the environment in Late Glacial times, it is difficult to make projections about the human carrying capacity during the Upper Paleolithic period but it can be assumed that the carrying capacity was quite high. In contrast, most modern hunter-gatherers live in environments with comparatively low animal biomasses. The small size of their social groups in part reflects this paucity. Extrapolations from the !Kung San of the Kalahari Desert of Africa, for example, to the Upper Paleolithic of Europe are thus questionable.

*Upper Paleolithic period hunting and gathering peoples inhabited richer and more varied environments than do modern hunter-gatherers.* By the late Pleistocene, hunting and gathering peoples occupied a large portion of the Earth's surface from the tropics to the subarctic in both the Old and the New Worlds. After the close of the epoch, food-collecting subsistence systems began to be replaced in prime environments by those based on agriculture and herding. By historic times, modern hunting and gathering peoples persisted only in circumpolar, desert, steppe, or heavily forested environments which were decidedly marginal from the standpoint of agriculture or pastoral nomadism.

*Upper Paleolithic period peoples must have subsisted entirely upon the hunting and gathering of wild foodstuffs; very few ethnographically known hunter-gatherers do so.* Examples of hunting and gathering peoples living entirely independent of surrounding food-producing economies are comparatively rare in the ethnographic literature. The majority of the hunter-gatherers known to science have (or had) established symbiotic ties, trading arrangements, or patron/client relations with agricultural peoples by the time their cultures were studied. In other instances, the food collectors had been conquered or exploited by settled peoples. In addition, European expansion beginning in the sixteenth century subjected many of them to missionizing, colonization, warfare, and dependency on market exchange. Leacock (1982: 160) points out that, as a consequence, "in most instances, peoples with a gatherer-hunter heritage have not lived solely as gatherer-hunters for a long time." They are far from perfect analogues for Paleolithic subsistence systems, which were presumably based entirely on food collection.

*The assumption that modern hunting and gathering peoples retain the institutions and behavior patterns of the Paleolithic period is unwarranted.* Food-collecting sociocultural systems have surely developed and changed over the millennia just as have more complex social formations. Most modern hunting and gathering peoples are descendants of peoples who felt the full brunt of European expansion and colonial acquisition. These people were dispossessed of their lands and subjected to the sustained impact of the market and the mission. As a result, many experienced substantial cultural divestiture. Of course, this process did not begin in the sixteenth century. Formerly universal in their distribution, societies based on hunting and gathering subsistence have been gradually giving way to those based on agriculture and pastoral nomadism for the last eight thousand years. Many modern food collectors may be the descendants of pottery-using agricultural peoples who abandoned food production when they were driven from their former territories into marginal lands by stronger groups. For example, the Cheyenne, quintessential equestrian hunters of the North American Great Plains, originally practiced the characteristic mixed horticultural and hunting and gathering subsistence of other Native American peoples in the woodlands of the Great Lakes region. As noted above, they still were sowing catch crops of maize in various river valleys on the north-western high plains as recently as 1865 (Grinnell 1962: 250–53).

## ETHNOGRAPHIC ANALOGY AND THE NATURE OF SOCIETY

Given the unique circumstances in Europe during the late Pleistocene, there are probably no exact historic or modern analogues for Upper Paleolithic period society there. Evaluated in light of these special circumstances, however, ethnographic data can provide useful hypotheses about Upper Paleolithic sociocultural systems.

First, *the dietary contribution of hunting was probably more significant during the Upper Paleolithic period than among most ethnographically known hunters and gatherers.* A strict adherence to the basic model would lead to the conclusion that gathering, rather than big-game hunting, made the most significant contribution to the diet of Upper Paleolithic pedestrian hunters and gatherers. However, the inhabitants of Upper Paleolithic Europe may chiefly have been specialized hunters rather than generalized hunter-gatherers or foragers. At least four classes of evidence support such an inference: the abundance of game animals in Europe during the late Pleistocene; the volume of animal bone remains at European archaeological sites like Solutré, Moldova, Predmosti, and Dolni Vestonice; the large amount of usable meat on late Pleistocene game animals; and tooth-wear studies of late Upper Paleolithic period burials which indicate a high meat diet (Dahlberg and Carbonell 1961; Butzer 1971: 463). Further, the cold climate of Europe during the late Pleistocene would have been analogous to modern climate now found in regions of the earth above forty degrees latitude; historically, hunter-gatherers north of this latitude have derived a greater proportion of their food from hunting or fishing than from gathering (Martin 1974: 13).

Second, *human population densities were relatively high during the Upper Paleolithic period.* The large animal biomass characteristic of late Pleistocene Europe surely supported a greater density of hunters and gatherers than the comparatively impoverished environments of most ethnographically known food collectors. Huge quantities of butchered animal bones have been recovered at several Upper Paleolithic sites in Europe. The horse was the primary prey of the Solutrean period occupants of the site of Solutré; the reindeer was the chief prey of the Magdalenian hunters who followed them in southwestern Europe. The woolly mammoth, present in southwestern Europe, dominated the subsistence efforts of the hunters at Predmosti

and Dolni Vestonice in Czechoslovakia, and at Moldova in the Ukraine.

The amount of usable meat produced by adult animals in each of these species is truly impressive: a modern ten-year-old adult African elephant can yield up to 3,000 pounds [1361 kilograms] (Fairservis 1975). When fully dressed out, modern reindeer produce about 125 pounds [57 kilograms] of usable meat (T. E. White 1953: 397). The horses of Pleistocene Europe were relatively small and probably were comparable in weight to the modern pony-sized Przwalski's horse, the last wild horse species known to roam Eurasia. Przwalski's stallions currently in the Minnesota Zoo in Apple Valley, Minnesota, weigh around 1000 pounds (454 kilograms), mares around 800 pounds (363 kilograms). Perhaps 50 percent of this weight would be usable meat. A full-sized male American bison yields around 900 pounds [408 kilograms] of meat, a female 400 pounds [181 kilograms] (T. E. White 1953: 397), and the modern European bison probably produces similar amounts. Aurochs or wild cattle very likely yielded slightly less usable meat than modern cattle, calculated by Wu Leung (1971, cited in Webster 1981: 581) as producing slightly less than 500 pounds [225 kilograms]. Assuming a rate of waste and spoilage of 20 percent per animal, the meat from the major prey species exploited by Upper Paleolithic peoples would produce roughly the following:

| animal | usable meat less 20% waste | kcal./kg. | kcal./animal |
|---|---|---|---|
| mammoth[1] | 1,089 kg. | 2,000 | 2,178,000 |
| male bison[2] | 326 kg. | 1,500 | 489,000 |
| reindeer[3] | 46 kg. | 1,500 | 69,000 |
| male horse[4] | 181 kg. | 1,500 | 272,250 |
| auroch[5] | 180 kg. | 2,000 | 360,000 |

[1]Weight from Fairservis (1975) kcal./kg. estimated.
[2]Weight from T. E. White (1953) kcal./kg. estimated.
[3]Weight from T. E. White (1953) kcal./kg. estimated.
[4]Weight courtesy of Minnesota Zoo, Apple Valley, Minnesota. Kcal./kg. estimated.
[5]Weight and kcal/kg. from Wu Leung (1971).

Webster (1981: 580–81) suggests that the minimum daily calorie intake necessary to support a healthy individual ranges from around 1,700 kilocalories (determined for most modern human populations

to 2,700 kilocalories (the amount Kemp [1971] determined was needed by modern Eskimos engaged in strenuous activity and experiencing cold stress). Lee (1969: 89) and Jochim (1976: 61) use a figure of 2,000 kilocalories per day or 730,000 kilocalories per year as a suitable average individual requirement. Let us assume that twenty-five people, each needing 2,700 kilocalories (67,500 kilocalories daily total), obtained 75 percent [50,625 kilocalories] of their caloric intake from meat. A single mammoth kill could support them for 43 days, a male bison kill could support them for 10 days, an auroch for 7 days, a horse for 5 days, and a reindeer for 1 day. If meat constituted only 50 percent of their diet and if their caloric intake averaged 2,000 kilocalories, the same twenty-five people would need 25,000 kilocalories from meat per day and could be supported for 87 days by the mammoth kill, 20 days by the male bison, 14 by the auroch, 11 days by the horse, and 3 days by the reindeer. Of course, spoilage would quickly become a factor as the days following the actual kill lengthened into weeks.

Such quantities of meat—and the calories they contain—are truly prodigious. In general, large animals occupy correspondingly large home ranges and are highly mobile within them (Clutton-Brock and Harvey 1978). Late Pleistocene big-game herds would not always have been present for the taking, and in their absence, Upper Paleolithic hunters must have hunted smaller species like ibex, deer, boar, porcupine, or hare. Nonetheless, impressive bone remains at sites like Predmosti indicate that, when big-game animals were available, Upper Paleolithic peoples slaughtered them with alacrity.

More importantly, ethnographically known foragers like the !Kung San or the Shoshone—who have contributed so much to the vision of the food collecting life incorporated in the basic model—had few species comparable to the mammoth, horse, bison, or aurochs available to them and never confronted large herds of herbivores. It is therefore more likely that the population densities of the semisedentary food collectors in the rich environment of the Northwest Coast of North America, the historic equestrian bison hunters of the North American Great Plains, or perhaps reindeer nomads like the medieval *Saami* (Lapps) of Scandinavia were closer to those of the Upper Paleolithic peoples of southwestern Europe than are the densities of pedestrian foragers of the Earth's wet tropics or arid zones. For example, the population density of the !Kung San is 0.06 (Lee 1969), and that of the Shoshone a bare 0.03 persons per square kilometer,

while on the Northwest Coast of North America, the Chinook had a density of 1.49, the Haida 0.95, and the Tlingit 0.10 people per square kilometer (Kroeber 1953: 137, 135).

Third, *at least by the end of the Upper Paleolithic period, subsistence systems were based on seasonally timed combinations of specialized big-game hunting, salmon fishing, and broad-spectrum hunting and gathering that allowed people to live in comparatively large, nucleated communities during some period of the year.* The woolly mammoth, reindeer, various species of bison, and other major big-game animals of late Pleistocene Europe were probably migratory and thus could not be hunted intensively on a year-round basis. Of these animals, only the movements of the modern reindeer have been observed directly in modern Europe. The woolly mammoth is extinct and wild herds of bison have long since disappeared from Europe, so the precise nature of their ancient seasonal movements and herd dynamics remains unknown. Hypotheses about all of these herd animals have been developed based on their fossil remains and on observations of related species of modern wild-herd animal populations in Africa, North America, and elsewhere.

For example, the behavior of the woolly mammoth has been reconstructed through observation of modern African and Indian elephant populations, by comparative studies of the teeth of fossil and living forms, and by dissection of frozen mammoth remains from Siberia (Fairservis 1975: 90). It is assumed that herds of these late Pleistocene animals moved in response to seasonal changes in temperature, water, and graze in a manner broadly analogous to that of modern African elephants. With the onset of the rains, African elephants undertake long migrations to the open grassland country. During this season the elephants scatter over the plains and are difficult to locate. At the end of the rainy season, the elephants return to the shaded forest country to browse on woody plants during the dry season, concentrating in large herds, which are easy for hunters to find.

European woolly mammoth teeth are hypsodent and finely plated, which suggests they were primarily adapted to grazing on the tough northern grasses. Fairservis assumes that, like other northern *Herbivora*, woolly mammoths obtained the bulk of their annual sustenance during the short summer season and stored up reservoirs of fat which they drew upon during winter. When winter snows covered the grasses, the mammoths probably browsed on twigs, bark, leaves, and branches of trees and other woody plants available in sheltered locations. Thus the seasonal movements of the mammoth in Europe very probably paralleled those of the modern African elephant: both would have migrated in herds during the spring, scattered in the summer, migrated in the fall, and concentrated in the winter. Fairservis (1975: 91) concludes that the vast bone accumulations at Moldova, Dolni Vestonice, Predmosti, and elsewhere in Europe are the remains of kills made by Upper Paleolithic peoples when the mammoth herds were concentrated in sheltered, tree-lined river valleys during the late fall or winter. Given the harsh winter conditions in late Pleistocene Europe, much of the meat obtained could have been stored or preserved for an extended period after the hunt.

The evidence for seasonal exploitation of the reindeer during the Magdalenian period was summarized in chapter 1. The data suggest that the natural *abris* of the Dordogne and other places in southwestern Europe served as winter habitations for hunters who interdicted the migratory reindeer herds on their way up country for calving in the spring and/or down to the coast for mating in the late fall. The pattern of reindeer movement is very like that of the African elephant: spring migration followed by summer dispersal, fall migration followed by winter concentration.

A slightly different pattern of seasonal movement was observed among North American bison on the Great Plains during the late nineteenth century. With the greening of the grass in the spring they concentrated on the plains in vast herds. As spring wore on into summer and the grass began to wither, the great herds began to break up into smaller groups. During winter, bison were dispersed throughout the plains seeking sheltered locations such as river valleys. Kurten (1968: 186) asserts that the mode of life of the European steppe bison probably resembled that of the North American bison.

In contrast, nonseasonal patterns probably characterized the movements of wild horse and auroch populations in late Pleistocene Europe. Although long extinct in Europe, wild descendants of late Pleistocene Przewalski's horse ranged freely on the Gobi Desert of Asia into the present century. According to Kurten, before modern hunting severely reduced their populations, the Gobi wild horses "formed large herds led by an experienced stallion; the same holds for the European tarpan or wild horse of Russia and Poland, which became extinct in 1918" (Kurten 1968: 150). Feral horses or "mustangs" have ranged freely over (diminishing) portions of western North America since their reintroduction onto the continent by the Spanish. Historic and modern accounts of these feral horses indicate that they behave in a fashion similar to their wild European cousins. As Dobie notes,

> the mustang stallion was both polygamous and constant. Guarding his mares the year round against all enemies and keeping them for himself against all opponents made him fiercely possessive and domineering. His band was the normal mustang unit. In the Southwest it took the Spanish name, *manada.* Only at foaling time did the mares drop out to be alone, often for hardly a day, until their colts grew strong enough to run. The identity of the *manada* endured as long as the vigor of its master endured. Depending upon his vigor and aggressiveness, it might number anywhere from three to fifty. Perhaps as old tales tell, a rare master-stallion now and then assembled a hundred or more mares. A band of thirty was considered extra large; one of fifteen to twenty was usual, but bands of a half dozen or so were common. (1934: 128)

As a consequence of their polygamous mating pattern, mustang stallions unable to find and keep mares formed loose bands of their own that often shadowed the stallion and his mares. Dobie goes on to state that herds of mustangs on the Great Plains exhibited little seasonal movement:

> Mustangs never migrated from north to south and back like the buffaloes. Nor did they migrate sporadically in the manner of squirrels, wolves and some other quadrupeds. They did not drift before winter winds as longhorn cattle on the open range sometimes drifted. Had they habitually kept together in vast droves, depletion of grass would have made constant change of grazing grounds necessary. Droughts and scarcity of grass from excess horse populations caused irregular shifting. If rains fell on a restricted area, mustangs from far away would find the fresh grass. . . . With a continent over which to roam, every band of mustangs habitually kept to a range seldom more than twenty miles across. (1934: 112)

Thus, according to Dobie, these feral horses occupied fairly small and stable territories more or less year round, except when forced by local environmental conditions to move. Whether or not horses behaved in a similar fashion during the late Pleistocene in Europe is a matter of conjecture.

The behavior of wild cattle or aurochs during the late Pleistocene is more difficult to model, since the last auroch died in 1627 (Kurten 1968: 189). Nonetheless, Kurten asserts that aurochs probably did not migrate across country on a seasonal basis. Rather, he concludes that they were "confined to more densely overgrown grasslands and open woodlands" (Kurten 1968: 188). Kurten's reconstruction seems consistent with the historical accounts of feral Spanish cattle or "longhorn" populations of nineteenth-century Texas. According to Dobie (1941: 147), the longhorns of Texas occupied territories or ranges from which they were driven only with difficulty. The bulls seem to have separated from the cows during the winter and to have formed herds of their own. In the springtime, bulls and cows reunited for breeding. Although wild cattle could have been hunted year-round, such undertakings were never without danger. Early accounts of longhorn bulls collected by Dobie indicate that they were exceedingly fierce, quick, willing to attack without provocation, and hard to kill. In the eyes of one contemporary observer, the wild cattle of both Texas and California were "more dangerous to footmen than grizzly bears" (Dobie 1941: 21). If anything, the aurochs of late Pleistocene Europe were probably more formidable.

In sum, Upper Paleolithic peoples lived in an environment that contained diverse and abundant game-animal populations. Because the seasonal movements of mammoth, bison, and reindeer were probably fairly predictable, hunters could have scheduled their exploitation on a regular and sequential basis throughout the year. The seasonal hunting of these three big-game species could have been timed to complement exploitation of the spring upstream migration runs of anadromous fish such as the Atlantic salmon. Finally, due to their nonmigratory behavior, both aurochs and horses would probably have been important backup prey during seasons when migratory species were not available.

Poiner believes that the degree of sedentism in hunting and gathering societies is directly correlated with the resource abundance, species diversity, and exploitative predictability. As a consequence, she concludes that "most sedentary groups live in regions with marked seasonal variability" (Poiner 1971: 47–50, 150, cited in Hayden 1981: 378). Upper Paleolithic hunters and gatherers exploited just such environments. While they no doubt moved periodically on a seasonal basis, the richness and predictability of their environment probably enabled Upper Paleolithic peoples to live in comparatively large, nucleated sedentary communities during some portion of the year. An ethnographic subsistence and settlement system that may parallel those of the Upper Paleolithic period was pursued in historic times by the *Saami* or *Samek* (Lapps) of the northern regions of Fenno-Scandinavia. Until the nineteenth century, the *Saami* practiced a variety of food-collecting strategies, including fresh- and salt-water fishing, sea-mammal hunting, small-mammal trapping, reindeer hunting, and reindeer herding or tending. If the fairly recent *Saami* practice of herding semidomesticated and domesticated reindeer is set aside, the seasonal schedule of the *Saami* was organized into essentially three seasonal poses: intensive fishing and sea-mammal hunting in the spring and summer, intensive trapping and reindeer hunting in the fall, and broad-spectrum subsistence activities in the winter. The largest indigenous organizational form among the *Saami* was the territorial and population unit termed the *sii'da*. The *sii'da* was a form of exogamous band organization directed by a council that consisted of the male family heads under the leadership of a headman, the *sii'da-ised*, and a "sheriff" and two "jurors" (Graburn and Strong 1973: 16). *Sii'da* members shared "common objects of worship" (Sammallahti 1982: 108), jointly built and maintained fishing weirs, provided communally for the poor and sick, owned land and other resources in common, cooperated in group hunting and seasonal migration, and annually lived together in winter villages (Graburn and Strong 1973: 16).

*Sii'da* cooperation was especially important in the communal hunting of wild reindeer among the so-called "Mountain *Saami*" of northern Norway. The great fall hunt, or *ordu*, which took place in the highland margins of the Mountain *Saami* territory, required the collaboration of many families inside the *sii'da*, as well as coordination of activities between two or more *sii'das*. Cooperative reindeer hunting among the *Saami* commonly involved the construction of extensive, converging wooden or stone fences that facilitated the concentration of reindeer, and allowed hunters to drive them into pens, blind canyons, or pitfalls, and then to dispatch them with spears. Permanent stone blinds for archers were constructed along game trails (Graburn and Strong 1973: 18; Barth 1982). While the labor costs involved in the construction and maintenance of these "delayed-return" capital investments were high, they contributed greatly to the efficiency of *Saami* hunting.

Fourth, *Upper Paleolithic society developed more complex forms of political and social organization than the band.* This expectation originates from two sources: Upper Paleolithic peoples were not reduced to occupying marginal environmental zones as are modern foragers, but were able to exploit some of the richest biomes ever known on Earth, and, as a consequence, the population size and degree of seasonal sedentism of these peoples was probably higher than that of modern band-level peoples. Again, if this expectation is correct, the equestrian nomads of the Great Plains or the fishing, hunting, and foraging societies of northern Scandinavia or the Northwest Coast of North America may be better sources of analogy than pedestrian foragers. The ethnographic record of these regions contain examples of food-collecting peoples who developed social formations which—at least seasonally—surpassed the band level of organizational complexity, structure of authority, territorial control, and population density.

**Summary.** The ethnography of modern hunting and gathering peoples remains an important source of insight into Paleolithic period culture. The contrasts between modern hunter-gatherers and those of the Paleolithic may be great, but they are surely of a lesser magnitude than the differences between food collectors generally and peoples who produce food by agricultural or agro-industrial means. Analogies between present and past hunting societies—tempered as they must be with the recognition of their limitations—can provide us with a set of expectations about life in the Upper Paleolithic period that can, in turn, be phrased as questions of the form: "If the nature of Upper Paleolithic society was X, what sort of configurations would be expected in the archaeological record?"

The basic model of food-collecting societies laid out at the beginning of this chapter provides us with expectations about life in the Upper Paleolithic period that seem, if not incontrovertible, then at least highly probable:

1. technology was simple;

2. subsistence systems were dependent upon wild food resources, which tended to be dispersed spatially and to fluctuate seasonally in their availability;

3. group population size was determined by the amount of wild foodstuffs collectible during the season of minimum availability;

4. kinship was the most important principle of social organization;

5. economic distribution and exchange was based—largely, at least—on generalized, and sometimes balanced, reciprocity; and

6. individuals owned their tools but social groups collectively owned land and other resources.

However, the basic model provides some questionable expectations about other major characteristics of hunting and gathering life. The range of variation in historic and ethnographically known food collectors and the unique nature of the Pleistocene environment suggest that students of the past interested in reconstructing the sociocultural systems present in southwestern Europe during the Upper Paleolithic may have *underestimated*:

1. population size and density;
2. degree of seasonal sedentism;
3. extent of dependence upon hunting over gathering;
4. amount of delayed consumption, delayed-return activities, and accumulated foodstuffs; and
5. political complexity.

When peoples like the Cheyenne, the Tlingit, and the *Saami* are used as sources of analogy, we are led to the expectations that Upper Paleolithic peoples:

1. based their political economies on specialized big-game hunting subsistence systems supplemented by fishing, trading, and to a lesser extent, by plant gathering;
2. engaged in large communal hunts on an annual basis;
3. coped with seasonal surpluses of foodstuffs in some institutional and ceremonial manner;
4. lived for at least a portion of the year in sedentary settlements;
5. achieved a population density comparable to that of the historic equestrian hunters or fishing-hunting-foraging peoples; and
6. annually formed larger and more complex political units than the band (cf., Soffer 1985: 476–93 for similar conclusions about Upper Paleolithic period life on the central Russian plains and Zvelebil [1986] for the Mesolithic period in postglacial Europe).

We would also expect that the religious calendar of these peoples was closely synchronized with their subsistence schedule. As such, annual periods of group aggregation and/or periods of prolonged sedentism would have signaled a quickening in the religious lives of these peoples and an intensified religious ritual activity. With these expectations in mind, let us turn to the question of ethnographic analogy and religious practice.

## ETHNOGRAPHIC ANALOGY AND THE RECONSTRUCTION OF RELIGIOUS PRACTICE

Knowledge of the ethnography of modern hunting and gathering people does not lead directly to knowledge of Upper Paleolithic period social and cultural life. At best, the examination of modern food collectors can provide a set of expectations or predictions about hunters and gatherers in prehistory. Let us construct a "basic model" of religious behavior based on the corpus of historic and recent hunting and gathering peoples, and use it to predict behavior during the Upper Paleolithic period in southwestern Europe.

First of all, *ethnographically known food collecting societies lack religious specialists just as they lack specialists in other aspects of their social life and political economy.* Despite this absence, when circumstances demand it, individuals with particular skills, knowledge, or capabilities may be called upon to engage in specialized labor on behalf of the group. Food collectors tend to rely on part-time religious practitioners or shamans in their religious lives. These individuals are thought to be particularly adept at dealing with the spiritual world and act as healers, diviners, mediums, and sorcerers, often in exchange for a fee. Practitioners of this kind utilize altered or special states of consciousness; what Lewis (1971: 18) calls "ecstatic encounters" or "the seizure of man by divinity." However, religious belief and ritual are seldom left completely in the hands of the shamans. Among food producers with more complex and productive political economies, lineages, clans, sodalities, or age-grades (hierarchical associations based on age) are often responsible for organizing and for performing communal or public religious rituals of passage or intensification.

Second, *an ability to enter altered states of consciousness is highly prized and is common in food-collecting populations.* For example, Lewis-Williams (1982: 434), citing a host of ethnographers who have worked among the !Kung San, states that today "about half the !Kung men and a third of the women become trancers." A substantial majority of the !Kung can induce the extraordinary mental states necessary for out-of-body travel, communication with the spirit world, and curing.

The equestrian hunters of the North American Great Plains showed a similar avidity for altered states of consciousness. To obtain such states, young men fasted rigorously and wandered for days in the wilderness without clothing or sleep. Vision quests of this kind sometimes resulted in contact with powerful supernatural beings who then became the individual's familiar and sponsor. Peoples like the Crow and the Cheyenne considered such supernatural help to be vital if an individual were to achieve success in warfare, curing, love, or the hunt. Yet, Lowie states that although

> all persons coveted a revelation, not all were able to obtain one. Those who did not succeed naturally did not wish to be thereby doomed to failure throughout life. The Crow and some other tribes resolved the dilemma by permitting a successful visionary to sell part of his power to less fortunate tribesmen, adopting them as his supernatural patron had adopted *him*. (1963: 175)

The specific examples of the !Kung San and the Plains Indians illustrate a phenomenon that is in fact quite general among food collectors.

Third, *among hunter-gatherers, the rules governing hunting procedures, the treatment of game animals, and the distribution of meat tend to be buttressed by religious sanction.* Recent ethnographic studies of peoples like the !Kung San and the M'buti have led most modern anthropologists to abandon the view that food collectors live precariously on the brink of starvation. Nonetheless, such collectors have little direct control over the sources of their sustenance. Although gathering may be relatively certain and risk free, even the most experienced hunter deals in probabilities. Knowledge and skill does not guarantee the hunt will be successful. Therefore, just as ritual prohibitions and magic surround those areas where personal prowess is not enough—open sea fishing and trading in the Trobriand Islands or batting and pitching in American big-league baseball—ritual prohibitions tend to govern hunting activities among foraging peoples. In a controlled comparison of four African hunting and gathering societies (the !Kung San, the M'buti, the Hadza, and the Baka Pygmies), Woodburn notes

> there are a whole series of prohibitions and injunctions associated with hunting (especially the hunting of large game), with the dismemberment of the carcass and the sharing of the meat. Fulfillment of these injunctions and prohibitions brings good fortune and breach of them is believed to have the most serious consequences. (1982a: 188)

Although such prohibitions and injunctions serve to maintain social conformity and control in a key area of subsistence and exchange, they are certainly never comprehensive and rigid nor systematically enforced. This is due in part to the egalitarian spirit of food collecting societies, plus the fluid and changing membership of band social groupings. Nonetheless, chronically uncompliant behavior in hunting or meat sharing presents a fundamental threat to both the moral and material basis of the food collecting political economy and cannot be tolerated indefinitely. Lee (1984: 96) recounts an instance among the !Kung San in which a long-time transgressor was finally put to death with the compliance of virtually an entire band. The legitimacy of the act was recognized by the dead man's kinsmen as they demanded no compensation from those involved in his murder. Systems of prohibitions, injunctions, and enforcement surely surrounded the hunting of big game in southwestern Europe during the Upper Paleolithic period.

Fourth, *communal rituals among hunter-gatherers tend to mirror or to express the social relations that organize and energize their subsistence systems.* Godelier (1975: 11) considers communal rituals that relate to production or which confer power over animals to be symbolic forms of work. Such rituals are structured so as to be "formally identical to the generalized and reciprocal cooperation which exists . . . within the relations of production." In this sense such rituals reproduce "in the field of symbolic and ideological practice the cooperation of the social process of production."

Anthropologists commonly divide rituals into two general classes: rites of passage and rites of intensification. Ethnographically, both types of rites are practiced in band societies. An example of the isomorphism between symbolic work and material work in rites of intensification is found in the *Molimo* ceremony of the M'buti of the Ituri Forest of Africa. The *Molimo*, which "calls for vigorous hunting during the daytime and equally vigorous singing and dancing at night" (Turnbull 1965: 144), is held by the various bands of Ituri Forest peoples after a death or when they deem that subsistence or interpersonal problems within the local group make it necessary. According to Godelier, the *Molimo* both symbolizes the reciprocal and interdependent nature of the subsistence practices of the Ituri Forest peoples, and stimulates continued production by fostering interdependence through reciprocal exchange. As Turnbull (1982) points out, the *Molimo* ceremony also strengthens social solidarity by providing a mechanism for avoiding and reducing interpersonal conflict between band members.

Although the *Molimo* rituals are held irregularly as needed by the Ituri forest peoples, other hunter-gatherers hold intensification ceremonies as "periodic rites" that are scheduled on a regular basis to coincide with seasonal changes in the environments. The isomorphism between subsistence relations and ritual relations can often be discerned in these periodic rites as well. As Coon (1977: 343) notes, "seasonal changes bring with them associated changes in the activities of the people concerned and consequently in their relations with each other." Some of the social and subsistence relations that change at these intervals include the duration and intensity of social interaction, the size of the social unit, and the degree of cooperation needed between individuals and nuclear families within the group. Seasonal rites recognize the occurrence of these changes and facilitate transitions from one set of social and economic relations to another. Among contemporary hunters and gatherers, food-sharing among and within groups tends to be an important part of seasonal rites. When periodic rites are scheduled to coincide with annual periods of low resource availability, such food-sharing reallocates available foodstuffs and reduces shortage among segments of the population that may be under stress (Hayden 1981: 387).

Of course, we will never know to what degree communal rituals of Upper Paleolithic peoples expressed the social relations at the center of their subsistence systems. We can hypothesize nonetheless that such relations found expression and symbolization in the mobiliary and parietal art of the period. No doubt the scholars labeled "environmentalists" in chapter 5 would find such a hypothesis acceptable. Jochim's (1983) thesis seems particularly conformable with this view. Recall that he asserts that 1) reindeer hunting and salmon fishing have profoundly different implications for social interaction, nucleation, and population among hunter-gatherers; 2) that mobiliary art objects are the material remains of regional *inter*-group communication networks developed by societies focusing their subsistence systems on reindeer hunting; 3) that the great parietal art caves are the material remains of localized *intra*-group religious systems that fostered social solidarity and conflict resolution in societies focusing their subsistence on salmon fishing; and 4) that changes in the growth and distribution of these two artistic traditions through time in Europe record the alterations between these two types of subsistence during the Upper Paleolithic period. Upper Paleolithic period art for Jochim—like ritual for Godelier (1975: 11)—symboli-

cally and ideologically fosters and reproduces the cooperation necessary to the social and subsistence processes. For Jochim, and for the
other environmentalists, art is part of the symbolic work of a society.

Fifth, *the communal rites of passage of hunter-gatherers tend to
emphasize the initiation of adolescents into adulthood.* People at all
levels of social complexity practice communal rites of passage of one
kind or another marking the life crises of birth, puberty, marriage,
and death. However, according to Service,

> of the various life crisis rites, those involving the initiation of adoles-
> cents or puberty rites are the most distinctive at the band level. Birth,
> marriage, and burial rituals are individualized, occur sporadically, and in
> the case of birth and death, at least, they happen when they happen. The
> physiological onset of adulthood, on the other hand, is gradual, and a
> year or two of difference is not significant, so that it is possible to have
> one big celebration for children of somewhat different ages from several
> families. Thus the rites of initiation to adulthood seem more socially
> significant and larger in scale than the others. To put it another way, the
> initiation rites seem to be of group interest, whereas birth, marriage, and
> death are of more concern to the immediate family, less so for the more
> distant relatives. (1979: 67)

Coon (1977: 366) asserts that it is common in hunting and gathering societies for girls to be initiated singly, "while boys' rites are
conducted collectively, in most cases during great seasonal ceremonies when food is abundant." In any case, initiation ceremonies
mark adolescents' assumption of their respective adult sex roles and
generally highlight the distinctive, yet complementary nature of
these roles. Sex is the most important determinant of an individual's
place in the division of labor within the egalitarian political economy
of most food-producing societies. The prominence of puberty rites
among hunter-gatherers and the consistent emphasis of these rites
on the contrasts and complementarity of the sexes can be understood
in Godelier's materialist terms. These rites are charged with reproducing and reinforcing the essential differentiation and cooperation needed in the hunting and gathering subsistence process. Thus,
they too are part of the symbolic work of food-collecting sociocultural systems.

Two trends in the archaeological record of the Upper Paleolithic
period may reflect a changing "symbolization of work" regarding sex
and the sexual division of labor during the period: 1) the appearance
of Venus figurines and carved vulvae in Upper Paleolithic contexts as
early as 29,000 B.P.; and 2) the regular appearance of women in Upper

Paleolithic burial populations in contrast to their absence from those of the Middle Paleolithic period. Do these events indicate an increased importance of women in Upper Paleolithic political economy and are these changes perhaps a reflection of the increasing importance of gathering? On a contrary note, it is important to recall the apparent absence of such symbols of femininity as vulvae carvings and figurines from Solutrean archaeological contexts. Does this mean that the Solutrean religious ideology symbolized the relations between the sexes in a very different—perhaps more archaic—manner than did the ideologies of the preceding and following cultural traditions of the Upper Paleolithic?

Seventh, *the scale and elaboration of the mortuary practices among food collectors is determined by the degree of their sedentism, the nature of their seasonal schedule, and whether or not they practice a delayed-return form of subsistence.* Coon (1977: 369–70) provides a brief overview of the numerous ways developed by hunting and gathering peoples for disposing of their dead. These methods include simple exposure or abandonment; the insertion of the corpse into natural caves, crevasses, or hollow trees; cremation; and burial, either directly in the earth or under rock slabs. Coon notes that "however hunting and gathering peoples dispose of bodies, they usually do so individually in separate places, for graveyards are an artifact of sedentary life" (1977: 370). In the terms adopted here, Coon is speaking largely of the mortuary practices of pedestrian foragers. Of such simple procedures for the treatment and disposal of the dead, Woodburn says: "They go beyond, but not very far beyond, the directly practical requirements for getting rid of a rotting corpse." In his view, hunters and gatherers with simple procedures and practices for dealing with the dead are generally also those with immediate-return economies, social organization, and values. Elaborate funeral rituals and mortuary behavior are found only among those hunter-gatherers who have delayed-return political economies (Woodburn 1982a: 202).

The appearance of Neanderthal burials in the Middle Paleolithic period is generally seen as reflecting the development of a new level of consciousness or the emergence of a belief in an afterlife; the apparent increase in the number of burials during the Upper Paleolithic is often interpreted as due to population increase. However, if Coon's generalization can be extended back into prehistory, these burials—especially when they occur in groups—may actually indicate a lengthened annual period of sedentism or the development of a more predictable seasonal schedule that allowed groups to return regularly to favored locations. In addition, the increasing elaborateness of the burials in the Upper Paleolithic may reflect the emergence of more elaborate funeral beliefs and practices, which in turn are correlated with the development of a greater emphasis on delayed-return forms of socioeconomic behavior. If some or all of the great painted caves of southwestern Europe were ceremonial centers used seasonally, they also reflect more predictable scheduling and longer periods of sedentary life within the seasonal subsistence rounds.

# 7. An Interpretation

As in our example of the archaeology of Christianity, the patterning of Upper Paleolithic period material remains provides the most reliable point of departure for our reconstruction. Of course, these remains have been subjected to extensive "C-Transforms" and "E-Transforms" during and after their accumulation in the archaeological record over the last ten thousand to thirty-five thousand years.

## RECONSTRUCTION OF THE RELIGIOUS "PRACTICE": MATERIAL PATTERNING

The Upper Paleolithic archaeological context created in southwestern Europe by these two sets of transforms has six attributes which bear upon a reconstruction of the religion of the period:

1. The material patterning which appears to reflect religious activity most directly is found in Upper Paleolithic period mortuary remains, parietal art, and certain mobiliary art objects.

2. Compared with the preceding Middle Paleolithic period, mortuary remains of the Upper Paleolithic period exhibit a) an apparent increase in the overall number of individuals receiving formal burial treatment; b) a far greater likelihood that women and children will be buried; c) a dramatic increase in the number, diversity, exotic origin, and quality of grave goods interred with burials; and d) inter-regional and intra-regional variability in the manner of the interments.

3. A great uniformity occurs in the styles of both parietal and mobiliary art throughout the Upper Paleolithic period. However, while various forms of mobiliary art are reported throughout the inhabitable portions of Europe and Eurasia, the known occurrences of parietal art are largely limited to southwestern Europe.

4. Within southwestern Europe, a pronounced spatial dichotomy exists between the location of human habitation and the location of parietal art. While we can never know with certainty whether or not the habitation sites were once decorated, the absence of occupation debris from the interior of most parietal art cave sites allows us to conclude that these locations were not regularly inhabited.

5. Parietal art cave sites vary from one another as to the quantity of parietal art that they contain and the scale and elaborateness of their decoration.

6. The natural interiors of parietal art caves exhibit evidence of having been decorated and utilized in systematically different ways. Specifically, areas of the caves that were more remote or difficult to reach appear to have been sought out, decorated, and utilized in a different manner from those areas that were large and easy to reach. Such differential decoration and use may be interpreted as a kind of "architectural order."

These six generalizations about the patterning of material remains of the Upper Paleolithic period lead to the following tentative conclusions regarding the nature of religious practice in southwestern Europe at that time.

**Burials and Cult Types.** The greater elaboration and variability of Upper Paleolithic period mortuary remains, compared with burials of the preceding Middle Paleolithic period, suggest that society in the latter period was becoming structurally more differentiated than it had been previously. The variations in mortuary treatment among individuals is particularly interesting. Such variations may indicate that individuals occupied different roles and performed distinct, specialized functions in their societies. As Dole (1973: 248) notes, we can measure the development of societies to higher and higher levels of sociocultural complexity by charting their structural differentiation and functional specialization and by noting the manner in which these structures and functions become integrated into new and higher levels.

Since the organizational elaboration of religious activity is correlated with the overall complexity of the sociocultural system, the increasing social specialization and differentiation seen in burials may indicate that a corresponding increase in the complexity of organization of religious life occurred then as well. Religious elaboration is reflected in four areas: the nature of religious practitioners; the number and duration of religious ritual events and performances; the degree of elaboration of these performances; and the number of individuals taking part in them.

The ethnographic record indicates that the type of religious practitioners present in a sociocultural system is a function of the degree of that system's social differentiation. In Wallace's (1966) taxonomy, shamanistic cults are characterized by the presence of the part-time religious specialist or shaman. One need not accept Lommel's (1967) thesis that the roots of Upper Paleolithic art are entirely of shamanic inspiration in order to conclude that such religious practitioners were present during the period and religious institutions of the period were of sufficient complexity to allow them to be classed at least on the level of Wallace's "shamanistic cults." The virtually universal occurrence of such part-time specialists in the anthropological record of the world lends credence to the view that they also were a part of Upper Paleolithic religious practice.

Communal cults are associated with sociocultural systems that have achieved a moderate population size and density and a fairly complex level of political and economic development, but have not reached the point at which they could support full-time religious specialists. The shaman as a part-time religious specialist remains important in communal cults, but members of age grades, men's and women's societies, kin or descent groups, or other social institutions are enlisted in the performance of communal rituals. Consequently, communal cults are characterized by more elaborate beliefs and ritual practices than shamanistic cults.

Are the burials and other archaeological evidence sufficiently differentiated however, to imply that the more complex communal cults had developed during this period? In and of themselves, the various classes of archaeological evidence that bear on the problem— burials, parietal and mobiliary art, artifactual material, habitation structures, and overall site size—are insufficient to provide an answer. However, when these data are considered *in toto* as a complex of traits and attributes, they imply an ingenious, even elaborate, cultural tradition. The continuity and apparent sophistication of this tradition argue persuasively for the presence in the Upper Paleolithic period of social and religious institutions of greater complexity than Wallace's shamanistic cult.

**Seasonal Schedules and Ceremonial Centers.** Parietal cave art sites in southwestern Europe vary in terms of quantity, scale, and quality of the art that they contain. Much of this variation is probably due to random factors such as the vagaries of cave geology or the chance elements of cave discovery. However, some of the scalar and formal variation among the caves may reflect differences in the ways in which these sites were used during the Upper Paleolithic period. Thus differences among the sites may provide clues to the way the various caves functioned in the systemic context of the religions of the time.

Using ethnographic analogy derived from modern studies of the world's hunter-gatherer groups, Conkey (1980b) provides an interpretation of the variations among a few Upper Paleolithic cave sites. Studies such as Conkey's draw upon observations that hunter-gatherers are generally obliged to

> follow an annual cycle characterized by periods of concentration and dispersion. The aggregation site is an *a priori* type of hunter-gatherer site. . . . In an ethnographic sample of 90 societies of "pedestrian foragers," Martin (1974) found seasonal dispersion and nucleation the dominant settlement pattern. (1980b: 609)

Conkey might also have noted that such a pattern of seasonal aggregation is common among the generally more complex equestrian hunters in Martin's study as well. For the most part, this pattern of seasonal settlement change relates to the ecological constraints under which hunter-gatherers operate. Supplies of wild plants and animals vary in annual availability and in spatial patterns of concentration and distribution. Hunter-gatherers must arrange movements and schedule activities accordingly. However, the actual patterns of seasonal dispersal and aggregation that emerge in hunter-gatherer sociocultural systems are not exclusively the result of ecological or subsistence factors. Conkey (1980b: 609–10) emphasizes that the importance of the "social and ritual components of aggregations should not be minimized." Further, referring to ethnographic examples, she notes that such large gatherings are inherently volatile and must be stabilized and integrated through reference to shared religious ideology and joint participation in group ritual. Conkey contends that the pattern of seasonal dispersal and aggregation known ethnographically among hunter-gatherers can be assumed to have been used at least by the late Upper Paleolithic period. Specifically, she suggests that the cave of Altamira in Spain would have been an ideal central place for the seasonal aggregations of otherwise dispersed family clusters in this region of the Cantabrian Coast during Magdalenian III times.

The physical characteristics of Altamira would seem to make it an ideal aggregation site. It is located near the coast of the Cantabrian Sea and yet is strategically positioned to allow its occupants to exploit woodland, valley, and mountain resources. Most importantly, of course, Altamira contains truly magnificent parietal art in galleries that are close to the surface and easily accessible. The parietal art at the site makes it intuitively satisfying to interpret Altamira as a key ceremonial locus on the seasonally timed subsistence route of the Upper Paleolithic peoples of this region—a kind of Ice Age precursor to the nearby historic pilgrimage site of Santiago de Compostela. Conkey attempts to adduce quantitative evidence that such aggregations not only could have taken place at Altamira, but in fact did take place in Magdalenian III times. She undertakes this by closely examining the variability in the "design elements" and "structural principles" in the mobiliary art recovered at the site. Her conclusion is that diversity of stylistic variability in mobiliary art indicates that the objects were made by people from diverse social groups who aggregated there seasonally.

Conkey argues that the high degree of variability that she observes in the design of mobiliary objects reflects the diverse backgrounds of individuals and the social distance that existed between different groups who occupied Altamira at different times during the Magdalenian III. It is critical to her argument that she show that such diverse mobiliary objects were drawn from roughly contemporary archaeological occupation strata. Perhaps the most damaging objection to her work, therefore, is Straus's (1980: 624–25) assertion that such poor temporal and stratigraphic controls were maintained during the original excavation of Altamira that it is impossible for Conkey to be certain that the mobiliary objects were contemporary. Thus she cannot reject the alternative hypothesis that the stylistic variability observed in these objects is due to stylistic change over time. Despite this criticism, Conkey probably is correct in the interpretation that Altamira was a locus of seasonally timed aggregation and religious and ceremonial activity. However, she will have to refine her analysis in order to convince her critics. Perhaps she might be more successful at some of the other parietal art caves, which, like Altamira, float in a sea of rockshelters and smaller, less elaborately decorated caves.

Altamira, Lascaux, Tito Bustillo, El Castillo, and some of the other giants—and perhaps also the newly discovered Cuevo del Juyo—may have served as ceremonial centers. According to Eliade (1959b), ceremonial centers exist in a wide range of religious contexts. He notes that although such centers are commonly the location of seasonally timed ceremonies of social renewal and intensification, they have another purpose as well. Eliade contends that ceremonial centers come to embody a "sacred canon" or religious model of the social order in their architectural layout, decoration, and ritual activity. Ceremonial centers are both the material manifestations of a group's cultural tradition and a guarantee of the persistence and continuity of that tradition through time. Eliade's concept of the ceremonial center presents us with a means of melding the internalist and environmentalist interpretations of Upper Paleolithic art.

The choice of a specific cave to be fashioned into a ceremonial center and the timing of its use were determined by the nature of the seasonal subsistence schedule and the cycles of human aggregation and dispersal that such a schedule dictated. The sacred canons contained and expressed within such ceremonial cave centers would thus have been linked to economic realities in the lives of the people using them in direct and palpable ways. We can further speculate that the sacred canon provided meaning and reinforcement to the specific social and economic relations of the hunting and gathering system in which it emerged. Presumably, this was accomplished through the metaphorical expression of social and ideological realities. As noted above, Godelier considers the cooperation found in certain classes of rituals to be "formally identical to the generalized and reciprocal cooperation which exists . . . within the relations of production. It reproduces in the field of symbolic and ideological practice the cooperation of the social process of production" (Godelier 1975: 11). Art can operate in a like manner; Lewis-Williams's (1982) analysis of the parietal painting of the San peoples of southern Africa led him to conclude that art symbolizes and reflects the cooperative nature of economic activities among these desert foragers. It seems likely that the message encoded in the Upper Paleolithic "sacred canon" in the caves of southwestern Europe was partly economic in character. A discussion of the possible nature of that canon follows in the final section of this chapter.

**Social Integration and Revitalization.** Finally, what does the uniformity of the parietal and mobiliary art styles found throughout the Upper Paleolithic period in southwestern Europe tell us about the nature of religion there at the time? First of all, such uniformity allows us to reject the view that the motive behind the production of these paintings and objects was simply *art pour l'art;* that is, they were not created solely for their own sake by artists seeking to express personal aesthetic visions or emotions or to give pleasure to beholders. Speaking generally of the graphic arts of historic and recent hunting and gathering peoples, Service (1979: 70) states that the artist is not creative because "the style or pattern must be followed exactly simply because it is ritualized—any deviation breaks the spell just as surely as it does in an act of magic or sorcery." The dearth of evidence for individual creativity and originality in the paintings and objects suggests that these works were deeply embedded in the ritual life of the period. It supports the "classical" view that both art and its production were part of an attempt to control nature and society by supernatural means.

Uniformity of style also conforms nicely with the related hypothesis that the art of the period facilitated social integration and economic interaction. This thesis, advanced in various forms by Gamble, Jochim, and Conkey, is unconcerned with the aesthetic qualities of the art or with its religious meaning. Instead, these scholars emphasize the notion that shared religion fostered cooperative interactions or information sharing among widely separated Upper Paleolithic peoples. Religion provided these peoples with a common ideology and a universal symbolic grammar for expressing it. According to these scholars, art was uniform over a wide area of Europe because such uniformity fostered general intercommunication and selective advantage accrued to hunting groups with information about game movements over a wide area. As Moore puts it, information is after all a resource in its own right; "it is something that must be gathered either directly through searching or indirectly through the social processes that distribute information among individual decision makers (Moore 1983: 177). The problems of information collection and processing are just as real and just as critical to the maintenance of social life as is the collection of foodstuffs and raw materials—and societies must be structured accordingly.

Such an analysis of Upper Paleolithic art—and by extension, the religion of the period—is similar to the approach adopted by Rappaport in his Tsembaga Maring work. That is, religion is seen primarily in terms of its material effects, its systemic interconnections, and its contributions to the overall adaptation of any sociocultural system to the environment. On the other hand, functional analyses of this kind tend to be synchronic; they see religion simply as a fixed and conservative part of the sociocultural system.

Of course, religions are not exclusively conservative phenomena, and for this reason synchronic analyses cannot do them full justice. Religions also emerge as revitalization movements in times of social stress and cultural disintegration and often lead to profound transformations in sociocultural systems. Conceivably, the uniformity of Upper Paleolithic period art in Europe relates to the emergence and spread of such a revitalization. Fagan (1983: 122) suggests that the Venus figurines—which, by Gamble's lights, were produced during a narrow, two-thousand-year-long period—represent the material expression of such a movement. Christianity, after all, began as a revitalization movement, and its rapid spread is reflected in the spatial distribution of the material remains of its cult buildings and symbols. Ultimately, the cult became a conservative element fostering social integration in the sociocultural systems of which it was a part.

## RECONSTRUCTION OF THE RELIGIOUS THEORY: FORMAL ANALYSIS

The great painted caves of southwestern Europe occupy an important and distinctive status in contemporary studies of the Upper Paleolithic period. The pride of place accorded parietal art is due in part to the curious fact that works of undeniable beauty were fixed in dark and often inaccessible locations. Yet their attraction is by no means solely attributable to this unusual juxtaposition. More importantly, the caves and their painted decorations attract us because they represent the most dramatic and successful Paleolithic example of a uniquely human activity: the transformation of the natural environment for cultural and intellectual ends. In this they offer material evidence of the attempt by Upper Paleolithic peoples to impose their mental system and their sense of order and design on the intractable, resisting, and elemental structure of the earth: to sculpt the material world, as it were, into some conformity with the pattern of their minds. The degree to which they achieved this goal is hard to judge, but complete success was no more within their grasp than it is within ours.

What insights into the immutable design of Upper Paleolithic thought, ethos, and worldview remain to be discovered in the formal analysis of their art and symbolism? The elusive nature of thought and belief makes the extraction of that design or theory from an artistic context perilous and painfully difficult, and many scholars conclude, with Sieveking (1979: 208–9), that we can never know the meaning of Upper Paleolithic art, or even more pessimistically with Halverson (1987: 66), that the representations have no meaning at all in any ordinary sense of the word. Yet it has been the purpose of this book to demonstrate—without minimizing or dismissing the difficulties—that we *can indeed* penetrate the ancient systems of meaning that formed the basis of Upper Paleolithic art and in the process gain tentative and partial understanding of the religious life of the period.

**Pairs, Hands, and Codes.**  To the Structuralists, binary thought, or the tendency to divide reality into dichotomous pairs, is a universal attribute of the human mind. For them, the presence of consistent dichotomous pairings in Upper Paleolithic art and thought is taken for granted. Unfortunately, for the rest of us such an assertion must be demonstrated, not merely assumed, and the question of whether or not consistent dichotomous pairings were present in Upper Paleolithic thought remains a very real issue.

The apparent spatial dichotomy between the location of human habitation and the location of most parietal art in the Upper Paleolithic period settlement pattern is potentially instructive in this regard. Parietal art *may* once have decorated the surface of rockshelter habitation sites, but it is clear that most subterranean cave galleries were never inhabited for any extended period. This suggests that Upper Paleolithic peoples made an important spatial distinction between "living space," in the light and above ground where their everyday activities took place, and "ceremonial space," in the dark galleries below the earth's surface where extraordinary actions took place. This spatial distinction could have been a way to symbolize and make manifest the conceptual dichotomy drawn by Paleolithic peoples between the sphere of the profane and the sphere of the sacred.

A dichotomous division is also apprehensible in the interiors of the parietal art caves themselves. Leroi-Gourhan (1965b, 1982), Pfeiffer (1982b) and others report that cave art is found in accessible and central loci on one hand and in inaccessible or remote locations on the other. According to Leroi-Gourhan, the imagery in these two types of locations is different. He interprets this difference as reflecting the binary cosmological order that governed the structuring of the caves' overall decoration. In a later book, he interprets the difference in a functional manner: the inaccessible loci have become "sanctuaries," that is, chapels or cells reserved for the select few, while the accessible and central locations are seen by him as "temples," naves or central halls open to the many (Leroi-Gourhan 1982: 75).

Indirect evidence of binary thought is found at Gargas and at other sites containing negative and positive hand-print paintings. Huntington and Metcalf (1979: 18) note that the use of the right hand to symbolize good and the left hand evil is a nearly universal human trait. They suggest that this is due to the binary form of moral evaluation—good or evil—and the fact that human beings are both two-handed and generally right-hand dominant. In addition, Hertz (1960) points out the widespread association between death and the left hand. In this light, it is interesting to note that the representations of both whole and mutilated human hands painted or traced on walls of the Upper Paleolithic site of Gargas are overwhelmingly of *left* hands (Hadingham 1979: 148). Further, these hands were painted with either red or black pigments, two colors that also have virtually universal associations and oppositions. Victor Turner (1967: 88–91) refers to a "basic color triad" in human thought that associates the color red with power, life, and sex; the color black with death, mourning, and decomposition; and the color white with purity and fertility.

Thus when we break the hand prints down into their constituent attributes, we have a set of four binary oppositions:

1. red or black;
2. left or right;
3. positive or negative;
4. whole or "mutilated" (e.g., missing digits or bent fingers).

Each hand can be characterized by only one of each of the four dichotomous variables listed above. That is, it can either be left or right, positive or negative, red or black, mutilated or unmutilated. (Directionality could potentially be a fifth attribute, but virtually all of the reported hand prints are positioned with digits towards the ceiling.) Different combinations of these attributes on a given hand print have the potential for conveying different information, and the different "kinds" of hands could, of course, be strung together in sets to increase the complexity of their message. The potential complexity of this system could be fairly large; for example, our four binary sets of attributes can be combined to produce sixteen different kinds of hand prints $(2 \times 2 \times 2 \times 2 = 16)$.

In addition, any hand print can potentially represent a value of between 0 and 5 based on the number of digits shown. If instead of being a binary variable, "mutilated or unmutilated," the number of fingers shown on a hand print was meant to be read as a numerical value from zero to five, then the possible number of different kinds of hand prints is forty $(2 \times 2 \times 2 \times 5 = 40)$. The panels of hand prints have generally been taken as reflecting many separate and individual acts of painting or ritual participation, all of which occurred more-or-less unrelated to one another. So they may have been. However, it is also possible that the panels of supposedly unrelated hand prints at Gargas and elsewhere display rather sophisticated messages of some kind conveyed in binary code.

If such a coding is present in the hand prints, it is likely that information was conveyed in a similar manner by the various other classes of Upper Paleolithic period symbols. To test this hypothesis, it will be necessary to determine whether or not a consistent co-occurrence exists between certain colors and various classes of symbols such as tectaforms, claviforms, and so forth, or between colors and naturalistic images. References to such co-occurrence can be found scattered throughout the literature. For example, Kurten (1968: 189) notes that the cave painters at Lascaux tended to depict auroch bulls in black and cows in red. However, the search for such correlations will have to be undertaken on a regional scale and in a systematic manner. If it exists, evidence of such a systematic co-occurrence of color and form may provide a window into Upper Paleolithic art and thought. Turner's interpretation of the basic color triad would be a useful first step in decoding the hand prints and other symbols. Another step might be to make use of the interpretive methods found in the writings of the nineteenth-century Swiss anthropologist, J. J. Bachofen. In his classic essay, *An Essay on Ancient Mortuary Symbolism*, Bachofen noted the constant juxtaposition of symbols of life with rites and symbols of death. He concluded that the "funeral rite glorifies nature as a whole, with its twofold life and death giving principle. . . . That is why the symbols of life are so frequent in the tomb" (Bachofen 1967: 39). The Upper Paleolithic juxtaposition of the colors of life (red) and death (black) with the left and right hands perhaps suggests a twofold, funeral symbolism of the kind found by Bachofen among the Classical Greeks and Romans.

Leroi-Gourhan, of course, makes a strong case for similar artistic juxtapositions. For him, "male" symbols, weapons, and certain species of animals are counterpoised in Upper Paleolithic art against "female" symbols, prey animals, and wounded human and animal figures. Unfortunately, weaknesses in his methods of data collection have rendered his conclusions controversial. The issue will not be resolved in the absence of more rigorously controlled research. However, if Leroi-Gourhan is correct in identifying a consistent co-occurrence of certain symbols with naturalistic representations of certain animal species, it may be possible to further decode the message of parietal art. To do so it will be necessary to plot the color distributions in Leroi-Gourhan's data and to reconstruct closely the behavioral attributes of the key species in his system. This last technique has been used most successfully by Marshack. The behavioral characteristics of the animals used, together with color associations, may provide important clues as to the meanings the parietal art panels had for Upper Paleolithic peoples.

**Long Time Passing.** The work of Leroi-Gourhan presents the first dramatic challenge to the classical interpretation of Upper Paleolithic art and religious thought. He asserts that the parietal art of southwestern Europe was systematically composed of a limited set of principles that governed the association or pairings of certain images and symbols, and the relative placement of these images and symbols on the walls and in the different galleries of the caves. He concludes that this artistic and spatial order was the material reflection of the intellectual or metaphysical order in the minds of the Upper Paleolithic people who painted the caves, and that this metaphysic was centered on the fundamental duality of male and female.

It has proven easy over the years to dismiss Leroi-Gourhan's argument as merely another interpretation of art as an expression of subliminal sexual interests or forces and to link him in this sense with the Freudian school of art criticism. Of course, there is some justice in this identification. Freudian interpretations of art, which first appeared in 1916, in *Leonardo Da Vinci: A Study in Psychosexuality*, continue to be influential in our own time. For Freud and his followers, both art and religion constituted unconscious projects of the human family and the Oedipal struggle into the realm of conscious life. To the Freudian, "sexual concerns are an integral part of religious beliefs and consequently are reflected in art, which itself is tied into the dominant religious-symbolic system of society" (Silver 1979: 282).

Thoroughgoing Freudians would go much farther than Leroi-Gourhan in identifying sexual themes in Upper Paleolithic art and religion. For example, they would probably find more symbolic genitalia in the tectiforms, claviforms, and spaghetti signs than does Leroi-Gourhan. The paintings of predatory bears and lions in the outer galleries would be identified by them as thinly veiled images of the over-arching father figure of the Oedipal struggle. They would observe the deep and wide grooved "vulva signs" carved at the mouths of many of the painted caves of southwestern Europe and would note the dark, damp, and womblike galleries of the caves themselves. Emergence from such caves, they would surely conclude, was designed to create a powerful reenactment of the birth trauma in even the least avid Upper Paleolithic infantile regressor.

Mercifully, Leroi-Gourhan does not go this far. Instead, he merely points to the evidence of dichotomous pairing in Upper Paleolithic art as indicating that the cognitive system of these peoples interpreted the world as organized in terms of the principle of sexual duality. Of course, the sexual principle in human thought is closely and logically connected to the concept of fertility and regeneration. If Upper Paleolithic religious thought really did center on the sexual dichotomy, the associations between sexuality and regeneration might allow us to hypothesize that the Upper Paleolithic worldview was based on the doctrine of "eternalism." According to Eliade (1959), this doctrine is found in religions throughout the world. Such religions "seek a regeneration, a cyclical recurrence or eternal return, of all creation: cosmic, biological, historical, human" (Haber 1959: 12). Change is seen as illusory, and eternal repetition is viewed as the nature of the cosmos.

Such a doctrine contrasts markedly with the concept of time and reality found in most Western religious worldviews. Although there are elements of symbolic regeneration in both Judaism and Christianity, for example, such elements are not central to either faith. Instead, both these religions take what Haber (1959) calls a "patristic" view of time. In them, time is seen as beginning with Creation and the Age of the Patriarchs and moving, not in a cyclical or endlessly regenerative trajectory, but along a unique, *linear* progression with a discrete beginning, middle, and end.

Granting for a moment that Upper Paleolithic period art and religion is based on a sexual dualism, what other evidence is consistent with the hypothesis that the people of this period held a regenerative and cyclical worldview? At least two strands of evidence point in that direction: Marshack's interpretation of some mobiliary marks as a notational system for recording the lunar cycle; and the apparent conjunction of the moon (and by implication, its cycle) with the human female (and by implication, the menstrual cycle and the cycle of human birth, growth, and death).

Let me suggest that the Upper Paleolithic worldview probably represented a fusion of understanding of two separate, empirically knowable phenomena of the natural world: the passage of time and the nature of human—especially female—sexuality. Both of these natural phenomena are characterized by dramatic surficial or formal changes that can be observed and predicted with great ease and precision by virtually anyone. The moon waxes, then wanes, then disappears, then waxes again; women are born, enter their menses, become pregnant, give birth, and die. The palpable nature and cyclicality of these two phenomena make them attractive and convenient models for thinking about nature in general. It is easy to see how they might become "grand analogies," useful in explaining the universe, in rationalizing it, and in investing it with meaning in terms readily and widely understood.

In such a worldview, the world is not random and inexplicable. Rather, it is based on the same principle of dynamic opposition and yet ultimate complementarity found in human sexuality. In such a worldview, reality is not all change and flux. Rather it is the experience of a grand cycle, like the smaller cycles observed in the menses of women, or in the changes of the seasons, or in the phases of the moon. An ethos that emphasizes the careful observation of these changes would fit conformably with such a worldview. Records of the moon's passage that time the changing of the seasons and allow the prediction of the behavior and movements of animals would serve to confirm the aptness of the cyclical world picture.

**The Birth of Venus** With a nod to Botticelli, whose unique vision of Antiquity provides the title of this section, let us turn to the formal analysis of the celebrated female or "Venus" figurines recovered so widely in European Upper Paleolithic archaeological contexts. As noted in chapter 4, these figurines have been reported from the Pyrenees to the Urals and were shaped in media as varied as stone, ivory, and fired clay. They appear to be definitely missing only from the Solutrean tradition. The swollen bellies and exaggerated breasts, hips, and buttocks of some of these figurines have commonly led to the entire class of objects being interpreted as fertility images or mother-goddesses. Since this interpretation conforms nicely with the hypothesis advanced above, that Upper Paleolithic period thought conjoined the sexual and regenerative principles to create an "eternalist" worldview, it is tempting to accept the mother-goddess hypothesis more or less *in toto*. However, a number of well-crafted studies in recent years have forcefully questioned—and perhaps refuted—the view that the Venuses were simply or solely goddesses.

Harding (1976), for example, finds the image of the Venus figurine far from divine. In fact, he considers the proportions of the figurines to be so distorted that he suggests they depict females with a rare pathological condition known as "massive hypertrophy of the breasts." In a similar interpretation, Kopper and Grishman (Ice Age Idols 1978) see the figurines as embodying the physical symptoms of another disease called "Cushings syndrome" or "hyperadrenocorticism." This syndrome, which is due to the excessive production of the steroid hormone cortisone, leads to obesity, thin extremities, a hunched back with a large fat deposit or hump, and a moonlike face. Individuals with this disease tend towards states of high excitability and euphoria. Kopper and Grishman suggest that such symptoms might have been taken as an additional sign that a woman afflicted with the disease had shamanic powers. Both of these studies imply that the figurines represent real individuals—marked or punished by the gods, perhaps—but not divine in themselves.

Are these ubiquitous little Venus figurines likely to be realistic representations of extremely rare physical ailments or are we better served by interpreting them as projections of the more ordinary interests and values of Upper Paleolithic people? If the latter view is the more plausible, perhaps we should look upon the Venuses as ancient "Rorschach tests" that contain information about the personalities of both their creators and their "public." The essential idea of such tests is that "all human behaviors are determined, among other factors, by the personality of the agent. All behavior is expressive of—is a "projection" of—the agent's personality" (Wallace 1950: 241). The problem is to isolate behavioral traits that can be correlated with personality categories. In one method of correlation, the investigator asks the subject to draw a human figure and then attempts to correlate the specific form of that figure with elements of the subject's personality.

In a similar manner, sporadic attempts have been made by archaeologists to use ancient art as a "projection" of the personalities of the artist and of his society (for example, Davies 1969; Levey 1966; McClelland 1958, 1961; Rippeteau 1972; Wallace 1950). The results of such studies have been mixed, but the idea remains intriguing. With regard to Upper Paleolithic period art, it is worth noting that the most salient physical characteristics of the Venus figurines are also those areas of the human body whose representation is considered to have significant interpretive implications in the "Draw-a-Figure" personality projection test. For example, according to Machover,

> Whether the breast is given a low, pendant line, suggesting that the figure is a mother-image representation, or whether it is given the high, firm line of a youthful female figure is significant. The accentuated bosom is usually in the context of a strong and dominant mother-image, in the drawings of both male and female subjects. (1949: 70)

Wallace (1950: 256) expands on this and suggests that the tendency to portray female breasts as excessively prominent and pendulous is evidence of a "tendency to regress to an oral-dependent attitude." At the same time, Wallace (1950: 256, citing Machover's work) sees the tendency to portray female figures without arms or with excessively short arms as evidence that the drawer feels rejected by his mother. Finally, Machover finds that the way a subject draws the face on his figure is a projection of the style of his social relations. Therefore,

> the subject who deliberately omits facial features in a drawing showing careful and often aggressive delineation of contour and detail of other parts of the figure, is one who is evasive about the frictional character of his interpersonal relationships. This treatment is a graphic expression of avoidance of the problem. Superficiality, caution, and hostility may characterize the social contacts of such an individual. (Machover 1949: 40–41)

We might thus interpret the Venus figurines as representing projections of personalities shaped by strong, dominant, and rejecting mothers who engendered feelings of dependency in their children. These artists perhaps experienced frictional relations with their fellows and tended to deal with them in superficial, cautious, and hostile fashion. Of course, we can never know whether twentieth-century interpretive criteria can be applied validly to the personality projections of the Upper Paleolithic period. Further, even if they can, we can never know to what extent the personality characteristics of the artists who carved the Venuses were shared by their "public." Wallace (1950: 243) asserts that if we confine our interpretation to those elements common to the artistic tradition in general, we can be fairly certain that we are dealing with a projection of the society's modal personality rather than that of the individual artist.

It is very possible, however, that these interpretations of the figurines are misperceptions due to the design convention used by the Upper Paleolithic carvers. According to André Leroi-Gourhan,

> the leading convention that characterizes these statuettes is the way breast, abdomen, and pelvic regions are grouped approximately within a circle. The rest of the body—toward the head and the feet—tapers gradually, even dwindles away along the vertical poles of the circle. As a result most of the figurines can be inscribed within a lozenge. (1968: 90)

This convention has the effect of emphasizing the sexual characteristics of the figurines at the expense of their other attributes. Once a twentieth-century viewer accustoms himself to that ancient idiom it is possible to see a good deal of complex and significant variation between the figurines. In a recent study, Rice (1982) systematically compares some 188 Upper Paleolithic period Venuses in terms of five body attributes: breasts, stomachs, hips, buttocks, and faces. She concludes that, far from exclusively representing pregnant women, the figurines include images of young girls, nonpregnant "middle-age" females (roughly fifteen to thirty-five years old), and old women past child-bearing age. Significantly, the percentage of each of these classes represented in her corpus of figurines closely approximates the age and pregnancy distributions found in contemporary hunter-gatherer populations (1982: 408). Since she finds the statuettes depict females "throughout their adult life-span, not just in their reproductive stage," Rice rejects the classic view that the Venuses were goddesses carved solely to glorify fertility or to insure or sanctify it. Instead, she suggests the Venus figurines

> represent some combination of secular pragmatism and sacred mysteriousness, rather than either exclusively. Because the Venuses represent

women of different ages in proportion to their probable actual frequency in the population, there is little basis for assuming an exclusively sacred function; if anything, a stronger case can be made for the statuettes representing women in real-life roles and yet ethnographic parallels argue against an exclusively pragmatic interpretation. (Rice 1982)

The archaeological context of the figurines may strengthen Rice's interpretation. The majority of those Venuses for which contextual information is available were recovered in association with habitation debris or in what apparently were "domestic settings" (Gamble 1982: 96).

Finally, it is worth recalling that the Upper Paleolithic period is the first time in prehistory that females were commonly buried with grave goods. Although male burials are substantially more common in the archaeological record, for the first time in prehistory some females received burial treatment similar to that accorded to males and perhaps were able to achieve social status on a par with men during this period (Harrold 1980: 207). In their own way, do the Venus figurines reflect a parallel increase in the significance of women—or at least of femaleness—in the Upper Paleolithic spiritual realm? If they do, much of the parietal and mobiliary art of the period reflects a "sacred canon" which symbolically reproduces the social processes of production and asserts that the duality and complementarity of the sexes were essential to the social and economic persistence of society.

## THE GODS BEFORE HISTORY

The richness of the late Glacial environment of southwestern Europe must have enabled Upper Paleolithic hunting and gathering subsistence systems to support human populations in densities beyond those of recent pedestrian foragers and equal to or greater than those achieved in historic times by equestrian hunters on the Great Plains or fisher-forager-hunters on the Northwest Coast. Although forced to make scheduled moves in response to annual cycles of game and fish availability, Upper Paleolithic peoples probably lived in sedentary communities for extended periods of time during certain seasons in their annual round. The important rites of intensification and passage practiced by these peoples no doubt took place during these periods of extended sedentism and maximum social aggregation or group size. Male initiation rites were probably an important element in the religious cycle of these peoples and are likely to have been featured during the ceremonies held at times of maximum social aggregation. The larger cave art sites in Franco-Cantabria were probably ceremonial centers which served as the focus of the rites that occurred during these periodic aggregations. Like many historic and modern fisher-forager-hunters of the subarctic, Upper Paleolithic subsistence practices emphasized "delayed-return" activities in the form of storage, surplus accumulation, funeral ceremonialism, and artistic display. Because of their relatively high population densities and their annual periods of sedentary living, the complexity of their political and social organization—at least during seasons of maximum social aggregation—surpassed that of the "band."

The ethnographic record also suggests that the religious life of Upper Paleolithic societies depended upon shaman, part-time practitioners who vigorously and directly sought to confront the spirit world in "ecstatic encounters." Given the high value that historic and recent food collectors place on achieving these special or altered states of consciousness, there no doubt was widespread group or communal participation in the religious life of the Upper Paleolithic period. In addition to its ecstatic and extraordinary elements, the Upper Paleolithic religious ideology no doubt sanctioned the rules governing interpersonal relations, sex roles, hunting procedures, the treatment of game animals, and the distribution of meat. But the reverse was also true: the complex social and productive relations in the world of everyday experience were, in turn, reflected in the rituals of the Upper Paleolithic period as well as in the "sacred canon," the religious and symbolic model of the social order that lay behind that ritual life.

In a related manner, the material patterns in the archaeological record, together with the formal interpretations of those patterns, conforms with the expectations of two hypotheses. First, religion in Franco-Cantabria during the Upper Paleolithic period was a) based upon a complex intellectual and theological order and b) was ultimately experiential in inspiration. Second, two profound natural phenomena—a) a perceived cyclicality in the passage of time and b) the dialectic of human sexuality, especially the periodicity and fecundity of women—were generalized into universal principles or "grand analogies" that formed the basis of speculation and thought about nature, humankind, the universe, and reality. This model of social and material reality was embodied and reflected in the great parietal art caves of Franco-Cantabria.

Human life is fragile and transitory and its essential fact—the inevitability of death—can be countered only by birth, by more life. Human existence is both obvious and mysterious: we know it must end in death yet it is filled with signs and portents suggesting otherwise. Fragility and mystery—fear and hope—provoke the yearnings for fertility and immortality in humankind. To find that we share these yearnings even with peoples of as remote an age as the late Pleistocene is to recognize our kinship with all humanity.

To the Classical Greeks, fear and hope were the twin tyrants of humankind. No less than ourselves, the peoples of Ice Age Europe were tormented by these twin tyrants. Their reply to this torment is frozen in the mighty art of the Upper Paleolithic and has resonated down three hundred centuries into our own time.

# Bibliography

Adams, John W.
1973   *The Gitksan Potlatch: Population Flux, Resource Ownership and Reciprocity.* Toronto: Holt, Rinehart and Winston of Canada.
Anati, E.
1984   The state of research in rock art. *Bolletino del Centro Camuno di Studi Preistorici* 21:13–56.
1985   The rock art of Tanzania and the East African sequence. *Bolletino del Centro Camuno di Studi Preistorici* 23:15–68.
1986   Comment. *Current Anthropology* 27(3): 202.
ApSimon, A. M.
1980   The last Neanderthal in France? *Nature* 287:271–272.
Bachofen, Johann J.
1967   *Myth, Religion and Mother Right.* Translated by E. Mannheim. London: Routledge and Kegan Paul.
Bahn, Paul G.
1977   Seasonal migration in southwest France during the Late Glacial period. *Journal of Archaeological Science* 4:245–257.
1978a  Water mythology and the distribution of Paleolithic parietal art. *Proceedings of the Prehistoric Society* 44:125–134.
1978b  The "unacceptable face" of the West European Upper Paleolithic. *Antiquity* 52:183–192.
Bahn, Paul G., and Claude Couraud
1984   Azilian pebbles: an unsolved mystery. *Endeavour* 8(4): 156–58.
Bailey, Geoffrey N.
1983   Concepts of time in Quaternary prehistory. *Annual Review of Anthropology* 12:143–164.
Bandi, Hans-Georg
1980   After Breuil: review of A. Leroi-Gourhan's *Préhistoire de l'Art Occidentale (1965). The Quarterly Review of Archaeology* 1:9–11.
Barth, Edward K.
1982   Ancient methods for trapping wild reindeer in south Norway, In *The Hunters: Their Culture and Way of Life.* Edited by Ake Hultkrntz and Ornulf Vorren. *Tromso Museum Skrifter* 18: 21–46.

Beaumont, Peter B., Hertha de Villers, and John C. Vogel
    1978    Modern man in sub-Saharan Africa prior to 49,000 years B.P.: review and evaluation with particular reference to Border cave. *South African Journal of Science* 74:409–419.
Beck, Benjamin
    1980    *Animal Tool Behavior.* New York: Garland.
Bennett, C. L.
    1979    Radiocarbon dating with accelerators. *American Scientist* 67:450–457.
Bennett, John William, and Melvin Marvin Tumin
    1948    *Social Life: Structure and Function.* New York: Alfred A. Knopf.
Berelson, Bernard, and Gary A. Steiner
    1964    *Human Behavior: An Inventory of Scientific Findings.* New York: Harcourt, Brace and World, Inc.
Berenguer, Magín
    1973    *Prehistoric Men and their Art.* Park Ridge, New Jersey: Noyes Press.
Berggren, William A., Lloyd H. Burckle, M. B. Cox, H. B. S. Cooke, B. M. Funnell, S. Gartner, James D. Hays, James P. Kennett, N. D. Opdyke, L. Pastouret, N. J. Shackleton, Y. Takayanagi
    1980    Towards a Quaternary time scale. *Quaternary Research* 13:277–302.
Bidney, David
    1953    *Theoretical Anthropology.* New York: Columbia University Press.
Binford, Lewis R.
    1971    Mortuary practices: their study and their potential. In Approaches to the social dimensions of mortuary practices. Edited by James A. Brown. *Society for American Archaeology Memoir* 25:92–112.
    1972    *An Archaeological Perspective.* New York: Seminar Press.
    1973    Interassemblage variability—the Mousterian and the "functional" argument. In *The Explanation of Culture Change.* Edited by Colin Renfrew, pp. 227–254. Liverpool: Duckworth.
    1981    *Bones.* New York: Academic Press.
    1983    *In Pursuit of the Past.* New York: Thames and Hudson, Inc.
    1984    *Faunal Remains from Klasies River Mouth.* New York: Academic Press.
    1987    Searching for camps and missing the evidence?: Another look at the Lower Paleolithic. In *The Pleistocene Old World: Regional Perspectives.* Edited by Olga Soffer, pp. 17–32. New York: Plenum Press.
Binford, Lewis R., and Chuan Kun Ho
    1985    Taphonomy at a distance: Zhoukoudian, "The Cave Home of Beijing Man"? *Current Anthropology* 26(4): 413–442.
Binford, Lewis R., and Sally R. Binford
    1966    A preliminary analysis of functional variability in the Mousterian of Levallois. *American Anthropologist* 68(2):238–296.

Binford, Sally
1968   A structural comparison of disposal of the dead in the Mousterian and Upper Paleolithic. *Southwestern Journal of Anthropology* 24:139–151.
Binford, Sally R., and Lewis R. Binford
1969   Stone tools and human behavior. *Scientific American* 220:70–83.
Bishop, Walter W., J. A. Miller, and Sonia Cole, eds.
1972   *The Calibration of Hominoid Evolution.* Edinburgh: Scottish Academic Press.
Blanc, Alberto C.
1961   Some evidence for the ideologies of early man. In The Social Life of Early Man. Edited by Sherwood L. Washburn, *Viking Fund Publications in Anthropology* 31:119–136.
Blumenberg, Bennett
1983   The evolution of the advanced hominid brain. *Current Anthropology* 24(5): 589–523.
Boaz, Noel T.
1979   Hominid evolution in Eastern Africa during the Pliocene and Early Pleistocene. *Annual Review of Anthropology* 8:71–85.
Bordaz, Jacques
1970   *Tools of the Old and New Stone Age.* Garden City: The Natural History Press.
Bordes, François
1958   Nouvelles fouilles à Laugerie-Haute—premiers résultats. *L'Anthropologie* 62:205–244.
1959   Laugerie-Haute. *Gallia Préhistorie (Informations archéologiques)* 2:156–167.
1961   Mousterian cultures in France. *Science* 134:803–810.
1968   *The Old Stone Age.* New York: McGraw-Hill Book Company.
1972   *A Tale of Two Caves.* New York: Harper and Row, Publishers.
1973   On the chronology and contemporaneity of different Paleolithic cultures in France. In *The Explanation of Culture Change.* Edited by Colin Renfrew, pp. 217–226. Liverpool: Duckworth.
Bordes, François, and C. Thibault
1977   Thoughts on the initial adaptation of hominids to European glacial climates. *Quaternary Research* 8:115–127.
Bordes, François, and Denise de Sonneville-Bordes
1966   Protomagdalénien, ou Périgordien VII? *L'Anthropologie* 70:113–122.
1970   The significance of variability in Paleolithic assemblages. *World Archaeology* 2(1):61–73.
Bouchud, Jean
1954a   Le renne et le problème des migrations. *L'Anthropologie* 58:79–85.
1954b   Dents de renne, bois de rennes et migrations. *Bulletin de la Société Préhistorique Française* 51:340–345.
1966   *Essai sur le renne et la climatologie du Paleolithique moyen et supérier.* Perigueux: Imprimerie Magne.

Boughey, Arthur S.
1968   *Ecology of Populations.* New York: The Macmillan Company.
Bowen, David Q.
1978   *Quaternary Geology.* Oxford: Pergamon Press.
Brace, C. Loring
1962   Cultural factors in the evolution of the human dentition. In *Culture and the Evolution of Man.* Edited by Ashley Montagu, pp. 343–354. New York: Oxford University Press.
1979   Krapina, "classic" Neanderthals and the evolution of the European face. *Journal of Human Evolution* 8:527–550.
Brain, Charles K.
1981   *The Hunters or the Hunted? An Introduction to African Cave Taphonomy.* Chicago: The University of Chicago Press.
Brandon, Samuel G. F.
1975   *Man and God in Art and Ritual.* New York: Charles Scribner's Sons.
Breuil, Abbé Henri
1913   Les subdivisions du Paléolithique supérieur et leur signification. In *Congrès International d'Anthropologie et d'Archaéologie Préhistorique* (Geneva 1912), pp. 165–238.
1979   *Four Hundred Centuries of Cave Art.* Translated by Mary E. Boyle. New York: Hacker Art Books. Originally published in 1952 by Centre d'etudes et de documentation préhistoriques, Paris.
Breuil, Abbé Henri, and Raymond Lantier
1959   *Les hommes de la pierre ancienne.* Paris: Bibliotheque Scientific-Payot.
Bricker, Harvey M.
1976   Upper Paleolithic archaeology. *Annual Review of Anthropology* 5:133–148.
Brooks, Charles E. P.
1949   *Climate Through the Ages.* (Third ed.) London: E. Benn.
Burch, Ernest S., Jr.
1972   The caribou/wild reindeer as a human resource. *American Antiquity* 37(3): 339–368.
Burnett, Jacquetta Hill
1969   Ceremony, rites and economy in the student system of an American high school. *Human Organization* 28(1):1–10.
Butzer, Karl W.
1971   *Environment and Archaeology.* (Second ed.). Chicago: Aldine, Atherton.
1974   Geological and ecological perspectives on the middle Pleistocene. *Quaternary Research* 4:136–148.
1976   Pleistocene climates. In Ecology of the Pleistocene: a Symposium. Edited by R. C. West and W. G. Haag. *Geoscience and Man* 13: 27–44.
1977   Environment, culture and human evolution. *American Scientist* 65(5):572–584.

1981 Cave sediments, Upper Pleistocene stratigraphy and Mousterian facies in Cantabrian Spain. *Journal of Archaeological Science* 8:133–183.

1982 *Archaeology as Human Ecology*. New York: Cambridge University Press.

Butzer, Karl W., G. J. Fock, L. Scott, and R. Stuckenrath

1979 Dating and context of rock engravings in southern Africa. *Science* 203:1201–1214.

1980 Comment on: Red ochre and human evolution: a case for discussion, by E. E. Wreschner. *Current Anthropology* 21(5): 635.

Butzer, Karl W., and Glynn Isaac, eds.

1975 *After the Australopithecines: Stratigraphy, Ecology, and Culture Change in the Middle Pleistocene*. The Hague: Mouton Publishers.

Cabrera, V., and Frederico Bernaldo de Quiros

1977 The Solutrean site of Cueva Chufin (Santander, Spain). *Current Anthropology* 18:780–781.

Campbell, Bernard G.

1982 *Humankind Emerging*. 3d ed. Boston: Little, Brown and Company.

Chang, Kwang-Chih

1977 *The Archaeology of Ancient China*. New Haven: Yale University Press.

Chase, P., and H. Dibble

1987 Middle Paleolithic symbolism: a review of current evidence and interpretations. *Journal of Anthropological Archaeology* 6: 263–296.

Chollot-Varagnac, Marthe

1980 *Les Origines du Graphisme Symbolique: Essai d'Analyse des Escritures Primitives Prehistoire*. Paris: Singer Polignac.

Ciochon, Russell L.

1983 Hominoid cladistics and the ancestry of modern apes and humans: a summary statement. In *New Interpretations of Ape and Human Ancestry*. Edited by R. L. Ciochon and R. S. Corruccini, pp. 783–843. New York: Plenum Press.

Clark, J. D.

1974 Africa in prehistory: peripheral or paramount? *Man* (n.s.), 10:175–198.

Clark, J. G. D., and Stuart Piggott

1965 Prehistoric Societies. New York: Alfred A. Knopf.

Clark, J. G. D., and Michael W. Thompson

1953 The groove and splinter technique of working antler in Upper Paleolithic and Mesolithic Europe. *Proceedings of the Prehistoric Society* 16:109–129.

Clark, W. E. LeGros

1964 *The Fossil Evidence for Human Evolution*. 2d ed. Chicago: The University of Chicago Press.

Clarke, David L.

1978 *Analytical Archaeology*. London: Methuen, Inc.

Clutton-Brock, T. H., and P. H. Harvey
    1978    Mammals, resources and reproductive strategies. *Nature* 273: 191–195.
Codere, Helen
    1950    *Fighting with Property.* New York: Augustin.
Cohen, Mark Nathan
    1985    Prehistoric hunter-gatherers: the meaning of social complexity. In *Prehistoric Hunter-Gatherers; the Emergence of Cultural Complexity.* Edited by T. D. Price and J. A. Brown, pp. 99–119. New York: Academic Press.
Cohen, Norman, and Rufus Colin
    1957    *The Pursuit of the Millennium.* New York: Harper and Row, Inc.
Collins, Desmond, and John Onians
    1978    The origins of art. *Art History* I(1): 1–25.
Comte, Auguste
    1896    *The Positive Philosophy of Auguste Comte.* Translated by Harriet Martineau. London: George Bell and Sons.
Conkey, Margaret W.
    1978    Style and information in cultural evolution: toward a predictive model for the Paleolithic. In *Social Anthropology: Beyond Subsistence and Dating.* Edited by C. Redman, W. Langhorne, M. Berman, N. Versaggi, E. Curtin, and J. Wanser, pp. 61–84. New York: Academic Press.
    1980a   Context, structure and efficacy in Paleolithic art and design. In *Symbol as Sense: New Approaches is the Analysis of Meaning,* edited by M. L. Foster and S. H. Brandes, pp. 225–248. New York: Academic Press.
    1980b   The identification of prehistoric hunter-gatherer aggregation sites: the case of Altamira. *Current Anthropology* 21(5):609–630.
    1981    A century of Paleolithic cave art. *Archaeology* 34(4): 20–28.
    1983    On the origins of Paleolithic art: a review and some critical thoughts. In The Mousterian legacy: human biocultural change in the Upper Pleistocene. Edited by Erik Trinkaus. *British Archaeological Reports International Series* 164:201–227.
    1988    New approaches in the search for meaning: a review of research in "Paleolithic art." *Journal of Field Archaeology* 14:413–430.
Coon, Carleton S.
    1977    *The Hunting Peoples.* New York: Penguin Books.
Cronin, J. E., Noel T. Boaz, C. B. Stringer, and Yoel Rak
    1981    Tempo and mode in hominid evolution. *Nature* 292:113–121.
Crowell, John C., and Lawrence A. Frakes
    1970    Phanerozoic glaciation and the causes of ice ages. *American Journal of Science* 268:193–224.
Dahlberg, Albert A., and V. M. Carbonell
    1961    The dentition of the Magdalenian female from Cap Blanc, France. *Man,* 61:49–50.

Dalrymple, G. Brent
    1972   Potassium-argon dating of geomagnetic reversals and North American glaciations. In *Calibration of Hominoid Evolution.* Edited by W. W. Bishop, J. A. Miller, and Sonia Cole, pp. 107–134. Edinburgh: Scottish Academic Press.

Daniel, Glyn
    1967   *The Origins and Growth of Archaeology.* New York: Galahad Books.

Dart, Raymond A.
    1957   The Osteodontokeratic culture of *Australopithecus prometheus. Memoir of the Transvaal Museum* 10.

David, Nicholas C.
    1966   The Perigordian Vc: an upper Paleolithic Culture in Western Europe. Unpublished Ph.D. Dissertation, Department of Anthropology. Cambridge: Harvard University.
    1973   On Upper Paleolithic society, ecology and technological change: the Noaillian Case. In *The Explanation of Culture Change.* Edited by Colin Renfrew, pp. 277–303. Liverpool: Duckworth.

Davidson, I.
    1974   Radiocarbon dates for the Spanish Solutrean. *Antiquity* 48:63–65.

Davies, Evan
    1969   This is the way Crete went—not with a bang but a simper. *Psychology Today* 3:42–47.

Davis, Kingsley
    1949   *Human Society.* New York: MacMillan, Inc.

Davis, Margaret Bryan
    1976   Pleistocene biogeography of temperate deciduous forests. In Ecology of the Pleistocene: a Symposium. Edited by R. C. West and W. G. Haag. *Geoscience and Man* 13:13–26.

Debecker, Luc Jean-François
    1978   The world's largest and oldest art collection. In *In the Spirit of Enterprise: From the Rolex Awards.* Edited by G. B. Stone, pp. 11–15. San Francisco: W. H. Freeman and Company.

Delibrias, G., and J. Evin
    1974   Sommaire des datations 14C concernant la préhistoire en France. *Bulletin de la Société Préhistorique Française* 71:149–156.

de Lumley, Henry
    1969   A Paleolithic camp at Nice. *Scientific American* 220:42–50.
    1975   Cultural evolution in France in its paleoecological setting during the middle Pleistocene. In *After the Australopithecines.* Edited by Karl W. Butzer and Glynn Isaac, pp. 745–808. The Hague: Mouton Publishers.

Delporte, H.
    1970   Le passage du Moustèrien au Paléolithique supérieur. In *l'homme de Cro-Magnon.* Edited by G. Camps and G. Olivier, pp. 129–139. Paris: Arts et Métiers Graphiques.
    1976   Les sépultures Moustèriennes de la Ferraisse. In Les sépultures

néandertaliennes, pp. 8–11. IX Congrès UISPP Pretirage. Nice: CNRS.

1979   *L'image de la Femme dans l'art préhistorique.* Paris: Picard.

Dobie, J. Frank

1934   *The Mustangs.* Boston: Little, Brown and Company.

1941   *The Longhorns.* Boston: Little, Brown and Company.

Dole, Gertrude E.

1973   Foundations of contemporary evolutionism. In *Main Currents in Cultural Anthropology.* Edited by R. Naroll and F. Naroll, pp. 247–279. New York: Appleton-Century-Crofts.

Driver, Harold E.

1961   *Indians of North America.* Chicago: The University of Chicago Press.

Drucker, Philip

1955   *Indians of the Northwest Coast.* Garden City: The Natural History Press.

Drucker, Philip, and R. F. Heizer

1967   *To Make My Name Good.* Berkeley: University of California Press.

Dunnell, Robert C.

1978   Style and function: a fundamental dichotomy. *American Antiquity* 43:192–202.

Durkheim, Emile

1961   *The Elementary Forms of the Religious Life.* Translated by Joseph Ward Swain. First published in 1912. Glencoe, Illinois: The Free Press.

1965   *The Elementary Forms of the Religious Life.* Translated by Joseph Ward Swain. Collier Books, New York.

Edwards, Stephen W.

1978   Nonutilitarian activities in the Lower Paleolithic: a look at two kinds of evidence. *Current Anthropology* 19(1):135–137.

Eliade, Mircea

1958   *Patterns in Comparative Religion.* New York: New American Library.

1959a   *Cosmos and History: The Myth of the Eternal Return.* New York: Harper.

1959b   *Sacred and Profane: the Nature of Religion.* New York: Harcourt Brace, Inc.

1964   *Shamanism: Archaic Techniques of Ecstasy.* New York: Bollingen Foundation.

1978   *A History of Religious Ideas, Volume 1: From the Stone Age to the Eleusinian Mysteries.* Chicago: The University of Chicago Press.

Embleton, Clifford (Editor)

1984   *Geomorphology of Europe.* New York: John Wiley and Sons.

Emiliani, Cesare

1966   Paleotemperature analysis of Caribbean cores P 6304-8 and P 6304-9 and a generalized temperature curve for the past 425,000 years. *Journal of Geology* 74:109–126.

Ericson, David B., M. Ewinn, Goesta Wollin, and Bruce C. Heezen
    1961   Atlantic deep-sea sediment cores. *Bulletin, Geological Society of America* 72:193–286.

Ericson, David B., and Goesta Wollin
    1968   Pleistocene climates and chronology in deep-sea sediments. *Science* 162:1227–1234.

Fagan, Brian M.
    1983   *People of the Earth.* 3d ed. New York: Little, Brown and Company.

Fairservis, Walter A., Jr.
    1975   *The Threshold of Civilization; An Experiment in Prehistory.* New York: Scribners.

Falk, Dean
    1980   Language, handedness and primate brains: did the Australopithecines sign? *American Anthropologist* 82(1):72–78.

Feuerbach, Ludwig
    1957   *The Essence of Christianity.* New York: Harper Torchbooks.

Ford, James A.
    1954a  Comment on A. C. Spaulding's statistical techniques for the discovery of artifact types. *American Antiquity* 19:390–391.

    1954b  The type concept revisited. *American Anthropologist* 56(1):42–53.

Fortune, Reo Franklin
    1935   Manus Religion. *Memoirs of the American Philosophical Society* 3.

Frayer, David W.
    1978   Evolution of the dentition in Upper Paleolithic and Mesolithic Europe. University of Kansas, Publications in Anthropology 10.

    1980   Sexual dimorphism and cultural evolution in the late Pleistocene and Holocene of Europe. *Journal of Human Evolution* 9:399–415.

    1981   Body size, weapon use, and natural selection in the European Upper Paleolithic and Mesolithic. *American Anthropologist* 83: 57–73.

    1984   Biological and cultural change in the European late Pleistocene and early Holocene. In *The Origins of Modern Humans: A World Survey of the Fossil Evidence.* Edited by F. H. Smith and Frank Spencer, pp. 211–250. New York: Alan R. Liss.

Frayer, David W., and Milford H. Wolpoff
    1985   Sexual dimorphism. *Annual Review of Anthropology* 14:429–473.

Freeman, Leslie G.
    1966   The nature of the Mousterian facies in Cantabrian Spain. *American Anthropologist* 68(2): 230–237.

    1973   The significance of mammalian faunas from Paleolithic occupations in Cantabrian Spain. *American Antiquity* 38(1): 3–44.

    1975   By their works you shall know them: cultural developments in the Paleolithic. In *Hominisation and Verhalten.* Edited by Gottfied Kurth and I. Eibl-Eibesfeldt, pp. 234–261. Stuttgart: Gustav Fischer Verlag.

    1978a  Mousterian worked bone from Cueva Morin (Santander, Spain): a preliminary description. In *Views of the Past.* Edited by Leslie G. Freeman, pp. 29–51. The Hague: Mouton Publishers.

1978b The analysis of some occupation floor distributions from Early and Middle Paleolithic sites in Spain. In *Views of the Past.* Edited by Leslie G. Freeman, pp. 57–116. The Hague: Mouton Publishers.

1980 The development of human cultures. In *The Cambridge Encyclopedia of Archaeology.* Edited by A. Sherratt. New York: Crown Publishers.

Freeman, Leslie G., and J. Gonzalez Echegaray

1970 Aurignacian structural features and burials at Cueva Morin (Santander, Spain). *Nature* 226:722–726.

1981 El Juyo: a 14,000-year-old sanctuary from northern Spain. *History of Religions* 21(1): 1–19.

Freud, Sigmund

1947 *Leonardo Da Vinci: A Study in Psychosexuality.* New York: Random House.

Fried, Morton H.

1967 *The Evolution of Political Society.* New York: Random House.

Fried, Martha Nemes, and Morton H. Fried

1980 *Transitions: Four Rituals in Eight Cultures.* New York: Penguin Books.

Gamble, Clive

1982 Interaction and alliance in Paleolithic society. *Man* 17(1): 92–107.

Gargett, Robert

1989 Grave shortcomings: the evidence for Neanderthal burial. *Current Anthropology* 30(2): 157–190.

Gates, Lawrence W.

1976 Modeling the Ice-Age climate. *Science* 191:1138–1144.

Geertz, Clifford

1973 *The Interpretation of Cultures.* New York: Basic Books, Inc.

Gmelch, George J.

1971 Baseball magic. *Transaction* 8(8): 39–41.

Goddard, Thomas, and M. H. Fisch, trans.

1968 *The New Science of Giambattista Vico.* (Rev. ed.). Ithaca: Cornell University Press.

Godelier, Maurice

1975 Modes of production, kinship, and demographic structures. In *Marxist Analyses and Social Anthropology.* Edited by M. Bloch, pp. 3–27. New York: John Wiley and Sons.

1977 *Perspectives in Marxist Anthropology.* New York: Cambridge University Press.

Goudie, Andrew

1977 *Environmental Change.* Oxford: Clarendon Press.

Gowlett, John A. J., J. W. K. Harris, D. Walton, and B. A. Wood

1981 Early archaeological sites, hominid remains and traces of fire from Chesowanja, Kenya. *Nature* 294:125–129.

Graburn, Nelson H. H., and B. Stephen Strong
  1973 *Circumpolar Peoples: An Anthropological Perspective.* Pacific Palisades, California: Goodyear Publishing Company, Inc.
Grinnell, George B.
  1962 *The Cheyenne Indians: Their History and Ways of Life.* New York: Cooper Square Publishers.
Grosswald, M. G.
  1980 Late Weichselian ice sheet of northern Eurasia. *Quaternary Research* 13:1–32.
Haber, Francis C.
  1959 *The Age of the World: Moses to Darwin.* Baltimore: Johns Hopkins Press.
Hadingham, Evan
  1979 *Secrets of the Ice Age.* New York: Walker and Company.
Hahn, Joachim
  1972 Aurignacian signs, pendants and art objects in central and eastern Europe. *World Archaeology* 3:252–266.
  1977 Aurignacian—das ältere Jungpaläeolithikum in Mittel- und Osteuropa. *Fundamenta* A9.
  1981 Recherches sur l'art Paleolithique depuis 1976. In *Aurignacien et Gravettian en Europe, Actes des reunions de la 10 eme Commission de l'U.I.S.P.P. Etudes et Recherches Archéologiques de l'Université de Liege* 13:79–82.
Hammond, Norman
  1974 Paleolithic mammalian faunas and parietal art in Cantabria: a comment on Freeman. *American Antiquity* 39(4):618–19.
Harding, J. R.
  1976 Certain Upper Paleolithic "Venus" statuettes considered in relation to the pathological condition known as massive hypertrophy of the breasts. *Man* (n.s.) 11:271–272.
Halverson, John
  1987 Art for art's sake in the Paleolithic. *Current Anthropology* 28(1): 63–89.
Haring, A., A. E. DeVries, and H. DeVries
  1958 Radiocarbon dating up to 70,000 years with isotopic enrichment. *Science* 128:472–473.
Harris, Marvin
  1979 *Cultural Materialism.* New York: Random House.
Harrold, Francis B.
  1980 A comparative analysis of Eurasian Paleolithic burials. *World Archaeology* 12(2):195–211.
  1981 New perspectives on the Châtelperronian. *Diputacío de Barcelona, Institut de Prehistória I Arqueologia, Monografies* LXII:1–51.
Hassan, Fekri A.
  1981 *Demographic Archaeology.* New York: Academic Press.
Hayden, Brian
  1981 Subsistence and ecological adaptation among modern hunter/gath-

erers. In *Omnivorous Primates: Gathering and Hunting in Human Evolution*. Edited by R.S.O. Harding and Geza Teleki, pp. 344–421. New York: Columbia University Press.

Heizer, Robert F.
  1962  *Man's Discovery of His Past: Literary Landmarks in Archaeology*. Englewood Cliffs, New Jersey: Prentice-Hall, Inc.

Herskovits, Melville J.
  1948  *Man and His Works*. New York: Alfred A. Knopf.

Hertz, Robert
  1960  *Death and the Right Hand*. Translated by R. and C. Needham. New York: The Free Press.

Hoebel, E. Adamson
  1978  *The Cheyennes: Indians of the Great Plains*. 2d ed. New York: Holt, Rinehart and Winston.

Hooten, Earnest A.
  1949  *Up From the Apes*. New York: MacMillan, Inc.

Hosteltler, John A.
  1970  *Amish Society*. (Revised ed.). Baltimore: The Johns Hopkins University Press.

Howell, F. Clark
  1957  Pleistocene glacial ecology and the evolution of "classic" Neanderthal man. *Southwestern Journal of Anthropology* 8:377–410.
  1965  *Early Man*. New York: Time-Life Books, Inc.
  1975  Neanderthal man: facts and figures. In *Paleoanthropology*. Edited by R. Tuttle, pp. 389–407. The Hague: Mouton Publishers.
  1984  Introduction. In *The Origins of Modern Humans*. Edited by F. H. Smith and Frank Spencer, pp. xiii–xxii. New York: Alan R. Liss, Inc.

Huntington, Richard, and Peter Metcalf
  1979  *Celebrations of Death*. Cambridge: Cambridge University Press.

Ice Age Idols
  1978  *The Sciences*. September: 4–5.

Issac, Glyn L.
  1982  Early hominids and fire at Chesowanja, Kenya. *Nature* 296:807.

Jacobi, R. M.
  1978  Northern England in the eighth millennium B.C.: an essay. In *The Early Postglacial Settlement of Northern Europe*. Edited by Paul Mellars, pp. 295–332. Pittsburgh: University of Pittsburgh Press.

James, Edwin O.
  1957  *Prehistoric Religion*. New York: Frederick A. Praeger.

James, Steven R.
  1989  Hominid use of fire in the lower and middle Pleistocene. *Current Anthropology* 30(1): 1–26.

Jelinek, Arthur J.
  1977  The Lower Paleolithic: current evidence and interpretations. *Annual Review of Anthropology* 6:11–32.

Jia, Lanpo
  1985  China's earliest Palaeolithic assemblage. In *Paleoanthropology and*

*Palaeolithic Archaeology in the People's Republic of China.* Edited
by Wu Rukang and J. W. Olsen, pp. 135–145. New York: Academic
Press.

Jochim, Michael A.
1976 *Hunter-Gatherer Subsistence and Settlement: A Predictive Model.*
New York: Academic Press.
1983 Paleolithic cave art in ecological perspective. In *Hunter-Gatherer
Economy in Prehistory: A European Perspective.* Edited by G.
Bailey, pp. 212–219. Cambridge: Cambridge University Press.

Johnson, Wayne A.
1983 Buffalo (Bison) nutrient contents and optimal cooking quality, In
*Buffalo Management and Marketing.* Edited by Dana C. Jennings
and Judi Hebbring, pp. 302–310. Custer, South Dakota: National
Buffalo Association.

Jowett, Benjamin, trans.
1943 *The Politics of Aristotle.* New York: Modern Library.

Judge, W. James, and Jerry Dawson
1972 Paleo-Indian settlement technology in New Mexico. *Science* 176:
1210–1216.

Kay, Richard F.
1985 Dental evidence for the diet of *Australopithecus. Annual Review of
Anthropology* 14:315–341.

Keane, Arthur S.
1981 Optimal foraging in a nonmarginal environment: a model of pre-
historic subsistence strategies in Michigan, In *Hunter-Gatherer
Foraging Strategies: Ethnographic and Archaeological Analyses.*
Edited by Bruce Winterhalder and Eric A. Smith, pp. 171–193. New
York: Academic Press.

Kemp, W.
1971 The flow of energy in a hunting society. *Scientific American* 237(5):
104–115.

Kennett, James P., and R. C. Thunell
1975 Global increase in Quaternary explosive volcanism. *Science* 187:
497–503.

King, Arden R.
1973 Review of Alexander Marshack: The Roots of Civilization and
Notation dans les gravures du paléolithique supérieur. *American
Anthropologist* 75:1897–1900.

Kirchner, Von Horst
1952 Ein archäologisher Beitrag zur Urgeschichte des Schamanismus.
*Anthropos* 47:244–286.

Klein, Richard G.
1969 The Mousterian of European Russia. *Proceedings of the Prehistoric
Society* XXXV.
1973 *Ice-Age Hunters of the Ukraine.* Chicago: The University of Chicago Press.
1980 Late Pleistocene hunters. In *The Cambridge Encyclopedia of Ar-*

*chaeology.* Edited by A. Sheratt, pp. 87–96. New York: Cambridge University Press.

1983    The stone age prehistory of southern Africa. *Annual Review of Anthropology* 12:25–48.

Koch, Klaus-Friedrich

1976    Feuding. In *The Encyclopedia of Anthropology.* Edited by D. E. Hunter and P. Whitten, p. 167. New York: Harper and Row.

Kopp, K. O.

1963    Schneegrenze und Klima der Wurmeiszeit and der Baskischen Küste. *Eiszeitalter und Gregenw* 14:188–207.

Kramer, Samuel N.

1959    *History Begins at Sumer.* Garden City: Doubleday and Company, Inc.

Krause, Aurel

1956    *The Tlingit Indians: Results of a Trip to the Northwest Coast of America and the Bering Sea.* Seattle: The University of Washington Press.

Kreiger, Alex D.

1960    Archaeological typology in theory and practice. In *Selected Papers of the Fifth International Congress of Anthropology and Ethnological Sciences,* pp. 141–151.

Kroeber, Alfred L.

1939    Cultural and Natural Areas of Native North America. *University of California Publications in American Archaeology and Ethnology,* vol. 38.

Kroeber, Alfred, and Clyde Kluckhohn

1952    Culture: A Critical Review of Concepts and Definitions. In *Peabody Museum of American Archaeology and Ethnology* 47(1).

Kukla, G. J.

1975    Loess stratigraphy of Central Europe. In *After the Australopithecines.* Edited by Karl W. Butzer and Glynn Isaac, pp. 99–188. The Hague: Mouton Publishers.

Kurten, Bjorn

1968    *Pleistocene Mammals of Europe.* Chicago: Aldine.

1971    *The Age of Mammals.* New York: Columbia University Press.

1976    *The Cave Bear Story.* New York: Columbia University Press.

Laming-Emperaire, Annette

1959    *Lascaux, Paintings and Engravings.* Harmondsworth: Penguin Books.

Laville, Henri, and Jean-Philippe Rigaud

1973    The Perigordian V industries in the Perigord: typological variations, stratigraphy, and relative chronology. *World Archaeology* 4:330–338.

Laville, Henri, Jean-Philippe Rigaud, and James Sackett

1980    *Rock Shelters of the Perigord: Geological Stratigraphy and Archaeological Succession.* New York: Academic Press.

Laville, Henri, and J-P. Texier
   1972   De la fin du Würm III au debut du Würm IV. Paleoclimatologie et implications chronostratigraphiques. *Comptes Rendus de l'Academie des Sciences de Paris* 275(D): 329–332.

Leacock, Eleanor
   1982   Relations of production in band society. In *Politics and History in Band Society*. Edited by Eleanor Leacock and Richard Lee, pp. 159–170. Cambridge: Cambridge University Press.

Leacock, Eleanor, and Richard Lee
   1982   Introduction. In *Politics and History in Band Society*. Edited by Eleanor Leacock and Richard Lee, pp. 1–20. Cambridge: Cambridge University Press.

Leakey, Lewis S. B., Philip V. Tobias, and John R. Napier
   1964   A new species of the genus *Homo* from Olduvai Gorge. *Nature* 202:7–9.

Leakey, Mary D.
   1971   *Olduvai Gorge Volume III: Excavations in Beds I and II, 1960–1963*. Cambridge: Cambridge University Press.

Leakey, Mary D., and Richard L. Hay
   1979   Pliocene footprints in the Laetolil Beds at Laetoli, northern Tanzania. *Nature* 278:317–323.

Leakey, Richard E. F., and Alan Walker
   1976   Australopithecus, Homo erectus, and the single-species hypothesis. *Nature* 261:572–576.

Leakey, Richard E. F., and Roger Lewin
   1977   *Origins*. New York: E. P. Dutton.

Leason, P. A.
   1939   A new view of the western European group of Quaternary cave art. *Proceedings of the Prehistoric Society* 5(1&2): 51–60.

Lee, Richard
   1968   What hunters do for a living, or, how to make out on scarce resources. In *Man the Hunter*. Edited by R. Lee and I. DeVore, pp. 30–48. Chicago: Aldine.

   1969   !Kung Bushmen subsistence—an input-output analysis. In *Environment and Cultural Behavior*. Edited by A. P. Vayda, pp. 47–79. New York: Natural History Press.

   1972   The !Kung Bushmen of Botswanna. In *Hunters and Gatherers Today*. Edited by M. G. Bicchieri, pp. 326–368. New York: Holt, Rinehart and Winston, Inc.

   1979   *The !Kung San: Men, Women, and Work in a Foraging Society*. Cambridge: Cambridge University Press.

   1984   *The Dobe !Kung*. New York: Holt, Rinehart and Winston.

Lee, Richard, and Irven DeVore, eds.
   1968   *Man the Hunter*. Chicago: Aldine Publishing Company.

Leger, M.
   1977   *Imprécision de la stratigraphie 'alpine' du Quaternaire. Approche écologique de l'Homme fossile*. Paris: Travaux du groups.

Leroi-Gourhan, André
1965a  *Préhistoire de l'art occidental.* Paris: Mazenod.
1965b  *Treasures of Prehistoric Art.* Translated by Norbert Guterman. New York: Harry N. Abrams, Inc., Publishers.
1968   The evolution of Paleolithic art. *Scientific American* 218(2): 58–70.
1982   *The Dawn of European Art: An Introduction to Paleolithic Cave Art.* Cambridge: Cambridge University Press.

Leroi-Gourhan, André, and Arlette Leroi-Gourhan
1965   Chronologie des grottes d'Arcy-sur-Cure (Yonne). *Gallia-Préhistoire* 7:1–64.

Leroi-Gourhan, Arlette
1982   The archaeology of Lascaux Cave. *Scientific American* 246(6): 104–112.

Leveque, F., and Bernard Vandermeersch
1981   Le nandertalien de Saint-Cesaire. *La Recerche* 12:242–244.

Levey, W. T.
1966   Early Teotihuacan: an achieving society. *Mesoamerican Notes* 7–8:25–68.

Levin, M. G., and L. P. Potapov
1964   *The Peoples of Siberia.* Chicago: University of Chicago Press.

Levine, Marsha
1983   Mortality models and the interpretation of horse population structure. In *Hunter-Gatherer Economy in Prehistory: A European Perspective.* Edited by Geoff Bailey, pp. 23–46. Cambridge: Cambridge University Press.

Lévi-Strauss, Claude
1963   *Totemism.* Boston: Beacon Press.
1966   *The Savage Mind.* Chicago: The University of Chicago Press.

Lewin, Roger
1981   Ethiopian stone tools are world's oldest. *Science* 211:806–807.
1986a  When stones can be deceptive. *Science* 231:113–115.
1986b  Anthropologist argues that language cannot be read in stones. *Science* 233:23–24.

Lewis, Ioan M.
1971   *Ecstatic Religion.* New York: Penguin Books.

Lewis-Williams, J. David
1982   The economic and social context of southern San rock art. *Current Anthropology* 23(4):429–449.

Lewis-Williams, J. D., and T. A. Dowson
1988   The signs of all times: entoptic phenomena in Upper Paleolithic art. *Current Anthropology* 29(2): 201–245.

Lieberman, Philip
1976   Interactive models for evolution: neural mechanisms, anatomy and behavior. In Origins and Evolution of Language and Speech. Edited by S. Harnad, H. D. Steklis, and J. Lancaster. *Annals of the New York Academy of Sciences* 280:660–672.

Lieberman, Philip, and E. S. Crelin
  1971   On the speech of the Neanderthal man. *Linguistic Enquiry* 11:203–222.
Lommel, Andreas
  1967   *Shamanism: The Beginning of Art.* New York: McGraw-Hill Book Company.
Loomis, Charles P.
  1957   *Community and Society: Gemeinschaft and Gesellshaft.* East Lansing: Michigan State University Press.
Loomis, Charles P., and J. Allan Beagle
  1951   *Rural Social Systems.* New York: Prentice-Hall, Inc.
Lorblanchet, M.
  1977   From naturalism to abstraction in European prehistoric rock art. In Form in Indigenous Art: Schematisation in the Art of Aboriginal Australia and Prehistoric Europe. Edited by Peter J. Ucko. Australian Institute of Aboriginal Studies, Canberra, *Prehistory and Material Culture Series* 13:44–56.
Lowie, Robert H.
  1948   *Primitive Religion.* New York: Liveright.
  1963   *Indians of the Plains.* American Museum Science Books Edition. New York: The American Museum of Natural History.
Lundelius, Jr., Ernest L.
  1976   Vertebrate palaeontology of the Pleistocene: an overview. In Ecology of the Pleistocene: a symposium. Edited by R. C. West and W. G. Haag. *Geoscience and Man* 13:45–59.
Lustig-Arecco, Vera
  1975   *Technology: Strategies for Survival.* New York: Holt, Rinehart and Winston.
Lynch, Thomas F.
  1966   The "Lower Perigordian" in French archaeology. *Proceedings of the Prehistoric Society* 32:156–198.
Macalister, Robert A. S.
  1921   *Textbook of European Archaeology.* Cambridge: Cambridge University Press.
Machover, Karen
  1949   *Personality Projection in the Drawing of the Human Figure.* Springfield, Illinois: Charles C. Thomas, Publisher.
McBurney, Charles
  1973   From the beginning of Man to 33,000 B.C. In *France Before the Romans.* Edited by Stuart Piggott, Glyn Daniel and Charles McBurney, pp. 9–29. Park Ridge, New Jersey: Noyes Press.
McCollough, C. Major
  1971   *Perigordian Facies in the Upper Paleolithic of Cantabria.* Unpublished Ph.D. Dissertation, Department of Anthropology, Philadelphia: The University of Pennsylvania.
McClelland, David C.
  1958   The use of measures of human motivation in the study of society. In

*Motives in Fantasy, Action and Society.* Edited by J. W. Atkinson, pp. 518–552. Princeton: Van Nostrand.

1961    The Achieving Society. Van Nostrand, Princeton.

Malinowski, Bronislaw

1954    *Magic, Science and Religion.* Garden City: Doubleday and Company, Inc.

Mankinen, E. A., and G. Brent Dalrymple

1979    Revised geomagnetic polarity time scale for the interval 0–5 m B. P. *Journal of Geophysical Research* 84:615–626.

Mann, Alan

1976    Ecology of early man in the Old World. In Ecology of the Pleistocene: a Symposium. Edited by R. C. West and W. G. Haag. *Geoscience and Man* 13:61–70.

Maringer, Johannes

1960    *The Gods of Prehistoric Man.* New York: Alfred A. Knopf.

Maringer, Johannes, and Hans-George Bandi

1953    *Art in the Ice Age.* New York: Fredrick A. Praeger.

Marshack, Alexander

1970    The baton of Montgaudier. *Natural History* 79:56–63.

1972a   Paleolithic notation. *Antiquity* 46:63–65.

1972b   Upper Paleolithic notation and symbol. *Science* 178:817–828.

1972c   *The Roots of Civilization.* New York: McGraw-Hill Book Company.

1976    Some implications of Paleolithic symbolic evidence for the origin of language. *Current Anthropology* 17(2): 274–282.

1977    The meander as a system: the analysis and recognition of iconographic units in Upper Paleolithic composition. In Form in indigenous art: schematisation in the art of aboriginal Australia and prehistoric Europe. Edited by Peter J. Ucko. Australian Institute of Aboriginal Studies, Canberra, *Prehistory and Material Culture Series* 13:284–317.

1981    On Paleolithic ochre and the early uses of color and symbol. *Current Anthropology* 22(2): 188–191.

Martin, M. Kay

1974    The foraging adaptation—uniformity or diversity? *Addison-Wesley Module in Anthropology* 56.

Martin, Paul S., and Richard G. Klein, eds.

1984    *Quaternary Extinctions: A Prehistoric Revolution.* Tucson: University of Arizona Press.

Melbin, Murray

1978    Night as frontier. *American Sociological Journal* 43(1): 3–22.

Mellars, P.

1965    Sequence and development of the Mousterian traditions in southwestern France. *Nature* 205:626–627.

1969    The chronology of Mousterian industries in the Perigord region. *Proceedings of the Prehistoric Society* 35:134–171.

1970   Some comments on the notion of "functional variability" in stone tool assemblages. *World Archaeology* 2(1): 74–89.

1973   The character of the Middle-Upper Paleolithic transition in southwestern France. In *The Explanation of Cultural Change.* Edited by Colin Renfrew, pp. 255–276. London: Duckworth.

Mithen, Steven J.

1988   Looking and learning: Upper Paleolithic art and information gathering. *World Archaeology* 19(3): 297–327.

Montet-White, Anta, et al.

1973   Las Malpas rockshelter: a study of the late Paleolithic technology in its environmental setting. *University of Kansas Publications in Anthropology* 4.

Moore, James A.

1983   The trouble with know-it-alls: information as a social and ecological resource. In *Archaeological Hammers and Theories.* Edited by J. A. Moore and A. S. Keene, pp. 173–191. New York: Academic Press.

Morgan, William N.

1980   *Prehistoric Architecture in the Eastern United States.* Cambridge: The MIT Press.

Moure-Romanillo, J. A., and M. Cano-Herrera

1979   Tito Bustillo Cave (Asturias, Spain) and the Magdalenian of Cantabria. *World Archaeology* 10(3): 280–289.

Movius, Hallam L., Jr.

1966   The hearths of the Upper Perigordian and the Aurignacian horizons at the Abri Pataud, Les Eyzies (Dordogne) and their possible significance. *American Anthropologist* 68(2): 296–325.

1969a  The Chatelperronian in French archaeology: the evidence of Arcy-sur-Cure. *Antiquity* 43:111–123.

1969b  The Abri de Cro-Magnon, Les Eyzies (Dordogne), and the probable age of the contained burials on the basis of the nearby Abri Pataud. *Annuario de Estudios Atlanticos* 15:323–344.

1974   The Abri Pataud program of the French Upper Paleolithic in retrospect. In *Archaeological Researches in Retrospect.* Edited by Gordon R. Willey, pp. 87–116. New York: Cambridge University Press.

Mukerji, Chandra

1983   *From Graven Images: Patterns of Modern Materialism.* New York: Columbia University Press.

Mumford, Lewis

1967   *Technics and Human Development.* New York: Harcourt Brace Jovanovich, Inc.

Murdock, George P., Clellan S. Ford, Alfred E. Hudson, R. Kennedy, John W. M. Whiting

1971   *Outline of Cultural Materials.* 4th rev. ed. New Haven: Human Relations Area Files, Inc.

Murphy, Robert F.
    1979    *An Overture to Social Anthropology.* Englewood Cliffs, New Jersey:
        Prentice-Hall, Inc.
Netboy, Anthony
    1968    *The Atlantic Salmon: A Vanishing Species!* Boston: Houghton
        Mifflin.
Netting, Robert McC.
    1977    *Cultural Ecology.* Menlo Park, California: Cummings Publishing
        Company.
Niebuhr, Reinhold
    1968    Introduction. In *The Religious Situation.* Edited by Donald R. Cul-
        ter. Boston: Beacon Press.
Nietschmann, Bernard
    1972    Hunting and fishing among the Miskito Indians, eastern Nicara-
        gua. *Human Ecology* 1:41–67.
Ninkovich, D., and Lloyd H. Burkle
    1978    Absolute age of the base of the hominid-bearing beds in eastern
        Java. *Nature* 275:306–307.
Norbeck, Edward
    1961    *Religion in Primitive Society.* New York: Harper and Row, Pub-
        lishers.
Oakley, Kenneth P.
    1957    *Man the Toolmaker.* Chicago: The University of Chicago Press.
Oberg, Kalervo
    1973    *The Social Economy of the Tlingit Indians.* Seattle: University of
        Washington Press.
Oswalt, Wendell H.
    1973    *Habitat and Technology.* New York: Holt, Rinehart and Winston.
    1976    *An Anthropological Analysis of Food-Getting Technology.* New
        York: John Wiley and Sons.
Pales, L.
    1981    *Les Gravures de la Marche, Vol. 2: Les Humains.* Paris: Ophyrs.
Parsons, Talcott
    1951    *The Social System.* Glencoe, Illinois: The Free Press.
Perper, Timothy and Carmel Schrire
    1977    The Nimrod connection: myth and science in the hunting model.
        In *The Chemical Senses and Nutrition.* Edited by Morley R. Kare
        and Owen Maller, pp. 447–459. New York: Academic Press.
Peyrony, Denis
    1933    Les industries aurignaciennes dons le bassin de La Vézère. *Bulletin
        Société Préhistorique Française* 30:543–559.
Peyrony, Denis, and Elie Peyrony
    1938    Laugerie-Haute, près des Eyzies (Dordogne). *Archives de l'Institut
        de Paléontologie Humaine, Mémoire 19.*
Pfeiffer, John E.
    1978    *The Emergence of Man.* Third Edition. New York: Harper and Row.
    1980a   Religious roots. *Science 80,* 1(8): 14–16.

1980b Icons in the shadows. *Science 80* 1(4): 72–79.

1982a *The Creative Explosion.* Ithaca: Cornell University Press.

1982b Inner sanctum. *Science 82* 3(1): 66–68.

Pilbeam, David

1984a The descent of hominoids and hominids. *Scientific American* 250(3): 84–96.

1984b Reflections on early human ancestors. *Journal of Anthropological Research* 40(1): 14–22.

Pilbeam, David, and Stephen J. Gould

1974  Size and scaling in human evolution. *Science* 186:892–901.

Platt, Colin

1978 *Medieval England: A Social History and Archaeology from the Conquest to 1600 A.D.* New York: Charles Scribner's Sons.

Poiner, G.

1971 *The Process of the Year.* B.A. Honors Thesis. Department of Anthropology, Sidney: University of Sidney.

Poirier, Frank E.

1977 *In Search of Ourselves.* 2d ed. Minneapolis: Burgess Publishing Company.

Polanyi, Karl

1957 *The Great Transformation.* Boston: Beacon Press, Inc.

Prasad, K. N.

1983  Was *Ramapithecus* a tool-user? *Journal of Human Evolution* 11: 101–104.

Price, T. Douglas, and James A. Brown, eds.

1985 *Prehistoric Hunter-Gatherers: The Emergence of Cultural Complexity.* New York: Academic Press.

Quechon, G.

1976  Les sépultures des hommes du Paléolithique supérieur. In *La Préhistoire Française, I: Civilisations paléolithiques et mésolithiques.* Edited by H. de Lumley, pp. 728–733. Paris: CNRS.

Rathje, William L., and Michael B. Schiffer

1980 *Archaeology.* New York: Harcourt Brace Jovanovich, Inc.

Rappaport, Roy A.

1968 *Pigs for the Ancestors.* New Haven: Yale University Press.

Redfield, Robert

1949 *The Folk Culture of Yucatan.* Chicago: The University of Chicago Press.

1953 *The Primitive World and its Transformation.* Ithaca: Cornell University Press.

1956 *Peasant Society and Culture.* Chicago: The University of Chicago Press.

1960 *The Little Community.* Chicago: The University of Chicago Press.

Reed, Robert C.

1976  An interpretation of some "anthropomorphic" representations from the Upper Paleolithic. *Current Anthropology* 17(1): 136–138.

Rice, Prudence C.
    1982    Prehistoric Venuses: symbols of motherhood or womanhood? *Journal of Anthropological Research* 37(4):402–414.
Rightmire, G. Philip
    1981    Patterns in the evolution of *Homo erectus*. *Paleobiology* 7:241–246.
Rippeteau, Bruce E.
    1972    The Need-Achievement test applied to the Hohokam. *American Antiquity* 37(4): 504–513.
Robbins, G. V., N. J. Seeley, D. A. C. McNeil, and M. R. C. Symons
    1978    Identification of ancient heat treatment in flint artifacts by ESR spectroscopy. *Nature* 276:703–704.
Robinson, J. T.
    1965    *Homo "habilis"* and the Australopithecines. *Nature* 205:121–124.
Rolland, Nicholas
    1981    The interpretation of Middle Paleolithic variability. *Man* 16:15–42.
Rosen, Stephen I.
    1974    *Introduction to the Primates: Living and Fossil.* Englewood Cliffs, New Jersey: Prentice-Hall.
Rosenfeld, Andrée
    1971    Review of Alexander Marshack: Notation dans les gravures du paléolithique supérieur. *Publications de l'institut de Préhistorie de L'Université de Bordeaux. Mémoire 8. Antiquity* 45:317–319.
    1972    Paleolithic notation. *Antiquity* 46:65.
Rosenfeld, Andrée, David Horton, and John Winter
    1981    Early man in north Queensland. *Terra Australis* 6.
Rouse, Irving
    1960    The classification of artifacts in archaeology. *American Antiquity* 25:313–325.
Rowe, John H.
    1961    Stratigraphy and seriation. *American Antiquity* 26:324–330.
    1962    Stages and periods in archaeological interpretation. *Southwestern Journal of Anthropology* 18(1): 40–54.
Sackett, James R.
    1966    Quantitative analysis of Upper Paleolithic stone tools. *American Anthropologist* 68:356–394.
    1981    From de Mortillet to Bordes: a century of French Paleolithic research. In *Towards a History of Archaeology.* Edited by Glyn Daniel and O. Klindt-Jensen, pp. 85–99. New York: Thames and Hudson, Ltd.
Sackett, James R., and J. Gaussen
    1976    Upper Paleolithic habitation structures in the Sud-Ouest of France. IXth Congress of the International Union of Prehistoric and Protohistoric Sciences, Colloquim XIII: Les Structures d'habitat au paléolithic supérieur, pp. 55–83.
Sahlins, Marshall D.
    1965    On the sociology of primitive exchange. In *The Relevance of Mod-*

*els for Social Anthropology.* Edited by Michael Banton, pp. 139–236. London: Tavistock Publications, Ltd.

1974 *Stone Age Economics.* London: Tavistock Publications, Ltd.

Sammallahti, Pekka

1982 Lappish (*Saami*) hunting terminology in an historical perspective. In The hunters; their culture and way of life. Edited by Ake Hultkrntz and Ornulf Vorren. *Tromso Museum Skrifter* 18:103–110.

Saxe, Arthur A.

1970 Social Dimensions of Mortuary Practices. Unpublished Ph.D. Dissertation, Department of Anthropology. Ann Arbor: University of Michigan.

Schaafsma, Polly

1971 The Rock Art of Utah. *Papers of the Peabody Museum of Archaeology and Ethnology* 65.

1972 *The Rock Art of New Mexico.* Santa Fe: State Planning Office.

Schaller, George B.

1972 Are you running with me, hominid? *Natural History* 81(3): 60–69.

Schmandt-Besserat, S.

1980 "Ocher in prehistory, 300,000 years of the use of iron ores as pigments," in *The Coming of the Age of Iron,* edited by T. A. Wertime and J. D. Muhly, pp. 127–150. New Haven: Yale University Press.

Schapiro, Meyer

1969 On some problems in the semiotics of visual art: field and vehicle in image-signs. *Semiotica* 1(3): 223–242.

Schneider, David

1968 *American Kinship: A Cultural Account.* Englewood Cliffs, New Jersey: Prentice-Hall, Inc.

Schvoerer, M. C., C. Bordier, J. Evin, and G. Delibrias

1979 Chronologie absolue de la fin des temps glaciaires en Europe. In *La fin des temps glaciaires en Europe.* Edited by Denise de Sonneville-Bordes, pp. 21–48. Paris: Editions du Centre National de la Recherche Scientifique.

Service, Elman R.

1962 *Primitive Social Organization: An Evolutionary Perspective.* New York: Random House.

1979 *The Hunters.* Englewood Cliffs, New Jersey: Prentice-Hall, Inc.

Shackleton, Margaret R.

1969 *Europe: A Regional Geography.* New York: Frederick A. Praeger, Publishers.

Shackleton, N. J.

1975 The stratigraphic record of deep-sea cores and its implications for the assessment of glacials, interglacials, stadials and interstadials in the Mid-Pleistocene. In *After the Australopithecines.* Edited by Karl W. Butzer and Glynn Issac, pp. 1–24. The Hague: Mouton Publishers.

Shimkin, Edith M.

1978 The Upper Paleolithic in north-central Eurasia: evidence and problems. In *Views of the Past.* Edited by Leslie G. Freeman, pp. 177–315. The Hague: Mouton Publishers.

Sieveking, Ann

1971    Paleolithic decorated bone discs. *British Museum Quarterly* 35: 209–229.

1975– The Upper Paleolithic cave site of Altamira (Santander, Spain).

1976    *Quaternaria* 19:135–148.

1976    Settlement patterns of the late Magdalenian in the central Pyrenees. In *Problems in Economic and Social Archaeology.* Edited by G. de G. Sieveking, I. H. Longworth and K. E. Wilson, pp. 583–603. London: Duckworth.

1979    *The Cave Artists.* London: Thames and Hudson, Ltd.

Silberbauer, George B.

1972    The G/wi Bushmen. In *Hunters and Gatherers Today.* Edited by M. G. Bicchieri, pp. 271–326. New York: Holt, Rinehart and Winston.

1981    Hunter/gatherers of the central Kalahari. In *Omnivorous Primates: Gathering and Hunting in Human Evolution.* Edited by R. S. O. Harding and Geza Teleki, pp. 455–498. New York: Columbia University Press.

Silver, Harry R.

1979    *Ethnoart.* Annual Review of Anthropology 8:267–307.

Small, Ronald J.

1972    *The Study of Landforms.* Cambridge: Cambridge University Press.

Smith, Fred H.

1984    Fossil hominids from the Upper Pleistocene of Central Europe and the origin of modern Europeans. In *The Origins of Modern Humans.* Edited by Fred H. Smith and Frank Spencer, pp. 137–209. New York: Alan R. Liss, Inc.

Smith, Fred H., and Frank Spencer, eds.

1984    *The Origins of Modern Humans.* New York: Alan R. Liss, Inc.

Smith, Philip

1964    *The Solutrean Culture.* Scientific American 211(2): 86–94.

1965    Some Solutrean problems and suggestions for future research. *Diputación Provincial de Barcelona, Instituduo de Prehistòria y Arqueologia. Monografias* 18:398–408.

1966    Le Solutreen en France. *Publications de l'Institut de Préhistoire de l'Université de Bordeaux, Mémoire* 5.

1973    Some thoughts on variations among certain Solutrean artifacts. In *Estudios dedicados al Professor Dr. Luis Pericot.* Edited by J. Malvquer de Motes, pp. 67–75. Barcelona: Instituto de Arqueologia y Prehistoria.

Smolla, G.

1960    Neolithische Kulturerscheinungen: Studien Zur Frage Ihrer Herausbildungen. *Antiquitas* (Series 2) 3:1–180.

Soffer, Olga
1985 *The Upper Paleolithic of the Central Russian Plain.* New York: Academic Press.
Sonneville-Bordes, Denise de
1960 *Le Paléolithique supérieur en Perigord.* Bordeaux: Imprimeries Delmas.
1963 Upper Paleolithic cultures in western Europe. *Science* 142:347–355.
1973 The Upper Paleolithic: ca. 33,000–10,000 B.C. In *France Before the Romans.* Edited by Stuart Piggott, Glyn Daniel, and Charles Mc-Burney, pp. 30–60. Park Ridge, New Jersey: Noyes Press.
Spaulding, Albert C.
1953 Statistical techniques for the discovery of artifact types. *American Antiquity* 18:305–313.
1954 Reply to Ford. *American Antiquity* 19:391–393.
1960 The dimensions of archaeology. In *Essays in the Science of Culture in Honor of Leslie A. White.* Edited by G. D. Dole and R. L. Carneiro, pp. 437–456. New York: Thomas Y. Crowell Company.
Spencer, Baldwin
1914 *Native Tribes of the Northern Territory of Australia.* London: Mac-Millan.
Spencer, Baldwin, and Frank J. Gillen
1927 *The Arunta.* 2 vols. London: Macmillan London and Basingstoke.
Spiess, Arthur E.
1979 *Reindeer and Caribou Hunters: An Archaeological Study.* New York: Academic Press.
Steward, Julian
1955 *A Theory of Culture Change.* Urbana: University of Illinois Press.
1969 Postscript to bands: on taxonomy, processes, and causes. Contributions to Anthropology: Band Societies. *National Museum of Canada Bulletin 228.*
Straus, Lawrence Guy
1975 *A Study of the Solutrean in Vasco-Cantabrian Spain.* Unpublished Doctoral Dissertation, Department of Anthropology. Chicago: The University of Chicago.
1976 A new interpretation of the Cantabrian Solutrean. *Current Anthropology* 17(2): 342–343.
1977a Of deerslayers and mountain men: Paleolithic faunal exploitation in Cantabrian Spain. In *For Theory Building in Archaeology.* Edited by Lewis R. Binford, pp. 41–76. New York: Academic Press.
1977b Thoughts on Solutrean concave base point distribution. *Lithic Technology* 6:32–35.
1978 Of Neanderthal hillbillies, origin myths and stone tools: notes on Upper Paleolithic assemblage variability. *Lithic Technology* 7:36–39.

1982    Carnivores and cave sites in Cantabrian Spain. *Journal of Anthropological Research* 38(1): 75–96.

1985    Stone age prehistory of Northern Spain. *Science* 230:501–507.

Straus, Lawrence Guy, Geoffrey A. Clark, Jesus Altuna, and Jesus A. Ortea

1980    Ice-age subsistence in Northern Spain. *Scientific American* 242(6): 142–152.

Stringer, C. B.

1974    Population relationships of later Pleistocene hominids: a multivariate study of available crania. *Journal of Human Evolution* 11:431–438.

1982    Towards a solution of the Neanderthal problem. *Journal of Human Evolution* 11:431–438.

Stringer, C. B., J. J. Hublin, and B. Vandermeersch

1984    The origin of anatomically modern humans in Western Europe. In *The Origins of Modern Humans*. Edited by Fred H. Smith and Frank Spencer, pp. 51–135. New York: Alan R. Liss, Inc.

Stringer, C. B., and P. Andrews

1988    Genetic and fossil evidence for the origin of modern humans. *Science* 239:1263–1268

Sumption, Jonathan

1975    *Pilgrimage: An Image of Mediaeval Religion*. Totowa, New Jersey: Rowman and Littlefield.

Suttles, Wayne

1962    Variation in habitat and culture on the Northwest Coast. *Proceedings of the 34th International Congress of Americanists*, pp. 522–537.

1968    Coping with abundance. In *Man the Hunter*. Edited by Richard Lee and I. DeVore, pp. 56–68. Chicago: Aldine.

Tainter, Joseph A.

1977    Modeling change in prehistoric social systems. In *For Theory Building in Archaeology*. Edited by Lewis R. Binford, pp. 327–351. New York: Academic Press.

Taranik, Linda L.

1977    *The Beauronnian at Solvieux: An Upper Paleolithic Industry from Southwestern France*. Unpublished Ph.D. Dissertation, Department of Anthropology. Los Angeles: University of California at Los Angeles.

Teilhard de Chardin, Pierre

1964    *The Future of Man*. New York: Harper and Row, Publishers.

Tobias, Phillip V.

1965    Early man in East Africa. *Science* 149:22–23.

1981    The emergence of man in Africa and beyond. *Philosophical Transactions of the Royal Society, London B* 292:43–56.

Toth, Nicolas

1985    The Oldowan reassessed: a closer look at early stone artifacts. *Journal of Archaeological Science* 12:101–120.

Trammel, William C.
  1984   *Religon, What Is It?* 2d ed. New York: Holt, Rinehart and Winston.
Tresguerres, J.
  1976   Azilian burial from Los Azules I, Asturias, Spain. *Current Anthropology* 17:769–770.
Trinkaus, Erik
  1989   Comment on Grave shortcomings: the evidence for Neanderthal burial, by Robert Gargett. *Current Anthropology* 30(2): 183–184.
Trinkaus, Erik, and William W. Howells
  1979   The Neanderthals. *Scientific American* 241(6):118–133.
Turnbull, Colin M.
  1961   *The Forest People.* New York: Clarion.
  1965   *Wayward Servants: The Two Worlds of the African Pygmies.* London: Eyre and Spottiswoode.
  1982   The ritualization of potential conflict between the sexes. In *Politics and History in Band Society.* Edited by Eleanor Leacock and Richard Lee, pp. 133–155. Cambridge: Cambridge University Press.
Turner, Victor W.
  1967   *The Forest of Symbols: Aspects of Ndembu Ritual.* Ithaca, New York: Cornell University Press.
Ucko, Peter J., and Andrée Rosenfeld
  1967   *Paleolithic Cave Art.* New York: McGraw-Hill Book Company.
Valladas, H., J. Reyss, J. L. Joron, G. Valladas, O. Bar-Josef, B. Vandermeersch
  1988   Thermoluminescence dating of Mousterian "Proto-Cro-Magnon" remains from Israel and the origin of modern man. *Nature* 331: 614–617.
Vallois, H.
  1961   The social life of early man: the evidence of the skeletons. In The social life of early man, edited by Sherwood L. Washburn. *Viking Fund Publications in Anthropology* 31:214–235.
Vandermeersch, Bernard
  1976   Les sépultures néandertaliennes. In *La Préhistoire Française, I: Civilisations paléolithiques et mésolithiques.* Edited by H. de Lumley, pp. 725–727. Paris: CNRS.
Van Gennep, Arnold
  1960   *The Rites of Passage.* Chicago: The University of Chicago Press. First published in 1909.
Vialou, Denis
  1983   Nouvelles recherches sur les representations parietales paleolithiques. *Bulletin de la Société Préhistorique Française* 80:264.
  1984   Des blocs sculptes et graves. *Histoire et Archéologie* 87 (Octobre): 70–72.
von Simson, Otto
  1956   *The Gothic Cathedral.* New York: Pantheon Books, Inc.
Walker, Alan, and Richard E. F. Leakey
  1978   The hominids of East Turkana. *Scientific American* 239(2): 54–66.

Wallace, Anthony F. C.

1950   A possible technique for recognizing psychological characteristics of the ancient Maya from an analysis of their art. *American Image* 7:239–258.

1952   Handsome Lake and the Great Revival in the West. *American Quarterly* (Summer): 149–165.

1956   Revitalization movements: some theoretical considerations for their comparative study. *American Anthropologist* 58:264–281.

1958   Dreams and the wishes of the soul. *American Anthropologist* 60: 234–248.

1961   Cultural composition of the Handsome Lake religion. In Symposium on Cherokee and Iroquois Culture. Edited by W. N. Fenton and John Gulick. *Bureau of American Ethnology, Bulletin* 180.

1966   *Religion: An Anthropological View.* New York: Random House.

1969   *The Death and Rebirth of the Seneca.* New York: Vintage Books.

Washburn, Sherwood L., and V. Avis

1958   Evolution of human behavior. In *Behavior and Evolution.* Edited by A. Roe and G. G. Simpson, pp. 421–436. New Haven: Yale University Press.

Wax, Murray, and Rosalie Wax

1963   The notion of magic. *Current Anthropology* 4(5):495–518.

Webster, David

1981   Late Pleistocene extinctions and human predation: a critical overview. In *Omnivorous Primates: Gathering and Hunting in Human Evolution.* Edited by R. S. O. Harding and Geza Teleki, pp. 556–594. New York: Columbia University Press.

Weiss, Kenneth M.

1973   Demographic Models for Anthropology. *Memoirs of the Society for American Archaeology, Number 27.*

West, R. G.

1977   *Pleistocene Geology and Biology.* 2d ed. London: Longman's Group, Ltd.

White, Leslie A.

1949a  Ethnological theory. In *Philosophy for the Future.* Edited by R. W. Sellars, and V. J. McFill, pp. 357–384. New York: M. Faber, Publisher.

1949b  *The Science of Culture: A Study of Man and Civilization.* New York: Farrar, Straus and Company.

White, Randall K.

1980   *The Upper Paleolithic Occupation of the Perigord.* Unpublished Ph.D. Dissertation, Department of Anthropology. Toronto: The University of Toronto.

1982   The manipulation and use of burins in incision and notation. *Canadian Journal of Anthropology* 2.

1982   Rethinking the Middle/Upper Paleolithic transition. *Current Anthropology* 23(2): 169–192.

1989   Visual thinking in the Ice Age. *Scientific American* 261(1): 92–99.

White, Theodore E.
  1953   A method of calculating the dietary percentage of various food
         animals utilized by aboriginal peoples. *American Antiquity* 18 (4):
         396–398.
Wiessner, Polly
  1982   Risk, reciprocity and social influences on !Kung San economics, In
         *Politics and History in Band Society.* Edited by Eleanor Leacock
         and Richard Lee, pp. 61–84. Cambridge: Cambridge University
         Press.
Willey, Malcolm M.
  1927   Psychology and culture. *Psychological Bulletin* 24:253–283.
Winner, Langdon
  1977   *Autonomous Technology; Technics-Out-of-Control as a Theme in
         Political Thought.* Cambridge: The MIT Press.
Wobst, H. Martin
  1974   Boundary conditions for Paleolithic social systems: a simulation
         approach. *American Antiquity* 39(1): 147–178.
  1975   The demography of finite populations and the origins of the incest
         taboo. *American Antiquity* 40(2): 75–81.
Woillard, Geneviére M.
  1978   Grande Pile peat bog: a continuous pollen record for the last
         140,000 years. *Quaternary Research* 9(1): 1–21.
Woldstedt, P.
  1958   *Das Eiszeitalter.* Stuttgart: Grundlinien einer Geologie der Quar-
         tärs.
Wolpoff, Milford H.
  1980   *Paleoanthropology.* New York: Alfred A. Knopf.
  1981   Cranial capacity estimates for Olduvai Hominid 7. *American Jour-
         nal of Physical Anthropology* 56:297–304.
Woodburn, James
  1980   Hunters and gatherers today and reconstruction of the past. In
         *Soviet and Western Anthropology.* Edited by Ernest Gellner, pp. 95–
         117. London: Gerald Duckworth and Company, Ltd.
  1982a  The social dimensions of death in four African hunting and gather-
         ing societies. In *Death and the Regeneration of Life.* Edited by
         Maurice Bloch and Jonathan Parry, pp. 187–210. Cambridge: Cam-
         bridge University Press.
  1982b  Egalitarian societies. *Man* 17:431–451.
Wreschner, E. E.
  1980   Red ochre and human evolution: a case for discussion. *Current
         Anthropology* 21(5): 631–644.
Wu Leung, W.
  1971   *Food Composition Tables for Use in Latin America.* Bethesda,
         Maryland: Interdepartmental Committee on Nutrition for Na-
         tional Defense and the Institute on Nutrition for Central America
         and Panama.

Wymer, John
  1982    *The Paleolithic Age.* New York: St. Martin's Press.
Wynn, Thomas
  1979    The intelligence of later Acheulean hominids. *Man* (ns) 14: 371–
       391.
Yellen, John E.
  1977    *Archaeological Approaches to the Present: Models for Recon-
       structing the Past.* New York: Academic Press.
Yesner, David R.
  1980    Maritime hunter-gatherers: ecology and prehistory. *Current An-
       thropology* 21:727–750.
Yinger, J. Milton
  1970    *The Scientific Study of Religion.* New York: Macmillan Publishing
       Company, Inc.
Yunis, Jorge J. and O. Prakash
  1982    The origin of man: a chromosomal pictorial legacy. *Science* 215:
       1525–1529.
Zvelebil, Marek
  1986    Postglacial foraging in the forests of Europe. *Scientific American*
       254(5): 104–115.

# Index

## ABOUT THE AUTHOR

D. Bruce Dickson attended Lawrence University, Northwestern University, and in 1973 received a Ph.D. in prehistoric archaeology from the University of Arizona. He has conducted extensive archaeological field research on prehistoric and historic sites in the American South and Southwest and Central America.

The author's most recent field research is focused on prehistoric human adaptation and environmental destruction and is centered in the remote and arid mountain region along the Big Bend of the Rio Grande in southwestern Texas.

He has organized several international, multidisciplinary conferences on the causes of social and cultural change. Currently he is developing an interdisciplinary field study program in Kenya and Tanzania on human and natural ecology in prehistory and history.

Dickson received a Distinguished Achievement Award for Teaching by the Association of Former Students of Texas A&M in 1983. Among the author's other published books are *Prehistoric Pueblo Settlement Patterns: the Pueblo Arroyo Hondo* and *The Transfer and Transformation of Ideas and Material Culture*, coedited with Peter Hugill.